I can count on one hand the people that have deeply influenced my life and thought. Dr. John Warwick Montgomery is one such person. Whether he's the index finger (#1) or the thumb (the get it done digit), I'm not sure. But chances are he's the ring finger—a symbolic gesture to his fidelity to Christ, a man to his Master. Whatever finger Dr. Montgomery represents, the reason he has so influenced my life is bound in the pages of his newest work, *Theology: Good, Bad, and Mysterious*. In these pages, Dr. Montgomery's voracious scope of knowledge and interests are on full display. From apologetics to theology, Dr. Montgomery's mental prowess is manifest in his keen insight and wit. As a fellow bibliophile, I was smitten by his chapter on "Choosing Books for a Theological Library." And as a cultural critic, I found his acumen on law, morality, race, and religion—quite engaging. My only advice is to use both your hands—all the digits—to pick up this fine work and read it! In its pages you'll find that Montgomery—in his 80 plus years on earth—has fulfilled what C.S. Lewis wrote in his essay *Why We Read*,[1] "We seek an enlargement of our being." Dr. Montgomery—through his writings and life—has expanded our being, and I'm thankful for it.

Brian C. Nixon, D. Phil
Author, artist, and musician

"How delightful to have in one volume the best, distilled arguments of one of the world's greatest contemporary apologists! Given Montgomery's range of interests that is so well presented here, there is literally 'something for everyone' that will advance their faith and that will help them respond to skeptic's challenges."

John A. Bloom, Ph.D., Ph.D., M.Div.
Director, MA, Science and Religion Program
Professor Physics
Biola University, La Mirada, CA

---

[1] Originally written in the epilogue from *An Experiment in Criticism*. As quoted, from *The Reading Life*, 3.

Lively, fresh and provocative ingredients, an always innovative presentation, and utterly consistent quality over a sustained time: That is why if the Michelin Guide recognized Christian Apologists then John Warwick Montgomery's provocative *Potpourri* would (once again) establish him as the Alain Ducasse of Apologetics. While Ducasse may be the proud possessor of more Michelin stars than any other Chef in the world, Montgomery's *Potpourri* shows that he too continues to take innovative approaches with topics of current concern in a heralded career that now spans over half a century of writing, teaching and debating. In this volume he creates intriguing presentations on mathematics and apologetics, terrorism, demon possession, racism, the Millennium, and populism (among other dishes), and in doing so shows he well deserves his long-held 3 Michelin stars for this apologetical equivalent of Ducasse's ground-breaking culinary potpourri: *Foie Gras and Black Truffle Ravioli*.

Craig Parton
Trial Lawyer, Price-Postel-Parma LLP of Santa Barbara, California and United States Director of the International Academy of Apologetics in Strasbourg, France

If any Christian has ever heeded the apostle Peter's words, "always be ready to give a defense [*apologia*] to everyone who asks you a reason for the hope that is in you" (1 Peter 3;15), it is John Warwick Montgomery. For sixty years, he has been the most prominent, internationally known defender of Christianity, ranging from defending the historicity of Christ/s bodily resurrection to biblical inerrancy. As a keen theologian and attorney, he has successfully countered internationally known skeptics in public debates and exposed the flaws of biased Bible critics in scores of his articles and books. For the benefit of readers, his latest book, *Theology: Good, Bad, and Mysterious*, alludes to many of those interesting, past encounters.

Alvin J. Schmidt, Ph.D.
Professor Emeritus of Sociology
Illinois College, Jacksonville, Illinois

The latest from the pen of polymath Dr. John Warwick Montgomery: Theology: Good, Bad, and Mysterious: A Theological and Apologetical Potpourri.

Even prior to reading the first essay, one notices that the author is identified as "Dr. Dr. Dr. John Warwick Montgomery!" And this designation does not include all of his impressive academic pedigree—not only earned doctorates in Bibliographical History, Theology, and Law, but some eight other university degrees as well! Talk about unusual breadth! Surely his writings are worth the serious reader's notice.

The potpourri of subjects in this, his latest book, is indeed broad. Of course (and mainly) the subject for which Dr. Montgomery is best known: Christian apologetics (including two essays illustrating the benefits of computer programming to apologetics!), But also: "Law and Morality: Friends or Foes?," the Occult, Johann Valentin Andreae, Johann Arndt, "On Innovative Theologians"––even a study on "Choosing Books for a Theological Library"!

I tell my university students, "Pay attention to each and every one of Montgomery's footnotes." Why? Because they are, in themselves, an education.

Dr. **Rod Rosenbladt**
Professor of Christian Theology and Apologetics
Concordia University Irvine, CA, USA

John Warwick Montgomery's collection of essays in this volume is exactly what it claims to be—a theological and apologetical potpourri. One of the most noticeable things about the volume is its variation of style and scholarly aims. The essays range from those that are blog-like and very brief to scholarly, in-depth discussions of fairly esoteric topics. Among the former are Montgomery's trenchant comments on a study purporting to show that religious children lose the ability to distinguish reality from fiction (since they have been taught to think that miracles are possible) and his satirical suggestion that the methods of higher criticism be applied to its own practitioners in order to debunk their existence. Among the latter are a detailed, interesting discussion of whether or not theologian Johann Valentin Andreae ever endorsed Rosicrucianism and a prescient meditation on the relationship between law and morality. The table of contents is enough to make one read a variety of the essays, musing, "I wonder what he thinks about *that* topic." Among the surprises (to me) in the volume were Montgomery's suggestion that perhaps those who have never heard of Christ before might be offered a God-given chance to accept or reject him in the split-second moment of death, a hypothetical possibility that he expressly distinguishes from a second chance after death but that he offers for apologetic purposes—to answer a challenge to the justice of God. Since I have independently suggested this possibility to various people (including myself) who have found this issue to be a real concern, I was pleased to see Montgomery bringing it up. It was also fascinating to see this highly empirical apologist stating in one essay that he has changed his mind and is open to a reconstructed version of the ontological argument for God's existence. The book is well worth browsing, which is exactly what a potpourri ought to be.

Lydia McGrew, PhD,
co-author of *Internalism and Epistemology: The Architecture of Reason* and author of *The Mirror or the Mask: Liberating the Gospels From Literary Devices*

John Warwick Montgomery

Theology: Good, Bad, and Mysterious

Christliche Philosophie heute – Christian Philosophy Today – Quomodo Philosophia Christianorum Hodie Estimatur

Volume 22

Vol. 1: John Warwick Montgomery. *Tractatus Logico-Theologicus.* (English Edition.)

Vol. 2: John W. Montgomery. *Hat die Weltgeschichte einen Sinn? Geschichtsphilosophien auf dem Prüfstand.*

Vol. 3: John W. Montgomery. *Jésus : La raison rejoint l'histoire.*

Vol. 4: Horst Waldemar Beck. *Marken dieses Äons: Wissenschaftskritische und theologische Diagnosen.*

Vol. 5: Ross Clifford. *John Warwick Montgomery's Legal Apologetic: An Apologetic for All Seasons.*

Vol. 6: Thomas K. Johnson. *Natural Law Ethics: An Evangelical Proposal.*

Vol. 7: Lydia Jaeger. *Wissenschaft ohne Gott? Zum Verhältnis zwischen christlichem Glauben und Wissenschaft.*

Vol. 8: Herman Bavinck. *Christliche Weltanschauung.* Thomas K. Johnson and Ron Kubsch (Ed.).

Vol. 9: John W. Montgomery. *La Mort de Dieu : Exposé et critique du plus récent mouvement théologique en Amérique.* Réimpression de l'édition 1971.

Vol. 10: David Andersen. *Martin Luther – The Problem of Faith and Reason: A Reexamination in Light of the Epistemological and Christological Issues.*

Vol. 11: Wim Rietkerk. *In dubio: Handbuch für Zweifler.*

Vol. 12: Patrick Werder. *Wenig niedriger als Gott: Der Mensch als Person von der Antike bis zur Gegenwart.*

Vol. 13: John Warwick Montgomery. *Christ As Centre and Circumference: Essays Theological, Cultural and Polemic.*

Vol. 14: Lydia Jaeger. *Als Mensch in Gottes Welt: Im Licht der Schöpfung leben.*

Vol. 15: Frederik Herzberg. *Theo-Logik: Über den Beitrag des Jansenismus zur formalen Methode in Theologie und Religionsphilosophie.*

Vol. 16: Hanniel Strebel. *Eine Theologie des Lernens: Systematisch-theologische Beiträge aus dem Werk von Herman Bavinck.*

Vol. 17: John Warwick Montgomery. *Fighting the Good Fight – A Life in Defense of the Faith.*

Vol. 18: Henry Hock Guan Teh. *Principles of the Law of Evidence and Rationality Applied in the Johannine Christology: An Argument for the Legal Evidential Apologetics.*

Vol. 19: John Warwick Montgomery. *Defending the Gospel in Legal Style – Essays on Legal Apologetics & the Justification of Classical Christian Faith.*

Vol. 20: S. Ross Hickling. *An Evidentiary Analysis of Doctor Richard Carrier's Objections to the Resurrection of Jesus Christ.*

Vol. 21: John Warwick Montgomery. *Tractatus Logico-Theologicus.* (French Edition / Édition française.)

Vol. 22: John Warwick Montgomery. *Theology: Good, Bad, and Mysterious – A Theological and Apologetical Potpourri.*

John Warwick Montgomery

Theology: Good, Bad, and Mysterious

A Theological and Apologetical Potpourri

WIPF & STOCK · Eugene, Oregon

Wipf and Stock Publishers
199 W 8th Ave, Suite 3
Eugene, OR 97401

Theology
Good, Bad, and Mysterious
By Montgomery, John Warwick
Copyright © 2020 Verlag für Kultur und Wissenschaft Culture and Science Publ.
All rights reserved.
Softcover ISBN-13: 978-1-7252-9442-4
Hardcover ISBN-13: 978-1-7252-9441-7
Publication date 12/4/2020
Previously published by Verlag für Kultur und Wissenschaft Culture and Science Publ., 2020

Contents

Introduction 11
Acknowledgements 13

Part One: Doing Apologetics 15
1. The Place of Reason 17
2. Is the Universe Computable? 29
3. God and Gödel 33
4. Mathematics and Apologetics: Leonhard Euler (1707–1783) 43
5. In re William Lane Craig 57
6. Lee Strobel's Case for Christ—the Case for *Whom*? 61
7. Computer Programming as an Assist to Apologetics 65
8. Resurrection and Legal Evidence 69
9. Did Jesus Physically Rise from the Dead? 73
10. Chronological Contradictions in the Gospels? 79
11. A More Consistent Application of Literary "Higher Criticism" 85
12. A Short and Easie Method with Postmodernists 91

Part Two: Theology, the Future, and the Occult 101
1. Law & Morality: Friends or Foes? 103
2. Millennium 125
3. Demon Possession: A Brief Commentary 139
4. The World View of Johann Valentin Andreae 145
5. John Arndt Revisited 163
6. Choosing Books for a Theological Library 167

Part Three: Casting a Wide Swath 203
1. Transhumanism? 205
2. Muslims As Two-Faced 209
3. The Stereotypic Clergyman 211
4. On Innovative Theologians 213
5. Racism in American Lutheranism 219
6. Do Christian Children lose Contact with Reality? 223
7. Those Who Have Not Heard the Gospel: A Construct ... 227
8. Freedom of Expression and Respect for Beliefs in France 231
9. Terrorism and Revolution: Are They Ever Justified? 235
10. Populism, Revolution and the Radical Reformation 239

Index of Names 243
Index of Places 250

Pour mes petits enfants

SARAH MONTGOMERY

WILLIAM WARWICK MONTGOMERY

Pas encore théologiens, mais qui sait?

Introduction

Yes, as this book's subtitle has it, it's a "potpourri." That expression can be defined as "a mixture of dried petals and spices placed in a bowl to perfume a room." But, having just published a little culinary masterpiece (*A Gastronomic Vade-Mecum*).[1] I am thinking in terms of the secondary definition: "an unusual or interesting mixture of ingredients."

Either way, you will surely enjoy this collection of essays. They are unusual and interesting—and they will perfume your thinking as to ultimate issues.

John Warwick Montgomery
12 April 2020
Easter Day: the Feast of the Resurrection

---

[1] Irvine, CA: New Reformation Press / 1517: The Legacy Project, 2019.

Acknowledgements

All but three of the articles collected here saw the light of day elsewhere, the exceptions being "A Short and Easie Method with Postmodernists," "Computer Programming as an Assist to Apologetics," and "John Arndt Revisited," which are published for the first time in this book.

"The Place of Reason, with a Personal Testimony" appeared originally in *His Magazine* (Inter Varsity Christian Fellowship, U.S.A.), January, February, and March, 1966.

"Is the Universe Computable?" and "God and Gödel" were first published in *Philosophia Christi* (Evangelical Philosophical Society, U.S.A.), Vol. 19, No. 2 (2017) and Vol. 20, No. 1 (2018).

"Mathematics and Apologetics: Leonhard Euler" was the lead article in the October, 2018, issue of *Faith & Thought* (The Victoria Institute, U.K.).

"Did Jesus Physically Rise from the Dead?" appeared in a volume of popular apologetics essays under the editorship of The Revd Todd Wilken and published by the Issues, Etc. broadcasting system (2019).

"Law and Morality: Friends or Foes?" was the author's Inaugural Lecture on being appointed Professor of Law and Humanities at Luton University (now the University of Bedfordshire), England, and was distributed as a booklet by that University (1994).

"Millennium" was published in the major revision (ed. Geoffrey W. Bromiley) of ISBE: *The International Standard Bible Encyclopedia* (Eerdmans, 1986).

"Demon Possession: A Brief Commentary" appeared first as an invited reaction to Mark Crooks's paper, "On the Psychology of Demon Possession: The Occult Personality," in a Special Issue of *The Journal of Mind and Behavior*, Vol. 39, No. 4 (Autumn, 2018), and subsequently in the online publication *The Global Journal of Classical Theology* [www.globaljournalct.com].

"The World View of Johann Valentin Andreae" was delivered as an invitational lecture at a Bibliotheca Philosophica Hermetica symposium in Amsterdam and first published in *Das Erbe des Christian Rosenkreuz,* ed. F. A. Janssen (Amsterdam: In de Pelikaan, 1988).

"Choosing Books for a Theological Library" appeared originally under the title, "A Normative Approach to the Acquisition Problem in the Theological Seminary Library," in the American Theological Library Association's *Summary of Proceedings,* Vol. 16 (1962).

"Freedom of Expression and Respect for Beliefs in France" was first published in *Amicus Curiae: Journal of the Society for Advanced Legal Studies* [U.K.], Issue 99 (Autumn, 2014).

The other republished essays in the present book appeared initially in various issues of *Christian News* (New Haven, Missouri, U.S.A.).

The author thanks the above publications for their willingness to allow his contributions a wider availability under a single cover.

Part One: Doing Apologetics

1. The Place of Reason

Last year His *printed several articles by John Montgomery showing the historical evidences for Christianity. Shortly afterward, we received some strong letters attacking the idea that historical evidence has any place in presenting the validity of Christianity.*

In response to this, Dr. Montgomery has written two articles specially designed to point out the importance of the historical roots of Christianity and the value of presenting historical evidence when we witness.

The Christian student has many valuable approaches he can take to help his non-Christian friend believe in Christ—the superior value system of Christianity, the relevance of Christianity to daily problems, the clear presentation of sin and its consequences, the study of Scripture with the non-Christian, the frequent use of sacrificial prayer, etc.

This present article and its sequel next month do not reject these weapons in our arsenal, but are intended to show that all arguments for Christianity rest on the basic one—that God entered history as a physical person, living, dying, and rising again in history.

Part One

My articles on the historical truth of the Christian faith[1] brought a number of appreciative letters, and two others. The two correspondents were both troubled by the same thing: my apparent endeavor to *prove* Christianity to the non-Christian. One of the students, from Göttingen University, Germany, wrote: "When one sets out to prove the validity of the Christian religion, there is no longer a place for faith. Faith is commitment, not to what can be made easy to swallow by sane arguments, but to that radical voice which calls directly to us, 'I am the resurrection and the life, whosoever lives and believes in me shall never die' (John 11:25)."

In these words, the Göttingen student expresses a tension that Christians have felt in every age: the tension between reason and faith, between knowing and believing, between head knowledge and heart commitment. So important is this issue, especially for Christian students on secular university campuses today, that I have been asked to deal with it in a series of

---

[1] His, December, 1964-March, 1965; now available as a *His* reprint.

two *His* articles. This article will examine the most important negative criticisms frequently voiced against "defending the faith"; in the next issue I'll suggest Biblical justification for the necessity of apologetics.

Under Fire

Apologetics, that branch of theology concerned with the defense of Christian truth, has fallen on hard times. Though traditionally considered one of the three major branches of systematic theology, it is hardly represented at all in seminary curricula today. In light of the conflicts among liberals, neo-orthodox and orthodox, one would expect that apologetics would have vociferous champions as well as opponents, but the surprising fact is that few theologians of any stripe show real interest. Quite the contrary. Across the theological spectrum apologetics is viewed with a distinctly jaundiced eye. A person like C. S. Lewis contrasts like the proverbial sore thumb with the numerous theologians who, though they have difficulty agreeing on much else, unite in their opposition to "proving Christianity." Let's examine briefly but critically the attitude of three major theological positions in this matter; after doing so, we'll be in a good position to discover why so much of present-day Christendom finds it difficult to "give an answer to every man who asks you a reason for the hope that is in you" (I Peter 3:15).

Protestant Modernism

Liberalism's displeasure with efforts to defend Christianity was made explicit by Willard L. Sperry in his book, *"Yes, But—": The Bankruptcy of Apologetics* (1931). For Sperry and the modernism he represented, Christians who argued for Biblical truth over against scientific judgments were hopelessly deluded. When science spoke, theology was to listen; and in cases where Biblical statements seemed to be contradicted by scientific opinion, the former ought properly to be rejected or recast in scientifically accommodating terms.

Two basic assumptions underlay Sperry's argument. First, he held with modernism that Christianity is basically not a religion of propositional, objective truth, but a way of life focusing on subjective feeling (Schleiermacher) and moral action (the "social gospel"). Thus the defense of doctrine was beside the point; science is the source of cognitive data about the world, and theology should bow to its judgments. Second, Sperry believed that Christianity was not qualitatively different from other religions of the world. Since all religious roads lead up the mountain of truth, one should not try to convince others of Christianity's special claims.

The fallacy of the modernist view of Christianity is now generally recognized in theological circles. The New Testament most definitely presents the Christian faith as a matter of concrete, cognitive truth. Whether one looks at Christ's demands ("Believe me that I am in the Father and the Father in me"—John 14:10-11) or at the explicit creedal affirmations of the apostles ("I delivered unto you first of all that which I also received, how that Christ died for our sins according to the scriptures . . . and that he rose again the third day according to the scriptures"—I Cor. 15:1-4), one sees that Christianity is not primarily a matter of feeling or even of action, but a religion of factual belief—factual belief which, only because of its objective truth, yields genuine religious experience and meaningful social action.

Moreover, *contra* liberalism, the Christianity of the New Testament is presented as qualitatively different from all other religions, past or future. "I am the way, the truth, and the life: no man comes to the Father but by me," said Jesus (John 14:6); "there is none other name under heaven given among men whereby we must be saved," His apostles preached (Acts 4:12).

Thus modernism's opposition to apologetics falls to the ground, for it is based on a misunderstanding of the nature of Christianity itself. A nonfactual religion is of course not capable of factual defense; but Christianity, grounded in the fact of God's entrance into human history in the person of Christ, is the factual and defensible religion *par excellence.*

Barth and Bultmann

Though Karl Barth was largely responsible for the demise of modernism, he is as displeased with attempts to defend Christianity as the modernists have been.

True, he has firmly maintained the objective factual character of the saving events in Scripture (the incarnation, death, and resurrection of our Lord, etc.), and he has proclaimed these events as unique and Christianity as the final religious truth.

But the impact of Barth's return to the Bible has been considerably weakened by his efforts to remove the key events of the plan of salvation from secular examination. Early in his career he asserted that the miraculous events of the gospel (virgin birth, resurrection, etc.) took place in a "meta-historical" or "suprahistorical" realm (*Geschichte*)—a realm not subject to the canons of ordinary historical (*historische*) investigation.[2] More recently he has preferred not to make this distinction between realms of history, but he still affirms that the miraculous events of Scripture cannot be validated apart from prior belief in them.[3] Consistent with this approach, Barth holds that neither the Bible itself nor the saving events recorded in it can be objects of "proof" to the unbeliever; it is only by faith that the Bible assumes its function as God's Word in a man's life.

Rudolf Bultmann and his followers have removed Christian truth even farther from objective verification. For them, the essence of the Christian message does not lie in historical accounts of Christ's miraculous saving activity. (Biblical miracles are either denied outright or regarded as meaningless and therefore irrelevant to modern man.) The New Testament accounts of Christ are "demythologized" so as to yield their "true" core: the existential experience of salvation.

Christianity then becomes the proclamation of existential experience of salvation in the present, not a defense of supposedly objective truth in the past. Truth is known only in "personal encounter" with the Christ of faith, and efforts to shift attention to rational proofs are to be rejected as religiously and psychologically unrealistic.[4]

Both Barth and Bultmann unhappily share modernism's conviction that objective, factual investigation of the Bible will destroy traditional belief in its truthfulness. For Barth this has meant the walling off of salvation events from historical scrutiny; for Bultmann, the desertion of objective, historical truth for subjective, psychological conviction. But the Scripture asserts without qualification that "the Word became flesh" (John 1:14), that the factual character of the resurrection could convince even the faithless (John 20:24-29), and that "none of these things" (Christ's saving work and miracles) were hidden or done in a corner (Acts 26:26). In actual fact, it is not the defense of the gospel that makes God's truth irrelevant, but the refusal to defend it in the objective terms of the New Testament proclamation.[5]

---

[2] See Montgomery, "Karl Barth and Contemporary Theology of History," *Evangelical Theological Society Bulletin*, VI (May, 1963), pp. 39-49.

[3] Cf. my remarks in "Faith, History, and the Resurrection: A Panel Discussion," *Christianity Today*, IX (March 26, 1965), pp. 655-59.

[4] On Bultmann's existential philosophy of history, see Montgomery, *The Shape of the Past* (Minneapolis: Bethany, 1975), pp. 120-22.

[5] Cf. my report of Barth's lectures at the University of Chicago in 1962: "Barth in Chicago: Kerygmatic Strength and Epistemological Weakness," *Dialog: A Journal of Theology*, I (Autumn, 1962), pp. 56-57.

1. The Place of Reason

Misguided Orthodoxy

Some Christians, though thoroughly opposed to contemporary dilutions of the gospel message, have joined the hew and cry against defending the faith. Two varieties of orthodox opposition to apologetics can be singled out: the presuppositionalist and the fideist. Doubtless our Göttingen student represents one or the other, if not both, of these viewpoints.

For the orthodox presuppositionalist, a radical break exists between the worlds of the Christian and the non-Christian—a cleavage so fundamental that the Christian cannot convince the non-Christian of Christian truth. Some presuppositionalists argue that non-Christians cannot even discover secular facts; others, that non-Christians, though they can determine secular facts apart from faith, cannot interpret them properly; and still others, that the non-Christian, even if he can be led to revelational facts, will not interpret them properly when he does meet them.

But all presuppositionalists, whether of a strict or mild variety, are convinced that the non-Christian is incapable of arriving at a proper interpretation of saving truth. From this it follows that the Christian is attempting the impossible if he tries apologetically to persuade the non-Christian of the objective truthfulness of the gospel story. The non-Christian lives in his presuppositional world, and the Christian in his; and no amount of rational argument can break down the wall between.

The fideist goes even farther. He says: Not only is it intellectually impossible to convince the unbeliever of the truth of Christianity; it is unspiritual to try. Only God convinces men of Christianity's veracity, and you or I can do no more than to preach His gospel. To endeavor to argue with the unbeliever is to substitute human wisdom for the Spirit's working (I Corinthians 1), and thus misunderstand the depth of human depravity and of man's need to rely solely on God.

Our answer to these orthodox objections to apologetics will carry over to the next issue. (Note how much deeper they strike than the anti-apologetic views of modernism, neo-orthodoxy and Bultmann's existentialism.) Here, however, we can point to the essential difficulties in these views.

The presuppositionalist finds it impossible for non-Christian and Christian to experience common ground in the matter of revelational fact and interpretation. But consider: In the realm of secular fact (e.g. the chemical composition of water, the historical crossing of the Rubicon by Caesar), both Christian and non-Christian are capable of discovering truth and interpreting it; all university life is predicated on this assumption, and advances in human knowledge are indisputable evidence that even unregenerate man can understand the factual nature of the world and rationally interpret the data of his experience.

Now if we say that the events of Christ's life (or the Biblical events in general) are not subject to comparable treatment, then whether we like it or not we are actually divorcing "Christian facts" from secular, non-religious facts. Yet this is precisely what the incarnation denies! In Christ God truly entered the human sphere; and if this is the case, the human events of His life objectively display His deity and are not adequately explainable apart from it. Such factual and interpretive conclusions will certainly arise when Jesus' life is subjected to the investigative techniques applied to other historical events—provided, of course, that unempirical bias (e.g., against the possibility of the miraculous) is not allowed to distort the documentary picture. Thus Christ's resurrection is capable of examination by non-Christians as well as by Christians, and its factual character, when considered in light of the claims of the One raised from the dead, points not to a multiplicity of equally possible interpretations, but to a single "best" interpretation (i.e. to an interpretation most consistent with the data), namely the deity of Christ (John 2:18–22).

Of course, sinful self-interest may tempt the non-Christian to avoid the weight of evidence, just as self-interest has so frequently corrupted investigation in other, purely secular matters; but selfish perversions of data or interpretation can be made plain in the area of revelational fact no less than in the non-revelational sphere. For Christian revelation occurred in time—in the secular world. To miss this point is to miss the character of the incarnation. God came to earth and by manifold proofs showed Himself to men. We do Him and our fellowmen a disservice when we imply that His presence among us was a docetic phantasm, open only to the subjective eye of faith and not to objective examination by every seeker for truth.

Yet are we not unspiritually arrogating to human reason a work that only God's Word and Holy Spirit can perform? Hardly, when it is God's word that records the historical facts and offers the soundest historical interpretations relating to Christ's gospel. As for the Spirit, He works through that very Word to convince men of God's truth, so in reality we bring men under His convicting aegis as we point them to the Biblical evidences for Christ's truth. More, however, needs to be said in this regard, and we shall do so as we consider the specific Biblical mandates for defending the faith.

Part Two

Last month's article dealt with Christian apologetics, that theological area devoted to the evidences for the truth of Christianity. Both it and this one were written in response to criticism against my article on the historical basis of the Christian faith. The critics maintained that we should not try to present historical reasons for believing in Christ. The February article began and ended with the question as to whether "proofs" for the gospel do not militate against "faith."

The question this month is whether the defender of the faith manifests psychological defensiveness in trying to support what only Holy-Spirit-produced faith can reveal as true. To answer this question (one that has especially troubled Christian students on secular campuses), we must take a close look both at the Biblical attitude toward verifying religious truth and at the contemporary university situation. It is in that academic context that the Christian student has the responsibility and privilege of bearing witness to his Lord.

Truth and the New Testament

In the deepest sense, the Bible identifies truth with the person of Jesus Christ, the God-man who came to earth to die for the sins of the world (John 14:6). Thus, knowing the truth ultimately depends on one's personal relationship to Christ: "If you continue in my [Christ's] word, then you are indeed my disciples, and you shall know the truth and the truth shall make you free" (John 8:31-32).

But the question immediately arises, what of those who hesitate to enter into such a personal relationship because they doubt the validity of Jesus' claims? Are they to be regarded as dishonest persons endeavoring to hide wilful opposition to Christ under the cloak of alleged intellectual doubts? If so, we would expect them to receive short shrift in the New Testament. Like the hypocritical Pharisees, they ought to be condemned as "whited sepulchres" in order that they might be brought to their senses and to a recognition of their moral perversity.

But this is not the case. Let's consider the key example of Thomas, whose confrontation with the risen Christ forms a climactic event in John's Gospel.[6] In 20:24-29, just prior to John's summing up of his purpose for writing his book, Thomas is presented as one who would not believe the

---

[6] Cf. Montgomery, "The Fourth Gospel Yesterday and Today," *Concordia Theological Monthly*, *XXXIV* (April, 1963), 197-222.

other disciples' testimony that they had seen the resurrected Christ. From this the conclusion is inescapable that Thomas, in spite of his contact with Jesus during His earthly ministry, had not yet become a Christian, since belief in the resurrection is an essential element of the saving gospel (Romans 4:23-25; I Corinthians 15).

Thomas demanded concrete, empirical proof of Jesus' claim to rise again after three days. He would not be convinced, he said, unless he could put his finger into Jesus' nailprints and thrust his hand into the wound made when Jesus' side was pierced.

And what did Jesus do? Did He reject Thomas' demand for objective proof on the ground (so often used by opponents of apologetics) that such demands are really sinful cover-ups for wilful refusal to believe? Not at all. Jesus appeared to Thomas and provided him with exactly the empirical evidence that he needed to become convinced of His deity. Thomas' cry, "My Lord and my God," is perhaps the strongest confession of Jesus' divinity in the entire Bible; and it was spoken because our Lord was willing, in His grace, specifically to satisfy Thomas' need for concrete evidence that He had risen from the dead.

Though Christ told Thomas that it would have been better for him to have believed without seeing (i.e., that he should have believed the testimony of his fellow disciples who had already seen the Lord), this rebuke was not given as a substitute for the proof Thomas needed. Rather, it followed both Jesus' appearance to Thomas and Thomas' affirmation of Jesus' deity. Only after Jesus brought Thomas to faith through graciously giving him evidence of His resurrection did He point out to him where his faith had been lacking.

Paul's Areopagus address in Acts 17 gives another clear example that in the New Testament the honest intellectual problems of unbelievers are respected and dealt with on their own ground. At Athens the apostle confronted Epicurean and Stoic philosophers. The cynical and self-indulgent Epicureans, whom E. M. Blaiklock has called the Sadducees among the Greeks,[7] were not Paul's focus of attention. Note that Paul's divine Master also had little patience with the intellectually dishonest Sadducees of Israel (cf. Matthew 22:29,34). But with the ethically sensitive Stoics it was different. In order to witness effectively to them, Paul began where they were—with their superstitious belief in an unknown god—and, through an

---

[7] Blaiklock, who was professor and chairman of the department of classics at the University of Auckland, New Zealand, made this point in delivering the Annual Wheaton College Graduate School Lectures, October 21-22, 1964.

appeal to truths expressed by their own poets (Paul quotes Stoic sentiments found in Cleanthes, Aratus, and Epimenides), he called for repentance and proclaimed judgment of the world "in righteousness by that man [Jesus] whom God has ordained, whereof he has given assurance to all men, in that he has raised him from the dead" (Acts 17:31).

Here we have one of the best New Testament examples of missionary and apologetic skill. "He who as a missionary will test the various elements in this speech will find that they all produce their effect," wrote missions specialist Warneck.[8] Indeed, as Richard Longenecker has recently emphasized, Paul's concern to be "all things lo all men" in order to bring them to a saving knowledge of Christ (I Corinthians 9:22) is the key to his entire ministry, and "from the days of the Fathers, Paul's Athenian experience as recorded in Acts 17 has been cited as the illustration of the 'all things to all men' principle as it worked out in the Gentile situation."[9] Like his Lord, Paul was willing to operate on the unbeliever's own terms. He did not position himself outside of the unbeliever's frame of reference and preach at him (Paul Tillich would say, "throw stones at his head"); rather, he literally became all things to all honest seekers, whether Jews or Greeks, so as to bring them to the light of Christ.[10]

How can Jesus and Paul take such an attitude toward truth, an attitude which encourages the believer to enter the non-Christian's frame of reference and convince him that the gospel is veracious? The New Testament does this primarily because, unlike much of contemporary theology, it sees the full implications of the incarnation. If, as we noted last time, God *really* became man in Jesus Christ, then His entrance into the human sphere is open to examination by non-Christian and Christian alike, and the honest doubter will find compelling evidence in support or Christ's claims. This is why the New Testament makes so much of the eyewitness contact the early church had with its Lord (cf. I John 1:1-4). The church of the New

---

[8] J. Warneck, *Paulus im Lichte der heutigen Heidenmission* (1914), pp. 73-74. Cf. Olaf Moe, *The Apostle Paul: His Life and Work*, trans. L. A. Vigness (Minneapolis: Augsburg, 1950), pp. 279-97.

[9] Longenecker, *Paul, Apostle of Liberty* (New York: Harper, 1964), p. 230.

[10] On the relation of the Areopagus address to I Corinthians 1, F. F. Bruce rightly says: "The popular idea that his [Paul's] determination, when he arrived in Corinth, to know nothing there 'save Jesus Christ, and him crucified,' was the result of disillusionment with the line of approach he had attempted at Athens, has little to commend it" (*Commentary on the Book of Acts* ["New International Commentary on the New Testament"; Grand Rapids, Mich.; Eerdmans, 1954], p. 365). See also N. B. Stonehouse, *Paul before the Areopagus* (Grand Rapids, Mich.: Eerdmans, 1957), where this point is made *in extenso*.

Testament is not an esoteric, occult, gnostic sect whose teachings are demonstrable only to initiates; it is the religion of the incarnate God, at whose death the veil of the temple was rent from top to bottom, opening holy truth to all who would seek it.

Apologetic Need

The world of the twentieth century, growing steadily smaller as communication revolutions succeed each other, displays a religious pluralism experientially unknown to our grandfathers, and remarkably similar to the heterogeneous religious situation in the Roman Empire in the first century. Sects and cults proliferate; philosophies of life, explicit and implicit, vie for our attention; and older, previously dormant religions, such as Buddhism and Islam,[11] are engaged in vigorous proselytizing. All about us ultimate concerns spring up, each claiming to be more ultimate, more worthy of our total commitment, than the other. In the university world the pluralistic cacophony is louder than perhaps anywhere else: materialism, idealism, pragmatism, communism, hedonism, mysticism, existentialism, and a hundred other options present themselves to the college student in classroom, bull-session, student organization, political rally, and social activity.

What is the non-Christian to do, when amid this din he hears the Christian message? Are we Christians so naive as to think that he will automatically, *ex opere operato*, accept Christianity as true and put away world views contradicting it? And if we call out to him, "Just try Christianity and you will find that it proves itself experientially," do we really think that he will not at the same time hear precisely the same subjective-pragmatic appeal from numerous other quarters?

What is he to do? Alphabetize the "ultimate concerns" and try them serially? If so, he must at least try agnosticism, atheism, Baha'i, and Buddhism (Mahayana and Hinayana!) before coming to Christianity, and as Arthur Koestler and others who have extricated themselves painfully from Marxist commitment will tell us, movement from one ultimate concern to another is a psychologically devastating experience. There is every chance that by the time the non-Christian comes to try Christianity, he will be so jaded psychologically that he will be incapable of recognizing ultimate truth when he actually meets it.

---

[11] Cf. Montgomery, "The Apologetic Approach of Muhammed Ali and Its Implications for Christian Apologetics," Muslim World, LI (April, 1961), 111–22; and author's "Corrigendum" in the July, 1961 Muslim World.

1. The Place of Reason

Evidently, what is necessary for effective Christian witness in a pluralistic university world is an objective apologetic—a "reason for the hope that is in you" that will give the non-Christian clear ground for experientially trying the Christian faith before all other options. Absolute proof of the truth of Christ's claims is available only in personal relationship with Him; but contemporary man has every right to expect us to offer solid reasons for making such a total commitment. The apologetic task is justified not as a rational substitute for faith, but as a ground for faith; not as a replacement for the Spirit's working, but as a means by which the objective truth of God's Word can be made clear so that men will heed it as the vehicle of the Spirit who convicts the world through its message.

The analytical philosopher Antony Flew, in developing a parable from a tale told by John Wisdom, illustrates how meaningless to the non-Christian are religious assertions incapable of being tested objectively:

> Once upon a time two explorers came upon a clearing in the jungle. In the clearing were growing many flowers and many weeds. One explorer says, "Some gardener must tend this plot." The other disagrees, "There is no gardener." So they pitch their tents and set a watch. No gardener is ever seen. "But perhaps he is an invisible gardener." So they set up a barbedwire fence. They electrify it. They patrol with bloodhounds. (For they remember how H. G. Wells' *The Invisible Man* could be both smelt and touched though he could not be seen.) But no shrieks ever suggest that some intruder has received a shock. No movements of the wire ever betray an invisible climber. The bloodhounds never give cry. Yet still the Believer is not convinced. "But there is a gardener, invisible, insensible to electric shocks, a gardener who has no scent and makes no sound, a gardener who comes secretly to look after the garden which he loves." At last the Sceptic despairs, "But what remains of your original assertion? Just how does what you call an invisible, intangible, eternally elusive gardener differ from an imaginary gardener or even from no gardener at all?"[12]

This parable is a damning judgment on all religious truth-claims save that of the Christian faith.[13] For in Christianity we do not have merely an allegation that the garden of this world is tended by a loving Gardener; we have the actual, empirical entrance of the Gardener into the human scene

---

[12] Antony Flew, "Theology and Falsification," in *New Essays in Philosophical Theology*, ed. Flew and Macintyre (London: SCM Press, 1955), p. 96.

[13] On the issue of theological verification, cf. Montgomery, "Inspiration and Inerrancy: A New Departure," *Evangelical Theological Society Bulletin*, VIII (Spring, 1965), pp. 45-75; and reprinted in several of the author's books, e.g., *Crisis in Lutheran Theology* (3 vols.; Irvine, CA: 1517 Legacy/New Reformation Press, 2017).

in the person of Christ (cf. John 20:14–15), and this entrance is verifiable by way of His resurrection.

We must present clear testimony to the Thomases and to the Stoics of our day that God did indeed come in the flesh and "showed himself alive after his passion by many infallible proofs" (Acts 1:3). Under no circumstances should we retreat into a presuppositionalism or a fideism which would rob our fellow students of the opportunity to consider the Christian faith seriously with head as well as heart. Our apologetic task is not fulfilled until we remove the intellectual offenses that allow so many non-Christians to reject the gospel with scarcely a hearing. We must bring them to the only legitimate offense: the offense of the cross. We must make clear to them beyond a shadow of doubt that if they reject the Lord of glory, it will be by reason of wilful refusal to accept His grace, not because His Word is incapable of withstanding the most searching intellectual examination.

When the Greeks of our day come seeking Jesus (John 12:20–21), let us make certain that they find Him.

2. Is the Universe Computable?

In a recent compendium of articles concerning the work of the consummate mathematical theorist and code-breaker Alan Turing, the following appears: "Alan Turing never said that the physical universe is computable, and nor do any of his technical results entail that it is. Some computer scientists and physicists seem infuriated by the suggestion that the physical universe might be incomputable; but it is an important issue, and the truth is that we simply do not know."[1]

Why should there be such a negative reaction on the part of "some computer scientists and physicists"?

Two reasons appear possible. We shall deal with each in turn.

First, the evidence for a completely materialistic, mechanistic (and therefore entirely computable) universe is so powerful that any other approach should be rejected out-of-hand.

However, it should be obvious that the universe is so vast that no argument asserting that only materialistic explanations are possible must *perforce* fail. At least since Einstein, the universe cannot be regarded as a tight playing field where we humans know all the rules (or can potentially discover them).

But have not the materialists been successful in showing the non-applicability of "spiritual" claims to explain phenomena? In the realm of spiritualism and professional magic, the successes have indeed been impressive. The debunking of spirit-explanations has been very important to the history, for example, of the Society for Psychical Research.[2]

The difficulty, however, lies in the welter of phenomena still inexplicable materialistically. One thinks, for example, of the after-death appearances of C. S. Lewis to New Testament scholar and translator J. B. Phillips:

> "The late C. S. Lewis, whom I did not know very well and had only seen in the flesh once, but with whom I had corresponded a fair amount, gave me an unusual experience. A few days after his death, while I was watching television, he 'appeared' sitting in a chair within a few feet of me, and spoke a few words which were particularly relevant to the difficult circumstances

---

[1] Jack Copeland, Mark Sprevak, and Oron Shagrir, "Is the Whole Universe a Computer," in *The Turing Guide*, ed. Jack Copeland, *et al.* (Oxford: Oxford University Press, 2017), pp. 445–62.

[2] See, Montgomery, *Principalities and Powers: The World of the Occult* (Minneapolis, MN: Bethany, 1973).

through which I was passing. He was ruddier in complexion than ever, grinning all over his face and, as the old-fashioned saying has it, positively glowing with health. The interesting thing to me was that I had not been thinking about him at all. [. . .] A week later, this time when I was in bed, reading before going to sleep, he appeared again, even more rosily radiant than before, and repeated to me the same message, which was very important to me at the time. I was a little puzzled by this, and I mentioned it to a certain saintly bishop who was then living in retirement here in Dorset. His reply was, "My dear J__ __, this sort of thing is happening all the time."[3]

Even more significant are the considerable number of historical miracle-claims *not reasonably capable of materialistic explanation*. Chief among them is the resurrection of Jesus Christ from the dead. We cannot here go into the detailed evidence (it is readily available elsewhere), but we note simply the presence of reliable witnesses (1) to Jesus' death and burial, and (2) to his resurrection appearances—of his physical body—during a forty-day period following his crucifixion.[4]

Only one such proof is enough to deep-six a universally applicable materialistic metaphysic.

So—if materialism cannot be established as a universal explanation of things, why become incensed over a non-computable universe?

To be sure, one might argue that the issue is not in fact *materialism*, but *mechanism*: regardless of whether everything is at root material, the universe is a machine and is therefore in principle computable.

Wittgenstein rightly observed that logic (and therefore mathematics and computation) does not show us the substance of the world; it is like the scaffolding of a building—it shows us the "shape" of the world, but not what it consists of.[5] 2+2=4, but we are not told from the mathematical formula (or by any computer program) what the 2's are: they could be trees—or they could be tooth fairies.

---

[3] J. B. Phillips, *Ring of Truth* [New York: Macmillan, 1967), pp. 118–19.

[4] See Montgomery, *History, Law and Christianity* (3d ed.; Irvine, CA: 1517 Legacy/New Reformation Press, 2014); and *Christ As Centre and Circumference* (Bonn, Germany: Verlag für Kultur und Wissenschaft, 2012).

[5] *Tractatus Logico-Philosophicus*, 6.124. "The 'scaffolding'" of the world (6.124a) is the same as the logical form of the world. In saying that logic exhibits (*darstellt*) this scaffolding, Wittgenstein is reminding us of his point, by now familiar, that logical propositions are concerned only with logical form and so, in a sense, have no subject-matter. Yet he insists that logic nevertheless has a 'connexion' with the world (6,124c), so that although logical propositions are not about the objects of the

2. Is the Universe Computable?

It follows that for a human being to show that the entire universe is computable, he or she would have to demonstrate that it is in fact no more than a machine (the same impossible problem as showing that the universe is nothing but materialistic), *and* that one has arrived at the nature of the cosmic program totally defining it.

Charles Babbage, in arguing for the legitimacy of miracle in a universe of physical laws, used the analogy of a computer that only rarely, and seemingly randomly, produces a strange, apparently miraculous, result. If one knew the complete program, the result would be perfectly understandable; but not otherwise. Babbage was saying that only God possesses the universal program (and thus miracles to us are not miracles to him).[6]

It follows that from a mechanistic point-of-view, human subjects would not be able to account for miraculous occurrences or be capable of arriving at a complete computational description of the universe. It is therefore irrelevant whether the computabilist is a materialist or a mechanist: in both instances, his *Weltanschauung* is fideistic, the product of blind faith.

This brings us to the second possible understanding of the "infuriation" produced by a non-computability viewpoint.

Is it not likely that the computablist is dreadfully threatened by the reality of a non-materialistic, non-mechanistic universe—one that he or she would not, even in principle, be able to explain? It has been said, "God created us in his image, and ever since we have been returning the compliment." That is to say: the self-centered, fallen human race wants to *be God*, and nothing is more irritating than having to admit that that will not work. Human egoism is in permanent tension with human finitude. We want to be God and to be able to explain—compute—everything. But our finitude (and the real history of things) makes this simply a non-option. So we have a psychological fit or two, and claim that—in spite of all the solid evidence to the contrary, *we really can* in principle explain the entire universe in its amazing complexity and diversity.

Suggestion: Grow up. Maturity consists of recognizing the way things in fact *are*; not endeavoring mythically to turn the universe into the kind of place we would like it to be, centered on ourselves. Freud had it back-

---

world, they still 'show something about the world' (6.124d)," (Max Black, *A Companion to Wittgenstein's 'Tractatus'* [Cambridge: Cambridge University Press, 1971], p. 329).

[6] See Montgomery, "Computer Origins and the Defense of the Faith," in his *Christ As Centre and Circumference* (op. cit.) and in 56/3 *Perspectives on Science and Christian Faith*, 189–203 (September, 2004).

wards (*Moses and Monotheism*): the myth-making is not on the part of religious believers; it is the mechanistic materialist who mythically creates a world of total computability and explainability that will pander to his or her ego and wish-fulfilment.

3. God and Gödel

This article represents a *mea culpa*—an admission of a change in the author's apologetics perspective on the ontological argument and the utility of mathematical proof for God's existence. A series of articles in *Christian Century* was titled, "How My Mind Has Changed."[1]

Though I myself have been published in that liberal theological magazine,[2] I never contributed to the mind-changing series. One might respond, "Of course not. You are a theological conservative, and conservatives never change their minds."

There is some truth in that retort, but it is not because Bible believers are egomaniacs who think that they never err. It is, rather, because they hold to a once-for-all, unchanging revelation that fixes the boundaries of one's theology. Indeed, the theological conservative, owing to a serious belief in original sin and its cognitively negative effects, is far more willing to admit fallibility than is the religious liberal—who so often assumes that his liberal ideology can't be wrong.[3]

Here is the position I have taken over the years on Anselm's ontological argument:

> Although a primitive form of the ontological argument for God's existence can be found in St. Augustine, St. Anselm of Canterbury provided its classic formulation in the 11th century. The argument purports to prove God's existence from the concept of God itself: God is "that than which no greater can be conceived"; he must therefore have all properties; and since existence is a property, God exists! The argument rests on the idealistic assumption that ideas have reality untouched by the phenomenal world (so rational idealists have been somewhat comfortable with it), but the overwhelming fallacy in the argument is simply that "existence" is not a property alongside other properties; existence is the name we give to something that in fact has

---

[1] The articles were published in book form as How My Mind Has Changed: Essays from the Christian Century, ed. David Heim (Eugene, OR: Wipf and Stock, 2012).

[2] John Warwick Montgomery, "Shirer's Re-Hitlerizing of Luther," Christian Century, December 12, 1962; reprinted in J. W. Montgomery, In Defense of Martin Luther (Milwaukee: Northwestern Publishing House, 1970).

[3] Cf. John Warwick Montgomery, "Bibliographical Bigotry," in Suicide of Christian Theology (Minneapolis: Bethany, 1970).

properties. To determine whether a something (God?) exists, we need to investigate the empirical evidences of its/his reality.[4]

As a consequence, I have roundly criticized attempts to present mathematical proofs of God's existence.[5] If mathematics is a special case of deductive logic, and therefore purely formal, it could not be capable of demonstrating any synthetic, empirical fact—including the existence of Deity (surely a factual matter, since any God worthy of the name would not be a mere logical formality, but a reality able to save real sinners from their factually fallen condition).

But I have been forced to rethink the entire issue as a result of a short piece in a little book of literary essays by a contemporary French philosopher.[6] He argues as follows:

> How did we know that we were so imperfect? From where came that sad realization that we didn't really know anything. [...] And yet, at the same time, we are conscious of perfection—a condition that has never been ours, but in comparison with which our situation is especially pitiable. The idea of the perfect is within us.

Delecroix illustrates with the analogy of a piece of paper torn in two. If we have only one half, we know that another half is needed to arrive at the complete sheet. But what gives us the idea of completeness or "perfection"? Why would we limit our addition to a certain size and not extend the paper to infinity?

> And I know when I try to add a piece that doesn't fit that it isn't right—that it clearly does not correspond to a proper sheet. [...] This idea of completeness was in us; we were not able to create it ourselves. That idea was placed there by a causal factor extrinsic to us. And that factor must exist, since it cannot be less than its real effects, that is to say, a perfect Being, infinite *per se*.

---

[4] Montgomery, "A Short History of Apologetics," in K. A. Swets and Chad V. Meister (eds.), Christian Apologetics: An Anthology of Primary Sources (Grand Rapids, MI: Zondervan, 2012), 21–8.

[5] E.g., my critique of Marvin L. Bittinger's The Faith Equation: Mathematical Evidence for Christianity, 2nd ed. (Altamonte Springs, FL: Advantage Inspirational, 2010). This critique appears in the Global Journal of Classic Theology 15, no. 1 (2018), http://www.globaljournalct.com.

[6] Vincent Delecroix, La prevue de l'existence de Dieu: monologues (Arles, France: Actes Sud, 2004), 26–8.

3. God and Gödel

Now, this is a kind of ontological argument, though dressed in empirical, existential clothing. It got me thinking. [. . .]

I have frequently employed Wittgenstein's description of mathematics as "scaffolding"—not the world, but showing the "shape" of the world, as scaffolding gives the shape of a structure but not what it is in fact made of.[7] But if the scaffolding precisely fits the building, does it not tell us something empirical about the building? Suppose mathematical formulae were to accord exactly with complex, empirical phenomena in the empirical world, would that not say something as to the reality to which the mathematics was pointing?

And that is precisely the case. Take just the example of the Fibonacci Sequence. The Sequence was known to classical Indian mathematicians and entered the West by way of the *Liber Abaci* (1202) of Leonardo of Pisa, known as Fibonacci. In the Fibonacci sequence, each number is the sum of the two preceding numbers: 3, 5, 8, 13, 21, 34, 55, 89, 144 . . .). Expressed as a sequence formula: $F_n = F_{n-1} + F_{n-1}$ . . .

Fine. But this formula turns out to describe a host of natural phenomena. Here are just a few examples: the lily has three petals; buttercups have five; the chicory twenty-one, and the daisy often has thirty-four or fifty-five. Or consider spiral patterns in nature: the number of a pineapple's diagonals is eight in one direction and thirteen in the other. Pinecones have either eight spirals from one side and thirteen from the other—or either five from one side and eight from the other. The heads of sunflowers display two sets of curves; the number of spirals is in general either twenty-one and thirty-four, or fifty-five and eighty-nine, or eighty-nine, and one hundred forty-four.

If the Fibonacci sequence were merely a formal notion, limited to validation by showing that it can be derived from the axioms of pure mathematics, it would hardly tell us anything about the empirical world. But, in

---

[7] Wittgenstein, Tractatus Logico-Philosophicus, 6.124. "The 'scaffolding' of the world (6.124a) is the same as the logical form of the world. In saying that logic exhibits (darstellt) this scaffolding, Wittgenstein is reminding us of his point, by now familiar, that logical propositions are concerned only with logical form and so, in a sense, have no subject-matter. Yet he insists that logic nevertheless has a 'connexion' with the world (6.124c), so that although logical propositions are not about the objects of the world, they still 'show something about the world' (6.124d)" (Max Black, A Companion to Wittgenstein's 'Tractatus' (New York: Cambridge University Press, 1971), 329). Cf. Montgomery, "A Computable Universe?," Philosophia Christi 19 (2017): 463–5; reprinted in Montgomery, Always Be Ready: A Primer on Defending the Faith (Irvine, CA: NRP Books/1517 The Legacy Project, 2018).

fact, it describes relationships in botany (and a host of other fields). Clearly, it does not tell us what kind of flowers or plants we are going to encounter, but it does tell that there is a world with a certain organization. That is to say, it gives us information as to the nature of the world's existence.

Now, if mathematics can assist us to know more about botany and other empirical fields of endeavor, why can it not in principle speak to the theological question of God's existence? Even if the critiques of Anselm's ontological proof are correct, could not a mathematical demonstration in ontological style having to do with God's existence be valid anyway?

The classic effort along this line is, of course, that of the great twentieth-century mathematician Kurt Gödel, who left it among his papers at his death.[8] The logical validity of Gödel's proof has recently been confirmed.[9]

The following is a corrected, contemporary version of the proof:[10]

A1 Either a property or its negation is positive, but not both:

$$\forall \phi [P(\neg \phi) \leftrightarrow \neg P(\phi)]$$

A2 A property necessarily implied by a positive property is positive:

$$\forall \phi \forall \psi [(P(\phi) \wedge \Box \forall x [\phi(x) \rightarrow \psi(x)]) \rightarrow P(\psi)]$$

T1 Positive properties are possibly exemplified:

$$\forall \phi [P(\phi) \rightarrow \Diamond \exists x \phi(x)]$$

---

[8] On Gödel, see John W. Dawson, Jr., *Logical Dilemmas: The Life and Work of Kurt Gödel* (Boca Raton, FL: CRC Press/Taylor and Francis, 2005); Dawson is one of the editors of Gödel's Collected Works. Cf. also Douglas Hofstadter, *Gödel, Escher, Bach* (New York: Vintage, 1980).

[9] Christoph Benzmüller and Bruno W. Paleo, "Formalization, Mechanization and Automation of Gödel's Proof of God's Existence," https://arxiv.org/abs/1308.4526. This abstract, uploaded to arXiv on August, 21, 2013, was the first communication of the computer-assisted formalization of Gödel's ontological proof. It has been superceded by Christoph Benzmüller and Bruno W. Paleo, "Automating Gödel's Ontological Proof of God's Existence with Higher-order Automated Theorem Provers," *Frontiers in Artificial Intelligence and Applications* 263 (2014): 93–8; available online at http://ebooks.iospress.nl/publication/36922. See the references (p. 98) for related work.

[10] Ibid.

3. God and Gödel

D1 A *God-like* being possesses all positive properties:

$$G(x) \leftrightarrow \forall\phi[P(\phi) \rightarrow \phi(x)]$$

A3 The property of being God-like is positive:

$$P(G)$$

C Possibly, God exists:

$$\Diamond\exists x G(x)$$

A4 Positive properties are necessarily positive:

$$\forall\phi[P(\phi) \rightarrow \Box P(\phi)]$$

D2 An *essence* of an individual is a property possessed by it and necessarily implying any of its properties:

$$\phi \text{ ess. } x \leftrightarrow \phi(x) \wedge \forall\psi(\psi(x) \rightarrow \Box\forall y(\phi(y) \rightarrow \psi(y)))$$

T2 Being God-like is an essence of any God-like being:

$$\forall x[G(x) \rightarrow G \text{ ess. } x]$$

D3 *Necessary existence* of an individual is the necessary exemplification of all its essences:

$$NE(x) \leftrightarrow \forall\phi[\phi \text{ ess. } x \rightarrow \Box\exists y\phi(y)]$$

A5 Necessary existence is a positive property:

$$P(NE)$$

T3 Necessarily, God exists:

$$\Box\exists x G(x)$$

Here is a very helpful explanation of Gödel's argument.[11]

> Gödel's ontological proof, an alleged proof of God's existence, is a proof in higher order S5 modal predicate logic. The proof proceeds by defining a concept of P-properties, where P is intended to be interpreted as Positive or Perfection or something along those lines.
>
> So let's first look at this concept of P-properties. They are constrained by 5 axioms:
>
> 1. $\{P(\phi) \wedge \Box \forall x[\phi(x) \Rightarrow \psi(x)]\} \Rightarrow P(\psi)$.
>
> This axiom states that if ϕ is a positive property and it is necessarily the case that having the property ϕ implies having the property ψ, then ψ is a positive property.
>
> It can be understood as the claim that only positive things follow from positive things. Good properties cannot entail bad properties.
>
> 2. $P(\neg \phi) \Leftrightarrow \neg P(\phi)$.
>
> This axiom states that any property ϕ either is positive or its negation is positive. In other words, the concept of positive properties partitions the set of all properties. There are no such things as neutral properties.
>
> 3. $P(G)$.
>
> This axiom states that the property G is a positive property. We will take a look at G later on, but its intended meaning is Godlike.
>
> 4. $P(\phi) \Rightarrow \Box P(\phi)$.
>
> This axiom states that positive property is necessarily positive. You might say this axiom embodies the claim of objective good. Positive and non-positive are the same in all possible worlds.
>
> 5. $P(E)$.

---

[11] John Gould, reply to "Can somebody explain Kurt Godel's proof of the existence of God?" Quora, April 22, 2017, https://www.quora.com/Can-somebody-explain-Kurt-Godel's-proof-of-the-existence-of-God.

3. God and Gödel

This axiom states that the property E is a positive property. We will take a look at that definition later, but its intended meaning is essential or indispensable. This basically states the claim that existence is better than nonexistence.

Now, the notions of possible and necessary in modal logic are defined in terms of possible world semantics. To say that something is possible is to say that there is a world reachable from this world where it is true. To say that it is necessary is to say that it is true in all worlds reachable from ours.

This is relevant to understanding the first theorem 'The possibility of Good':

$$P(\phi) \implies \Diamond \exists x \phi(x)$$

This theorem can be read as: if ϕ is a positive property then it is possible that there exists something which has that property.

Why is this true? Well, if ϕ were a positive property, but necessarily nothing had that property, in symbols $P(\phi) \land \Box \neg \exists x \phi(x)$, then in term of possible worlds, that would mean that there is no world reachable from ours that has an object that satisfies property ϕ. So in all such worlds $\phi(x) \implies \psi(x)$ is true, because $\phi(x)$ is false and *false* $\implies \psi(x) \equiv$ *true*.

Now ψ is an arbitrary property, and by axiom 1, it would then follow that such an arbitrary ψ must be a positive property. In particular we could choose $\psi \iff \neg \phi$. This however would directly contradict axiom 2, which states that if ϕ is positive then $\neg \phi$ is not. Therefore, under the assumption that ϕ is a positive property, it follows that $\neg \Box \neg \exists x \phi(x)$, which is equivalent to the theorem.

Now we move on to the definition of the predicate G, godlike.

$$G(x) \iff \forall \phi [P(\phi) \implies \phi(x)].$$

This definition can be read as: an entity is Godlike if and only if it has all good properties.

If we apply the previous theorem to the predicate G, we get the proposition

$$P(G) \implies \Diamond \exists x G(x), \text{ and we also have } P(G), \text{ by axiom 3}.$$

So we now have the following theorem "No hard atheism"

$$\Diamond \exists x G(x).$$

This can be read as: The existence of a godlike entity is possible.

Now the plot thickens with the definition of the essence of something. This is not an easy definition,

$$\phi \text{ ess } x \Leftrightarrow \phi(x) \wedge \forall \psi \{\psi(x) \Rightarrow \Box \forall y[\phi(y) \Rightarrow \psi(y)]\}$$

This definition can be read as follows: To say that a property ϕ is the essence of a thing x, is to say:

> x has property ϕ

for all other properties ψ that x might have, they must be necessarily implied by ϕ, which means that any object having property ϕ must also have property ψ, in all possible worlds.

So an essence of a thing is a property that entails all other properties. This definition is used in the following theorem "God has no Hair."

$$G(x) \Rightarrow G \text{ ess } x.$$

This theorem can be read as follows: if an entity is Godlike, then being Godlike is an essence of that object.

Now why is this true?

Well remember, to be godlike is defined as having all of positive properties that exist and none of the others. And axiom 4 tells us that any positive property is necessarily positive, which means that if a property is positive in a world, then it must be positive in any possible world.

So to have a positive property in this world is to have it in all possible worlds. And because any property implied by a positive property is positive, this means that in all possible worlds all of these consequences also hold. But that is the very definition of essence given above.

Now for the last definition. The definition of essentiality.

$$E(x) \Leftrightarrow \forall \phi [\phi \text{ ess } x \Rightarrow \Box \exists y \phi(y)].$$

This definition can be read as follows: to say that an entity x is essential in this world is to say that for all essences of x, there exists in all possible

3. God and Gödel

worlds some entity that has that property. In other words something is essential if it must exist in all possible worlds with its essences.

This definition and axiom 5 are used to prove the main theorem "God necessarily exists."

$$\Box \exists Gx\, G(x)$$

Any godlike entity has all positive properties, including the property of essentiality, which axiom 5 defines as a positive property. So by the very definition of essentiality any possible world must have an entity with the essences of this godlike entity, which by the No hair theorem is having the property G, i.e. to be Godlike.

So if there is something godlike in a world, then he necessarily exists in all possible worlds.

In symbols $\exists x\, G(x) \Rightarrow \Box \exists x\, G(x)$.

We also know from "No hard atheism theorem" that it is possible that there exists a god-like entity. So there is a possible world in which this godlike entity exists. And in that world he necessarily exists. Which means that in our world it is possible that this godlike entity necessarily exists, in symbols:

$$\Diamond \Box \exists x G(x).$$

Now we use one of the hallmark axioms of S5: $\Diamond \Box A \Rightarrow \Box A$, which gives us the conclusion.

Note well: one can no longer argue, as those attempting to refute Gödel's proof have consistently done, that its formal validity does nothing to show God's existence in the empirical, factual realm. True enough, the proof is another example of a mathematico-logical, axiomatic argument, the validity of which can be proven or disproven by showing the consistency or inconsistency of its conclusions with its premises. But just as the axiomatic character of the Fibonacci sequence does not belie its direct applicability to botanical and other empirical phenomena, so Gödel's proof can be another illustration that axiomatic, logical arguments can not only have formal validity but at the same time represent empirical reality.

    The scaffolding must tell us something factual about the actual building. Here, it does not give us the character of God, but it does give us his existence by way of an understanding of positive qualities. As for God's *nature*—his values, his creative demands, his saving work—a revelation from the Divine source is absolutely essential. A finite, fallen human race could never arrive at those essentials apart from a Word from God himself. But this does not preclude an ontological proof from the very idea of perfection, the summation of positive qualities.

Q.E.D.

4. Mathematics and Apologetics: Leonhard Euler (1707–1783)

Abstract: Regarded as the most productive mathematician in all of human history, Euler's personal Christian faith and confidence in an inerrant Scripture are seldom mentioned. This brief essay endeavors to set the record straight—describing a polymath whose worldview was 180° removed from that of his time, the so-called 18th-century "Enlightenment."

Introduction

Of Euler, the Marquis de Condorcet said in his funeral elegy for him in 1783: "Every mathematician is one of his disciples." This is no exaggeration, since Euler made fundamental contributions to a staggering number of mathematical fields and his accomplishments spilled over into the domains of physics and the applied sciences. One of the books published by the Mathematical Association of America for its Tercentenary Euler Celebration is titled simply, *The Genius of Euler.*[1]

Euler was also a convinced Christian believer who regarded Holy Scripture as God's inerrant revelation and believed that it could and should be defended intellectually. But that aspect of his life is systematically ignored by those who treat his thought and his ideas. One example: The Open University in England sponsored a series of four programmes on the history of mathematics that were broadcast on national television (BBC2) in 2017. No mention of Euler's religious beliefs was made at all—and the presenter, a British mathematician, at another point in the programme series, stated that he himself was not a believer: he clearly was more impressed by Gauss, a brilliant but self-centred mathematician who refused to help younger scholars and attributed their accomplishments to his own influence on them!

---

[1] The Genius of Euler, ed. William Dunham (Washington, DC: MAA, 2007). See also Dunham's Euler: The Master of Us All (Washington, DC: MAA, 1999).

We shall endeavor to set the record straight. A brief overview of Euler's life and work will be followed by illustrations, in his own words, as to how he defended the classic biblical faith of Christianity.[2]

Euler's Life in Summary

Euler lived in the first century of modern secularism, the 18th. That century, characterized as "the Age of Reason" by Thomas Paine, was a time when the most influential thinkers such as Voltaire jettisoned historic Christianity for varieties of the religion of "Nature." The Bible came to be regarded as a collection of ancient superstitions, the very opposite of anything factual or scientific. The natural world was all the revelation one needed—for it pointed to a Creator and to a natural morality.[3]

This, however, was not the way Leonhard Euler was brought up, and he never wavered in his lifelong belief in the truth of historic Christianity. He was born in Basel, German-speaking Switzerland, close the French border. His father was a Reformed pastor and his mother a pastor's daughter. His father wanted him to study for the ministry, but was persuaded by one the members of the Bernoulli family (a clan of distinguished mathematicians in their own right) that Leonhard's talent for mathematics was so remarkable that he simply had to make his career in the natural sciences.

Euler entered the University of Basel at the age of 13, graduated two years later, and went on to earn a master of arts degree in philosophy. But his attempts to obtain a professorship at the University of Basel were unsuccessful. Two of the Bernoulli brothers had succeeded professionally at Peter the Great's Imperial Russian Academy of the Sciences in St Petersburg, and when one of them died of appedicitis, Euler was invited to replace him. Thus began a lifetime association with the Russian crown and its successful attempts to build an academic culture comparable to that in western Europe.

Euler had a photographic memory, and conquered the difficult Russian language with no problem. It was noted later by others that he could quote the entire *Aeneid* of the Roman epic poet Virgil—even indicating which lines began and ended the pages he had memorized.

---

[2] As an introduction to Euler's life and work, see the detailed article on him, with excellent bibliography, by A. P. Youschkevitch in the Dictionary of Scientific Biography, ed. Charles Coulston Gillispie, et al., (16 vols.; New York: American Council of Learned Societies/Charles Scribner's Sons, 1970–1980), Vol. 4, pp. 467–84.

[3] See John Warwick Montgomery, *The Shaping of America* (Minneapolis: Bethany, 1976), Part I, chap. 2 ("The Enlightenment Spirit"), pp. 47–68.

4. Mathematics and Apologetics: Leonhard Euler (1707–1783)

Euler's tenure in Russia was interrupted owing to political intrigues and he spent some twenty-five years in Germany at Frederick the Great's Berlin Academy (1741–1766). However—in part surely because of Frederick's Enlightenment sympathies—they did not get along. Among Frederick's invitees to his Academy was *Voltaire*, who enjoyed making fun of Euler, the latter not being as effective a debater and social wit as Voltaire. The oft-repeated story that Euler drove Diderot out of Berlin by citing a mathematical formula to prove God's existence is entirely apocryphal.[4]

On receiving a magnanimous offer from Catherine the Great, one that included a handsome salary, a fine house, and promises to take care of the future of Euler's children, Euler returned to St Petersburg and remained there for the rest of his life—during the last 17 years of which he suffered from total blindness.

Euler's productivity in Berlin (as in St Petersburg) was enormous, and his most popular publication was a collection of the letters he wrote in the course of tutoring Frederick's niece, the princess of Anhalt-Dessau. These letters show how effectively he could explain abstruse scientific concepts to an educated but non-specialist audience. We shall return to these letters shortly, since they offer much insight into Euler's Christian convictions as well as his apologetic for the truth of the faith.

Euler was happily married for 40 years to the same woman. They had thirteen children, but only five reached adulthood. After his wife's death, he married her half-sister, who took care of him during his last years of total blindness.

Interestingly, Euler's mathematical productivity did not diminish as a result of the loss of sight. He commented that it removed "distractions" so that he could concentrate even more fully on his mathematical and scientific interests.

Euler was buried in a Lutheran cemetery. As a testimony to Euler's great reputation, his body was later removed to a Russian Orthodox monastery built by Peter the Great.[5]

---

[4] B. H. Brown, "The Euler-Diderot Anecdote," in *The Genius of Euler (op. cit.)*, pp. 57–59. The story is, sadly, accepted without question by authors who should have known better (e.g., E. T. Bell, *Men of Mathematics*).

[5] For more biographical detail on Euler's life and career, see Emil A. Fellmann, *Leonhard Euler*, trans. E and W. Gautschi (Basel: Switzerland: Birkhäuser Verlag, 2007).

Euler's Mathematical Accomplishments

Euler's mathematical and scientific productivity was simply enormous. If all of his surviving notebooks were printed, they would fill 60 to 80 quarto volumes.[6] Here we shall do no more than to summarize the major areas of his mathematical contributions.

Number Theory

Euler proved Fermat's little theorem and theorem on the sums of two squares—as well as Newton's identities. By his invention of the totient function he was able to generalize Fermat's little theorem (it would become "Euler's theorem").

Topology and Graph Theory

Euler developed a formula relating the number of faces, vertices, and edges of a convex polyhedron; this formula was a key element in the origin of modern topology. He also solved, in anticipation of modern topological theory, the hoary conundrum of the "Seven Bridges of Koenigsberg" by showing that there was no route by which one could cross each of the seven bridges only once and return to the point of origin.[7]

Analysis and Complex Analysis

Euler was responsible for introducing the concept of the function in general, the exponential function in particular, and logarithms in analytic proofs. He refined the power series: functions as sums of infinitely many terms. He invented the calculus of variations. The prime number theorem was the direct product of his work on the distribution of prime numbers and his proof of the infinitude of primes. Richard Feynman considered Euler's formula showing that for any real number Φ, the complex exponential function satisfies $e^{i\Phi} = \cos \Phi + i \sin \Phi$ "the most remarkable formula in mathematics," especially since the so-called Euler's identity" is a special case of that same formula: $e^{i\pi} + 1 = 0$ (a formula containing the five most

---

[6] The Euler Archive (eulerarchive.maa.org) contains some 850 entries, representing original works by Euler and their translations into other languages.

[7] See David S. Richeson, Euler's Gem: The Polyhedron Formula and the Birth of Topology (Princeton, NJ: Princeton University Press, 2008).

important mathematical constants, interlocking arithmetic, geometry, calculus, and the realm of imaginary numbers).[8]

Notation

Perhaps the most influential of Euler's contributions lay in his revolutionizing of mathematical notation. Our use of the sigma (Σ) notation for summation and e as the base of the natural logarithm are due to him (e is now termed "Euler's number"). He introduced f(x) for functions and the modern way of describing trigonometric functions. He began the use of i to represent the square root of -1.

We do not have the space here to describe Euler's influence in applied mathematics (including music). But his work in theoretical astronomy, especially the treatment of planetary motions, is particularly worthy of mention. His accomplishments included determining with remarkable precision the orbits of comets and other celestial bodies and calculating the parallax of the sun. His calculations also contributed to the development of accurate tables of longitude.

Suffice it to say that no mathematician before or since has had such a universal impact on the entire field and its future development.[9]

Euler As Christian Believer and Apologist

As indicated above, this aspect of Euler's life and thought has been sadly neglected. The only monograph appears to be a German thesis defended in 1851 by K. R. Hagenbach: *Leonhard Euler, als Apologet des Christenthums : Einladungsschrift zur Promotionsfeier des Paedagogiums d. 28. Apr. 1851*. Hagenbach, not so incidentally, would later be known for his widely-used *A Text-Book of the History of Doctrines* (no less than 20 editions published in English between 1861 and 2015).

Even the Marquis de Condorcet, who as a rationalist could not tolerate the introduction of theology into scientific thinking, had to acknowledge Euler's personal faith. Euler, he said, "would gather his children, his servants and those of his students who lived with him, for group prayer each

---

[8] Richard Feynman. "Algebra," The Feynman Lectures on Physics, Vol. I, chap. 22 (June, 1970). Feynman also says of the formula, "This is our jewel. Cf. Paul J. Nahin, Dr. Euler'd Fabulous Formula (Princeton, NJ: Princeton University Press, 2006).

[9] For a taste of Euler's early mathematical contributions, see C. Edward Sandifer, *The Early Mathematics of Leonhard Euler* (Washington, DC: MAA, 2007). Fascinating insights as to how Euler developed his proofs have been provided in Sandifer's *How Euler Did It* (Washington, DC: MAA, 2007).

evening. He would read them a chapter of the Bible and sometimes accompanied this reading with an exhortation."

Euler published a treatise defending the faith and the inerrancy of the Holy Scriptures over against freethinkers: *Rettung der Göttlichen Offenbahrung gegen die Einwürfe der Freygeister* (Berlin: A. Haude & J. C. Spener, 1747). This work was translated into English only in 2011, and it gives us a systematic insight into Euler's apologetic approach to the unbelief of his time.

Euler's theological commitments can be seen in his classic, *Lettres à une princesse d'Allemagne*.[10] The French edition by Condorcet omitted all of Euler's theological material (his references to God, salvation, and the Scriptures), since, from Condorcet's Enlightenment perspective, they were "anathema" to the teaching of science and rationalism.[11]

Let us begin with typical theological material from the *Letters*, afterwards proceeding to the *Rettung*.

The Letters are replete with acknowledgements of biblical truth. Divine creation is evident from such phenomena as the complexity of the human eye. Sin and the demonic are affirmed, as is the essentiality of the saving work of God to counter the effects of a fallen world.

In Letter 18, Euler argued for the necessity of special revelation:

> "How unfortunate would we be if God had abandoned us to ourselves with regards to the invisible world and our eternal salvation. On this important point, a revelation is absolutely necessary to us. We should make the most of it with the greatest veneration; and when this revelation presents us with things that seem inconceivable, we have but to remember the weaknesses of our mind, which strays so easily, even for the visible things."[12]

Letter 44 contains the following passage (again, omitted by Condorcet):

> "Atheists have the audacity to maintain that eyes, as well as the entire world, are but the product of chance. They find nothing in it that merits

---

[10] My valuable copy of the French text, in 2 vols. (Paris: L. Hachette, 1842), was obtained for a song from a Parisian bouquiniste along the Seine. Euler, whose academic writings were composed in German, his native language, or Latin, wrote these letters in French. We shall be citing a reprint edition of an early English translation by Henry Hunter, with the restoration of omitted passages as identified (1805) by the printer/bookseller Adrien Le Clère in his Annales littéraires et morales, Vol. 11 (and translated into English by Andie Ho).

[11] Dominic Klyve, "The Omnipresent Savant: Seeking the Original Text of Euler's Letters to a German Princess," Opusculum: The Euler Society Newsletter. Vol. 3, Issue 2 (Summer, 2011); available online in pdf-format.

[12] This passage was omitted by Condorcet in his French edition.

4. Mathematics and Apologetics: Leonhard Euler (1707–1783)

their attention, they acknowledge no mark of wisdom in the structure of the eye. Rather they believe to be very right to criticize its imperfections, because they can see neither in the dark nor through a wall, nor distinguish the smallest objects on bodies far away, such as the moon and other celestial bodies. They proclaim that the eye was not make on purpose, that it was formed by chance, like silt encountered in the countryside, and that it is absurd to say that we have eyes in order to be able to see; rather we should say that, having received eyes by chance, we take as much advantage of them as their nature allows. Your Highness will be indignant to learn that such beliefs exist, and yet these are all too common today among people who believe they alone are wise and who loudly mock those who find in the world the most prominent signs of a Creator who is sovereignly powerful and just. It is useless to get involved in a debate with these people. They remain unshakable in their belief and deny the most respectable truths. What the psalmist says is true: Only fools believe in their heart that there is no God."

Letter 90 defends prayer over against the freethinkers[13] and, in the second edition of the English translation, the editor restores a passage Condorcet excised:

"However extravagant and absurd the sentiments of certain philosophers may be, they are so obstinately prepossessed in favour of them, that they reject every religious opinion and doctrine, which is not conformable to their system of philosophy. From this source are derived most of the sects and heresies in religion; but in that case, divine truth ought surely to be preferred to the reveries of men, if the pride of philosophers knew what it was to yield. Should sound philosophy sometimes seem in opposition to religion, that opposition is more apparent than real; and we must not suffer ourselves to be dazzled with the speciousness of objection."

Euler's argument in favour of answered prayer runs as follows:

"When God established the course of the universe, and arranged all the events which must come to pass in it, he paid attention to all the circumstances which should accompany each event; and particularly to the dispositions, to the desires, and prayers, of every intelligent being; and that the arrangement of all events was disposed, in perfect harmony, with all these circumstances. When, therefore, a man addresses to God a prayer worthy of being heard, it must not be imagined, that such a prayer came not to the knowledge of God till the moment it was formed. That prayer was already

---

[13] Leonhard Euler, Lettere on Different Subjects in Physics and Philosophy Addressed to a German Princess, trans. Henry Hunter (2d ed., 2 vols; London: Murray and Highley, 1802), Vol. 1, pp. 345–46.

heard from all eternity; and if the Father of mercies deemed it worthy of being answered, He arranged the world expressly in favour of that prayer, so that the accomplishment should be a consequence of the natural course of events."

Euler's *Rettung—A Defense of Revelation*—consists of 53 numbered paragraphs. We shall quote a selection:[14]

XIX. Either there is a divine revelation or there isn't. Nobody yet has dared to maintain the absolute impossibility of a revelation, and the freethinkers are limited to uniting all their forces to eliminate the characteristics of a divine revelation from the Holy Scripture. God did not simply create man; because He simultaneously accorded them everything necessary to attain true happiness, it is distinctly clear that God must have a hand in the salvation of men. Consequently, if the revelation can contribute to the advancement of their happiness, then not only is the revelation not impossible, but it is even to be presumed that God proved kindness to man in this regard.

XXXII. Thus, if we find in the Holy Scripture, with the pure doctrine of God, the true source of all virtues and the most magnificent and powerful ways to lead us there, offered in the most explicit manner, it necessarily follows that this book will contribute to the advancement of our true happiness. And even if one does not want to attribute it to a divine origin, one is at least forced to acknowledge this unmistakable consequence: that the author of this book had not only some distinct ideas on the essence of true happiness, but that he also worked diligently to keep men from all vices and to lead them down the path of virtue. Would it not be just as absurd as it is unjust to want to denounce this author as crazy or even as a liar?

XXXIII. It follows that when authors of sacred texts, sensibly and with an integrity of which we are perfectly convinced, recount things that seem incredible to us, it would be most unjust to reject them simply and absolutely. The Holy Scripture tells us in a detailed manner about several things concerning the miracles performed by people glorying in a divine mission. Despite the incredibility of these miracles, believing in the arguments of the freethinkers, arguments which are born partly from a wild imagination and partly from ignorance, would be even more incredible, for it would mean that God had blinded men to lend support and credence to their masquerade.

---

[14] The translation is by Andie Ho (2011) and can be found in the Euler Archive (www.eulerarchive.maa.org).

4. Mathematics and Apologetics: Leonhard Euler (1707–1783)

XXXIV. The apostles and a multitude of Christians unanimously agree not only that Jesus Christ rose from the dead, but also that they have seen him with their own eyes since the resurrection and that they even communicated with Him. If one has paid attention to the doctrine and to the constancy with which it been maintained, one cannot say with any semblance of truth that one has believed nothing of what has been said in this regard and that it is thus an obvious lie. One would be even less likely to say that the apostles were seduced by false imagination and that their facts were nothing but an illusion. Either that or we will be forced to state that God had miraculously blinded them all at the same time in order to propagate a false doctrine.

XXXV. Using the evidence that the strongest of objections has been long refuted, it seems to me that the considerations I have proposed so far on the purity of the doctrine taught in the Holy Scripture and its perfect harmony with the happiness of man manage to destroy all doubts that incredulity alone is capable of forming, especially if one reflects at the same time on the nature of a true divine revelation which has already been stated. For such a revelation should not be accompanied by evidence that is too great, and it is enough that it includes all that can lead to the salvation of men who want to work diligently towards the reformation of their heart. This destroys without exception all the arguments that form unceasingly on the manner in which the Christian religion is spread throughout the world.

XXXVI. The resurrection of Jesus Christ is also an incontestable fact, and since such a miracle can only be the work of God alone, it is thus impossible to doubt the divinity of the Savior's mission. Consequently, the doctrine of Christ and his apostles is divine, and since its goal is our true happiness, we can be most assured of our belief in all the promises that the Gospel has made to us, both for this life and the one to come, and we can regard the Christian religion as a work of God who is tied to our salvation. It is not necessary to expand any further on these reflections, since it is impossible for anyone, once they are convinced of the resurrection of Jesus Christ, to retain the slightest doubt about the divinity of the Holy Scripture.

XXXVII. The freethinkers cannot put forward anything plausible against this bedrock on which the divinity of the Holy Scripture firmly rests. When they are forced to turn their attentions to this, they do all they can not to address the root of the question. They resort to all manner of loopholes to change the subject and attack other items, where they claim to find incomprehensible things and even contradictions. Most often, their reasoning does not have to do with the doctrines contained in formal terms in the Holy Scripture but with other writings from which only certain conclusions can be drawn. Although these conclusions are mostly legitimately derived, their process lacks rigor when, in raging against these conclusions, they try to persuade men that they are sufficient to entirely discredit the Holy Scripture.

XXXVIII. When the credibility of a writing is attacked using methods foreign to the bedrock on which the credibility rests, there is a certain indication of hidden malice. To judge by those who behave in this way, if there existed another divine revelation besides the Holy Scripture, they would not be any more inclined to believe in it, since divine truths can never allow any prejudices or passions which guide them. Thus, we can grant the freethinkers that the Holy Scripture must contain things that they do not agree with and which seem unreasonable to them. Contrarily, this agreement between the Scripture's doctrine and the ideas of the freethinkers is one of the most harmful things to the Holy Scripture.

XXXIX. As for the arguments formed by these adversaries and the apparent contradictions they claim are in the Holy Scripture, it would not be useless to begin by remarking that there is no science, no matter how solid its foundation, against which one cannot make objections just as strong or even stronger. There are also apparent contradictions which, at first glance, seem impossible to resolve. But since we are in a position to return to the primary principles of these sciences, this provides the means by which to destroy these arguments. However, when they are not seen through to the end, these sciences lose nothing of their certainty. Why would such similar reasons be enough to remove all authority from the Holy Scripture?

XL. Mathematics is regarded as a science in which nothing is assumed that cannot be derived in the most distinct way from the primary principles of our knowledge. Nevertheless, there have been people far above average who have believed to have found great problems in mathematics, whose solutions are impossible; by this they imagined themselves to have deprived this science of all its certainty. Indeed, this reasoning that they propose is so deceptively attractive that much effort and insight is required to refute them precisely. However, mathematics is not lessened in the eyes of sensible people, even when it does not clear up these problems entirely. So then what right do freethinkers unwaveringly think they have to reject the Holy Scripture because of a few nuisances which mostly are not nearly as considerable as the ones in mathematics?

XLI. In mathematics, one also encounters rigorously demonstrated propositions that, when not examined with the highest degree of attention, seem to contradict one another. I could produce several examples

4. Mathematics and Apologetics: Leonhard Euler (1707–1783)

here if their complexity did not require a deeper knowledge of mathematics than I suppose most readers to have. But I can at least say with assurance that these apparent contradictions are much more significant than those that are supposedly found in the Holy Scripture. Despite this, no one suggests dismissing the certainty of mathematics. This doubt does not even exist in those who do not have the capacity required to refute these contradictions and to demonstrate that they do not hold.

XLII. The other sciences have even more such inconveniences. They appear especially when we want to subject the primary principles of our knowledge to a more thorough examination. No one, for example, doubts that there are bodies in the universe. We are equally certain, or not, that they are composed of simple beings. But deciding upon one of these two opinions is so difficult that no one has yet been able to defend one of them in a way that fully satisfies those who support the opposing argument. If one wanted to conclude that neither of these two opinions represented the truth, it would be necessary to resort to denying the existence of the bodies. Although some fanatics have indeed taken this side, no man who uses his faculties of reasoning would imitate them.

XLIII. We have also seen people who absolutely deny all movement. They say that if a body moves itself, it must be either in the place it currently occupies or in another. The first case cannot happen, for as long as a body stays in its place, no movement can be attributed to it. The second is even more absurd, for how could a body move itself to where it is not? Perhaps there are a few people who are capable of resolving this sophism, but this will lead them to question the very least possibility of movement. Is it not then the greatest recklessness conceivable to utter an unappealable decision against the Holy Scripture as soon as one imagines to have encountered some difficulties whose solutions do not come to mind?

XLIV. Without going into a detailed examination of all the objections to the Holy Scripture, we can draw from all we have said thus far the certain conclusion that the enemies of this sacred book act most unjustly and inexcusably when, because of some difficulties that seem to them impossible to resolve, they dare deny the revelation entirely. Most of them are forced to admit that it would be entirely beyond their capabilities to respond to the objections that mathematics offers against the existence of bodies and the possibility of movement. Yet it has never occurred to them to reject the truth and to contest the existence of these things. Thus, it is a sure sign that the methods they use are not borne out of love for the truth, but originate from another source entirely, an impure source.

XLV. One thing that should be considered is that the Holy Scripture is limited to revealing to us things which we could not reason our ourselves, or at least not without great difficulty; for it would completely contradict the purpose of a divine revelation to only include knowledge that anyone could plainly see. But if the things themselves, which are the result of reason, are examined so closely that they sometimes seem to contain contradictions, then it necessarily follows that the revealed doctrine, which depends on principles superior to those of reason, contain ones that are at least as great and that it would be even more wrong to be scandalized by them.

XLVI. These reflections should well and truly destroy the objections of the freethinkers, but they seem to be much more substantial than they really are. The freethinkers have yet to produce any objections that have not long been refuted most thoroughly. But since they are not motivated by the love of truth, and since they have an entirely different point of view, we should not be surprised that the best refutations count for nothing and that the weakest and most ridiculous reasoning, which has so often been shown to be baseless, is continuously repeated. If these people maintained the slightest rigor, the slightest taste for the truth, it would be quite easy to steer them away from their errors; but their tendency towards stubbornness makes this completely impossible.

LIII. No matter how obvious and unwavering the principles on which we have just founded the divinity of the Holy Scripture, there is no hope that they are effective enough to save the freethinkers and libertines from their foolish behavior and to make them renounce their evil ways. On the contrary, the Holy Scripture assures us that their impudence will continue to increase, especially towards the end, and the exact fulfillment of this prophecy is not the least of the proofs of the divinity and the revelation. However, I hope with all my heart that these reflections will be the salvation of some people who are not completely corrupted and will return to the right path those who had the imprudence and misfortune to listen to dangerous ideas.

* * *

Euler's apologetic, like Pascal's, begins with the human condition: our need to find true happiness and our inability to achieve this by any kind of human effort. The natural world powerfully supports the existence and work of a Creator God. But, ultimately, it is biblical revelation that offers the only infallible solution to the human condition, and the arguments against it are puerile in comparison with those in its favour. Miracles, especially the resurrection of Jesus Christ from the dead, offer overwhelming proof of the divine truth of Scripture.

4. Mathematics and Apologetics: Leonhard Euler (1707–1783)

Euler employs his specialties in mathematics and the natural sciences to bolster his Christian claims. Difficulties and unsolved problems in the physical realm and in mathematics do not cause us to jettison them. Alleged errors and contradictions in Holy Scripture offer even less reason to reject the biblical message—which alone offers the route to genuine human happiness.

The *Defense* shows with utmost clarity the intimate connection between Euler's mathematics and his faith. Is this not another example of how biblical truth informs the most sophisticated intellectual endeavors, leading inexorably to a realization on the part of believers that the faith must be defended in a modern secular world?[15]

---

[15] Cf. John Warwick Montgomery, "Computer Origins and the Defense of the Faith," in his *Christ As Centre and Circumference* (Bonn, Germany: Verlag für Kultur und Wissenschaft, 2012), pp. 78-103. That article earlier appeared in *Perspectives on Science and Christian Faith: Journal of the American Scientific Affiliation*, September, 2004.

5. In re William Lane Craig

I attended the annual national meeting of the Evangelical Theological Society, held (November, 2018) in Denver, Colorado. The theme was "The Holy Spirit" and I presented a paper on that subject in a session with Angus Menuge and J. P. Moreland. As those two names suggest, the Evangelical Philosophical Society meets simultaneously with the E.T.S, and the featured E.P.S. speaker was William Lane Craig, presenting a defense of the vicarious atonement.

Many moons ago, I was Craig's first apologetics professor at the Trinity Evangelical Divinity School. In subsequent years, he has become one of the leading evangelical philosophers. In Scripture, we are given the Pauline model—that wherever Christ is preached, we are to rejoice (Philippians 1:15-18). And so I rejoice in Craig's debates and publications; but I am uncomfortable with his style and approach. I was particularly bothered by his E.P.S. address, based on his little book, *The Atonement* (Cambridge University Press, 2018). Let me explain my misgivings.

The lecture, like most of Craig's presentations, was dense to the extreme and reminded me of the scholastic arguments characteristic of medieval theology. I go with the Wittgensteinian adage that "anything that can be said can be said clearly." To be sure, this is a problem with most professional philosophers, but if one is also doing apologetics (as is Craig), extreme care needs to be exercised so that the results are more like the writings of C. S. Lewis than those of Thomas Aquinas. (See the section titled, "Apologetics ≠ Philosophy" in my article, "Apologetics for the 21st Century," included in my *Christ As Centre and Circumference*.)

On one occasion years ago, I attended a Craig presentation focusing on metaphysical questions such as the relationship of time to creation. (Craig loves these issues, but I have never found a single non-Christian whose objections to the faith lie at that level.) To Craig's irritation, I cited Saint Augustine, who, when dealing with the question as to what God was doing before he made heaven and earth, cited someone who responded facetiously, "Preparing hell for those who pry into mysteries" (*Confessions*, XI, 12). (Cf. James Fodor's overstated critique, *Unreasonable Faith: How William Lane Craig Overstates the Case for Christianity* [Hypatia Press, 2018].)

Craig's atonement paper focused particularly on legal analogies to vicarious punishment and substitution. Craig is not a lawyer or legally trained, and in his book he thanks an Edinburgh law professor for "directing him to legal literature on various subjects" and a legal practitioner "for help in obtaining court opinions." The result, sad to say, is poor legal argumentation and reliance on a narrow range of cases, most of them not of a leading nature. I myself, though holding a certificate in medical librarianship, do not possess an M.D. degree, and would not presume to write on the theology of, say, medical aspects of Jesus's crucifixion. Craig could have shown parallel humility.[1]

One example: Craig's lecture and book stress the concept of "legal fiction"—the occasional use in the Anglo-American common law of fictional categories (e.g., a corporation is regarded as having legal personhood). Craig does not seem to realize that this notion of legal fiction is not employed to any significant degree in the major Civil Law systems of continental Europe, and, more important, that such fictions do not constitute a source of law *per se* but derive their value solely from precedent and tradition. They must be used only to a limited degree and in strict accord with the established law. Thus in *Sinclair v. Brougham,* 1914 AC 378, the House of Lords refused to extend the fictional status of quasi-contract to a case of an *ultra vires* borrowing by a limited company, since to do so would have sanctioned the evasion of the rules of public policy forbidding a company to borrow *ultra vires.* "Piercing the corporate veil" is a common technique to bypass the legal fiction that a company is equivalent to an actual person.

Important secondary legal literature, deserving of careful treatment, includes, *inter alia*: Lon L. Fuller, *Legal Fictions* (Stanford University Press, 1967); Ch. Perelman and P. Foriers (eds.), *Les Présumptions et les fictions en droit* (Brussels: Ets Emile Bruylant, 1974); *La Fiction* ("Droits: Revue Française de Théorie Juridique," 21; Paris: Presses Universitaires de France, 1995).

In Craig's attempts to use vicarious liability, *respondeat superior,* and legal fictions to justify the biblical atonement, he does not seem to realize that, in law, all such instances require a real and substantive connection between the punisher (on earth, the State or Crown) and the person at fault who is therefore justly declared guilty and subject to punishment. The fact that one's fine can be paid by another is irrelevant. There must be a punishable act or omission and the one punished for it must be respon-

---

[1] One is reminded of the 18th-century minor dramatist Fettiplace Bellers, who, though entirely without a legal education, spent twenty years writing A Delineation of Universal Law (1754). A contemporary critic commented: "It is with a feeling of regret, mingled with something like reproach, that we find the labours of twenty years so wasted, and reflect upon the great expenditure of time and diligence that has been destitute of any useful result."

sible for that act or omission. This is the key issue in any attempt to analogize from what a human legal system does and what occurs in the divine economy of salvation. The best one can do is perhaps to theorize that placing the sins of the world on Christ's shoulders might be justifiable because God-in-Christ, though as to his human nature the Second Adam was indeed a sinless Lamb, as to his divine nature he created all things (John 1:1–3; Colossians 1:15–17) and, out of love, gave humanity freewill (which the human race misused)—thus making God-in-Christ, as to his divine nature, in a sense responsible for the sinful history of the race. Of course, this suggestion entails a cosmic mystery, hardly resolvable by any human system of jurisprudence.

Sadly, Craig passes rapidly and superficially over the great "Christus Victor" atonement motif, dominant in the Patristic age and revived during the Protestant Reformation—the theory that on the Cross our Lord conquered sin, death, and the devil—the powers of darkness arrayed against humanity. (See Gustaf Aulén's classic, *Christus Victor,* and this author's *Chytraeus on Sacrifice,* neither cited by Craig.)

Indeed, characteristic of the scholasticism of his presentation, Craig cites the Swiss Reformed theologian Turretinus (often called the "Thomas Aquinas of Calvinism"). How much better off Craig would have been to rely on Lutheran theologians, since they, unlike their Calvinist counterparts, are well aware that in the high matters of faith, mystery is unavoidable (as with the Holy Trinity, divine election, and the real presence of our Lord in the Eucharist). Calvinistic double-predestination and Arminian/Molinist, semi-pelagian "middle knowledge" both suffer from a fallacious insistence that high matters of faith can be rationally explained—if we just try hard enough. One of the glories of Lutheran theology is its willingness to accept whatever God reveals in Holy Scripture, even when we are incapable of explaining or justifying the teaching. And this is not irrationalism—for we can demonstrate factually the inerrant, revelational character of Scripture, thereby allowing facts to triumph (as in science) even when those facts do not yield to our best efforts at explanation (example: the wave-particle nature of light).

We end—inevitably—with Luther:

Could God, says Mr Wiseacre, find no other way to redeem the human race? Did His Son have to die a death so shameful? Why does God deliver His Son into the hands of His enemies? Surely, He might have sent an angel to overthrow the entire world, to say nothing of this band of Jews. No doubt God might easily have done this, for He is almighty. Besides, He is omniscient and also prudent, wise, and good enough not to require your wisdom in the least in order to determine what He wants to do. However, here the point is, not the ability but the will of God.[2]

* * *

If you begin your study of God by trying to determine how He rules the world, how He burned Sodom and Gomorrah with infernal fire, whether He has elected this person or that, and thus begin with the works of the High Majesty, then you will presently break your neck and be hurled from heaven, suffering a fall like Lucifer's. For such procedure amounts to beginning on top and building the roof before you have laid the foundation. Therefore, letting God do whatever He is doing, you must begin at the bottom and say: I do not want to know God until I have first known this Man; for so read the passages of Scripture: "I am Way, the Truth, and the Life"; again: "No man cometh unto the Father but by Me" (John 14:6). And there are more passages to the same effect.[3]

---

[2] WA 37, 325.
[3] WA 36:61 ff. (sermon of 6 Jan. 1532, on Micah 5:1).

6. Lee Strobel's Case for Christ— the Case for *Whom?*

When I take the TGV—the super-fast train from Strasbourg to Paris—on legal business, I always buy a copy of the weekly *Officiel des spéctacles* to see what is going on in the City of Light. On my latest trip, as I examined the list of films playing, what did I find? Amazingly, tucked away among the listings was "Jésus: L'enquête" (The Case for Christ)—described as the story of an atheist converted to Christianity.

Of course I could not resist. The film was not playing at the major theatres to which I ordinarily go; in fact, it was listed as playing in only three cinemas. I picked the one that was most centrally located, near the Arc de Triomphe on the Champs-Elysées. As it turned out, I constituted 50% of the audience (2 persons total in attendance).

The film is biographical: the conversion of American journalist Lee Strobel. What are the pluses and what are the minuses?

The Positive

Technically, "The Case for Christ" could hardly be bettered. The acting, the photography, the direction are all at the level of the best of Hollywood standards. The French subtitling was impeccable (though voice-dubbing would have been more effective). The producers were smart enough to enlist in a cameo role a known (though now long-in-the-tooth) Hollywood star, Faye Dunaway, in an obvious effort to capture an audience of non-religious film buffs.

There is much valuable apologetics material included in the film. Brief interviews occur with actors representing defenders of the faith such as Gary Habermas and William Lane Craig. (Habermas is a personal friend, and I was Craig's first apologetics professor—though I am never mentioned in the credits or otherwise.) The important *Journal of the American Medical Association* article confirming the death of Christ from crucifixion, over against "swoon theories"—an article I introduced into the apologetics arena years ago—plays an important role.

The Negative

The film is obviously the product of Baptists, and they cannot resist pushing their doctrinal orientation. Thus Strobel's wife goes through a full-scale, down-by-the riverside immersion baptism, and Strobel's post-conversion professorship at a Baptist institution is emphasized in the credits at the end of the film. Of course, we cannot object to Baptist money, and the film obviously cost someone an arm and a leg; but wouldn't it be nice if classical denominations, such as the Lutherans, spent money doing the same thing, only better? Problem is that the Lutherans are far more concerned with the internal life of their churches than with evangelism to a secular public—and have little interest in apologetics (doubts are apparently supposed to evaporate through preaching and liturgy).

The main problem with the film is that it is Strobel-Strobel-Strobel rather than Jesus-Jesus-Jesus. Strobel's real problem is not so much in the area of evidence as in the psychological sphere. He has a bad relationship with his father—and a psychologist whom he interviews points out that the great atheists such as Freud (who held that God is a projection of the father image) have all had bad relations with their fathers. Strobel's central concern is with his marriage: he believes that his wife's conversion somehow substitutes Jesus as husband for Strobel himself.

The contrast with the conversion of St Paul is striking. The account of that archetypical occurrence in the Book of Acts is thoroughly Christ-centered. Saul/Paul himself is a minor figure in the drama: "Now as he went on his way, he approached Damascus, and suddenly a light from heaven shone around him. And falling to the ground, he heard a voice saying to him, 'Saul, Saul, why are you persecuting me?' And he said, 'Who are you, Lord?' And he said, 'I am Jesus, whom you are persecuting.' (Acts 9:3–5).

It couldn't hurt our Baptist converts and filmmakers to read a little Luther. We suggest as a start—even though Baptists are not prone to the use of Creeds or Catechisms—the Reformer's explanation of the Third Article of the Apostles' Creed, from Luther's *Small Catechism*:

> I believe that I cannot by my own reason or strength believe in Jesus Christ, my Lord, or come to Him; but the Holy Ghost has called me by the Gospel, enlightened me with His gifts, sanctified and kept me in the true faith; even as He calls, gathers, enlightens, and sanctifies the whole Christian Church on earth, and keeps it with Jesus Christ in the one true faith; in which Christian Church He forgives daily and richly all sins to me and all believers, and at the last day will raise up me and all the dead, and will give to me and to all believers in Christ everlasting life. This is most certainly true.

Conclusion

Should you see *The Case for Christ*? In our time of pagan film production, very definitely. Should you take unbelievers to see it? Absolutely. There is enough good apologetics material there to assist the non-Christian to a conviction of the factuality of our Lord's historical existence, resurrection, and divine claims.

But be sure to refocus from Lee Strobel, his family, his accomplishments and those of his children, together with his Baptist connections—to *Jesus Christ*. Every conversion should be Christ-centered and should be presented as such. Anything else creates the tremendous danger that we will be substituting our human experiences for the work of the Holy Spirit, the sole source of a genuine passage from death to life.

7. Computer Programming as an Assist to Apologetics

Readers of my material will have gathered that I do a bit of programming.[1] Not very sophisticated programming, perhaps (Pascal, Turbo Pascal), but at least it's with a compiler and not with a mere interpreter, and it's not "object-oriented" (OOP) like the Micro:bit or Mecanoid kits. Owing to the rigorous syntax of Pascal, the programmer is forced to respect strict, logical reasoning.

In this short article, I shall offer an illustration of the potential benefits of programming to the apologetical task. We shall begin with an important point for program verification and then show its application to fundamental arguments in defense of biblical faith.

Program Verification

Two specialists write concerning the weakness inherent in the usual technique of verifying one's computer programs:

> Testing can only detect the presence of errors; it can never prove their absence. All we can say about the program is that for a wide range of carefully chosen data cases it has worked properly and, from this experience, we extrapolate to the statement that the program will work correctly under all circumstances, even for those test cases that were not explicitly tested. This extrapolation is really a "leap of faith" that is not based on either mathematical formalities or physical laws but on empirical observation and human judgment.[2]

An example of such limited testing is provided by oft-recurring advice to programmers to engage in "boundary testing." Since it is impossible or impractical to test all possible values, one tests values at just before or just after the limits of the propositions in one's program. "By a 'boundary' we

---

[1] See, for example, "Regeneration, Biological, Computational, Theological," in: Montgomery, *Defending the Gospel in Legal Style* (Bonn, Germany: Verlag für Kultur und Wissenschaft, 2017), pp. 373-82; and, in the present volume, *infra*, "A Short and Easie Method with Postmodernists" and "On Innovative Theologians."
[2] G. Michael Schneider and Steven C. Bruell, *Advanced Programming and Problem Solving with Pascal* (2d ed.; New York: John Wiley & Sons, 1987), pp. 499–500.

mean a point at which the rule for determining the answer changes."[3] To be sure, this kind of testing does nothing to show that values other than those on the boundaries will provide valid results.

For this reason, a more sophisticated kind of verification has been suggested. It is characterized as "informal," in that it does not necessarily reach the level of deductive certainty, but it is a substantial improvement as compared with the testing of individual values in a program. "The important thing... is not to make an assertion about the behavior of a single statement, but to study the behavior of entire programs."[4] A simple example of the applicability of this more rationally satisfying approach follows.

> Assume that we were writing the following fragment to sum up the first N elements in a list:
>
> i := 1;
>
> sum := 0;
>
> **while** i ? N **do** {not sure what is the correct relational operator}
>
> > **begin**
> >
> > sum := sum + X[i];
> >
> > i := i + 1
> >
> > **end**
>
> We are not completely sure right now whether the test condition in the loop should be $i < N$ or $i <= N$. A lazy way would be simply to write out whichever one you think is correct, knowing that boundary testing will detect an error if we are wrong.... The [more logical] reasoning that could be done about the previous code fragment might go something like the following:
>
> > When we enter the loop the value of i is 1. We add X[1] to sum, set i to 2, and end the iteration. After one pass, we have added one item from X and i is 2. After two passes, I see that we have added in two items from X and i is 3. Therefore, it must be the case that after k passes through the loop, we will have added X[1] ..... X[k] to sum and i will have the value k + 1.

---

[3] J. Winston Crawley, William G. McArthur, and Norman M. Jacobson, *Structured Programming Using THINK Pascal on the Macintosh* (Englewood Cliffs, NJ: Prentice Hall, 1992), pp. 77–79.

[4] Schneider and Bruell, *op. cit*, p. 501.

Thus, if I want to stop when I have correctly computed X[1] + . . . + X[N], then I will want to end the loop when i has the value N + 1 at the end of the loop. The correct condition to write in the while loop must be while i <= N.[5]

Application to Apologetics

Two of the most central issues in the defense of biblical faith are God's existence and the resurrection of Jesus Christ as proof of his deity and of the truth of his saving message.

Therefore, apologists go to great lengths to refute arguments such as:

G1: The multiverse makes God's existence unnecessary

G2: Life can be accounted for, not by divine creation but by the seeding of basic cells or life forms from outer space

R1: Jesus survived the crucifixion by natural means

R2: Someone else was crucified in Jesus' place

Let us suppose that, by analogy with the discussion of the pseudo-code fragment in the previous section, we are faced with the proposition

If ((G1 or G2) and/or (R1 or R2)) were true,
then biblical faith is false

and that we wish to test the stated condition. Should we endeavor to counter each of the sub-arguments, much as one would test boundary conditions in a computer program?

Such an approach would be grossly inefficient, since G- and R-type arguments create potentially infinite series. (G and R are by no means limited to two similar sub-arguments each. In a contingent universe, G^n and R^n are entirely realistic sub-arguments.) The four assertions G1, G2, R1, R2 in fact represent a single, common fallacy:

If ((G1 or G2 or G^n) and/or (R1 or R2 or R^n)) were true,
then *any and all* "natural" (non-supernatural) arguments totally lacking

---

[5] *Ibid.*, p. 508.

in evidential support would also be plausible, and it would then be impossible in religious argument to distinguish provable fact from improvable speculation.

Were that the case, religious explanation in general would fall under the epistemological axe of physicist Wolfgang Pauli, who wrote in the margin of a colleague's paper: "This isn't right. It isn't even wrong."

Therefore, instead of pursuing the refutation of individual arguments of the G and R variety, the apologist would do far better to see the total picture in the fashion of programmatic "informal verification" and decimate the underlying logic of all such arguments:

> **If** X is in principle empirically unable to be substantiated
> **then** X can be rejected out of hand.

No empirical evidence whatever of a multiverse or of the seeding of life on earth from outer space exists. No empirical evidence at all supports the notion that Jesus physically survived the cross or that someone else died in his place.

It follows inexorably from the inherent irrationality of such arguments that the universe requires a transcendent explanation and that Jesus' claims to deity must be taken with all seriousness.

Transcendent, divine creation is empirically confirmed by the application of contingency argumentation via the Second Law of Thermodynamics, as well as by strong empirical evidences of intelligent design in nature and in human life.[6]

Jesus' resurrection from the dead is empirically established by eyewitness accounts of his physical appearances from Easter morning to his public ascension into heaven, and is collaterally supported by the miracles he performed throughout his public ministry and by the many detailed prophecies of the Old Testament fulfilled during that ministry.[7]

A serious consideration of the approach to verification here outlined would make unnecessary the infinite pursuit of boundary discussions limited to non-empirical religious and philosophical speculation. Such a methodology might even contribute to raising the discipline of apologetics to the more respectable intellectual level it surely deserves.

---

[6] See Montgomery, *Tractatus Logico-Theologicus* (6th ed.; Bonn, Germany: Verlag für Kultur und Wissenschaft, 2019), sec. 3.85–3.87.

[7] In the present volume, *infra,* see the articles, "Resurrection and Legal Evidence" and "Did Jesus Physically Rise from the Dead?"

8. Resurrection and Legal Evidence

Ah, Easter! "Spring is sprung and all the little birds do hum." Cute bunnies. Easter egg hunts. Yummy chocolate *gâteaux*.

I am not a stick-in-the-mud Calvinist who would punch Santa Claus in the stomach and kill and eat the Easter bunny. But, of course, the problem is that if one puts the emphasis on the folklore aspects of Easter, one misses what the holiday is centrally about.

And the clergy often do little better than the pagans. An 18th-century "Enlightenment" sermon had the theme, "The Virtues of Early Rising," emphasizing the ethical model of Mary Magdalene at the tomb "early, while it was still dark." Horrors! *Easter sermons must present the factual miracle of the bodily resurrection of our Lord and the evidence for it.*

How do lawyers, the specialists on evidence, argue for or against particular scenarios? A fine example is presented in the criminal trials of one Jacques Viguier, professor of public law at the University of Toulouse, accused of murdering his wife. This *cause célèbre* began in February, 2000, with the mysterious disappearance of Viguier's wife. The two had had a stormy relationship, accompanied by infidelities. Viguier did not report the absence of his wife for several days and was generally uncooperative. (He was, after all, a *law professor*.) At the first trial, he was acquitted, but a second trial took place years later. (The French Code of Criminal Procedure, Art. 368, prevents one from being tried twice for the same offense—the principle of *non bis in idem*—but exceptions exist when fundamental judicial errors are thought to have occurred in the first trial or substantial, relevant new evidence has been discovered.)

The prosecution arguments were that the wife would not have disappeared voluntarily, leaving her children; none of her clothes were missing (only her wallet, not even the bag she carried daily on her person); her car was still at home; etc.

The defense, in its closing argument to the jury, said simply that the prosecution's case was purely circumstantial: not a shred of factual evidence connected Viguier with his wife's disappearance. Indeed, there was no corpus delicti and no proof that a murder had been committed—much less a kidnapping or any other criminal act.

In the film reconstruction of the case (*Intime conviction*, directed by Antoine Raimbault, 2017, following two published books by Viguier himself[1]),

---

[1] *Innocent* (2010) and *La République doit-elle vraiment guillotiner ses juges?* (2014).

the defense attorney tells the jury: "The police, the media, and the general public can speculate and hypothesize as to what happened, but you, as a jury, cannot. You must arrive at your *intime conviction* [solid belief/deep-seated conviction] of guilt or innocence solely on the basis of factual evidence. And not a shred exist to connect the accused to any crime." Result: Viguier was acquitted a second time. At the close of the film, a director's note appears on the screen, informing the audience that well over 10,000 people in France disappear without a trace each year.

Admittedly, the Civil Law criterion of *"intime conviction,"* like the English standard of "being satisfied so that you are sure," lacks the precision of the jury instruction defining Common Law proof to *a moral certainty beyond reasonable doubt* allowed in many American jurisdictions: "The accused must be found innocent unless you, the triers of fact, can to a reasonable and moral certainty eliminate by way of the admissible evidence all explanations of the crime other than that the accused did it."[2] But in the Viguier case, this standard was certainly upheld by the juries' verdicts to acquit.

So, what does all this have to do with the resurrection of our Lord? Simply this: *all the substantive, factual evidence points to a miraculous, physical resurrection, and all the arguments against it are purely circumstantial.*

I have dealt with this in detail in an essay reprinted in my recent book, *Defending the Gospel in Legal Style*.[3] There we list the arguments *pro* and the arguments *con* a physical resurrection on Easter morning.

Of the 20 key arguments *pro*, every single one is either directly factual or factually corroborative. Here's the list:

1. All events related to Christ's death and resurrection were reported by eyewitnesses or associates of eyewitnesses.
2. Jesus is said by these witnesses to have been born miraculously and performed numerous impressive miracles, including the raising of Lazarus, during his public ministry.
3. On several occasions, Jesus predicted his resurrection.
4. Jesus was tried publicly by Jewish and by Roman leaders, given a death sentence, and executed by crucifixion.
5. On the cross, a sword was driven into his side to assure the soldiers in charge that he was indeed dead.

---

[2] Montgomery, "The Criminal Standard of Proof, "in his *Defending the Gospel in Legal Style* (Bonn, Germany: Verlag für Kultur und Wissenschaft, 2017).

[3] Montgomery, "A New Approach to the Apologetic for Christ's Resurrection by Way of Wigmore's Juridical Analysis of Evidence," *ibid.*

8. Resurrection and Legal Evidence

6. Jesus' crucifixion occurred publicly in Jerusalem at the high season of the Jewish religious year.
7. Jesus' body was then placed in a well-known tomb belonging to a prominent Jewish religious personality.
8. Efforts were made by the Jewish religious leaders to prevent a stealing of Jesus' body and to surpress any rumours of resurrection.
9. On the first Easter morning, Jesus' disciples encountered a Jesus who was alive.
10. Jesus appearsed subsequently to his followers over a 40-day period, followed by his public ascension into heaven.
11. Jesus' disciples did not believe that he would rise prior to the event having occurred—as evidenced, for example, by "doubting Thomas."
12. Jesus' resurrection appearances were physical in nature (Jesus eating fish, Thomas able to touch wounds in Jesus' hands and side).
13. Paul testified to having seen and spoken to the risen Christ on the Damascus road.
14. Paul provided a list of named witnesses to the risen Christ and claimed that over 500 were still alive to testify to it in A.D. 56 (1 Cor. 15)—as well as claiming when on trial before the Roman governor that Christ's death and resurrection were "not done in a corner" (Acts 26:26).
15. Absence of motive to steal Jesus' body on the part of the Romans or the Jewish religious leaders, and every reason on their part not to do so.
16. Irrationalism of any argument that Jesus' disciples or followers would have stolen his body and then claimed he rose from the dead—thus inviting persecution and death.
17. Irrationality of any unnamed third parties stealing the body or inventing such a story.
18. No contemporary refutations or attempted refutations of the fact of the resurrection by those with means, motive, and opportunity to do so.
19. Explanations of the event other than that by Jesus and the firsthand witnesses have no cogency and should be rejected.
20. Jesus claimed to be God incarnate, raised up by his Father, and the unique Saviour through his death and resurrection.

In diametric opposition, the arguments *con* are in every instance either purely circumstantial or inferential. Here's a sampling:

1. Jesus did not die on the cross.
2. Victim was someone else.
3. He died later under other circumstances.
4. One cannot trust the documents/witnesses.
5. Disciples mistook someone else for Jesus.
6. Disciples had a mystical vision.
7. Disciples suffered from a collective hallucination.
8. Disciples stole the body.
9. Unnamed persons stole the body.
10. Jesus rose "spiritually," not physically.
11. Miracles just don't happen; people who die stay dead.
12. Any natural explanation is preferable to a supernatural, miraculous explanation.
13. Jesus was lying or lacking in self-knowledge/knowledge of the true explanation of his resurrection.

We admit that sound legal convictions can and have been based largely on circumstantial evidence, but in those cases the "circumstances" have had to be tied logically to concrete fact. Thus, the classic American case of *Commonwealth v Webster*,[4] in which a Harvard medical lecturer was convicted of murdering a medically-trained, successful business man to whom he owed considerable money. Though no body was discovered, there were human teeth, corresponding to those of the missing Dr Parkman, found in the accused's laboratory furnace. One has every right to draw logical inferences from known facts, but one must not substitute pure speculation for solid evidence and reliable testimony.

As Chief Justice Shaw declared in the *Webster* case, circumstantial argument, to be allowed, requires "establishing a connection between the known and proved facts and the fact sought to be proved." Indeed, "the circumstances taken together must be of a conclusive nature, leading on the whole to a satisfactory conclusion, and producing in effect a reasonable and moral certainty, that the accused, and no one else, committed the offense charged." No circumstantial argument against the de facto resurrection of Jesus Christ has ever been of that nature.

Conclusion: if we want our secular society to pay attention to Christian claims, believers need to take much more seriously the Petrine command: "Be ready always to give an answer to everyone who asks you a reason [Gk *apologia*] of the hope that is in you" (I Peter 3:15).

Joyeuses Pâques!

---

[4] 5 Cushing 295; 59 Mass. 295 (1850).

9. Did Jesus Physically Rise from the Dead?

Unbelievers have often said that Jesus could not have survived death on the cross. Let's see if that's so or not—and why the right answer to the question is of utmost importance.

Objections to a Physical Resurrection

Typical of those objecting to Jesus' physical resurrection was a German theologian, Karl Venturini, who, early in the 19th century, said that Jesus had not really died on the cross, but had "swooned." According to this "swoon theory," the disciples thought that Jesus had been resurrected, but, really, he had just fainted and later woke up.

What do you think? My view is that if you can believe *that,* you shouldn't have any problem believing in Jesus' resurrection from the dead, since such a "swoon" would have been more miraculous than the resurrection!

Why? Here are just a few reasons: (1) The Roman soldiers crucifying Jesus knew their business: they had conducted many, many crucifixions in that cruel time of history. (2) According to the accounts, the soldiers pierced Jesus' side with a sword after taking the body down from the cross—to make sure that he was dead—and out came blood and water, showing that he was no longer living. (3) Would the disciples not have known the difference between a gloriously risen Christ and someone who had been subjected to torture for hours and nailed to a cross? (4) What would have happened to Jesus afterwards? Would he have hid himself away somewhere? Gone into retirement? In fact, Jesus was the last person to lie about himself or deceive others about himself. (By the way, you might like to read the most careful medical study of Jesus' death, as published some years ago in the *Journal of the American Medical Association,* where the authors conclude that "Jesus was dead when taken down from the cross" [*JAMA,* Vol. 255, pp. 1455-63 (1986)].)

Let the Historical Records Make the Decision

Venturini is a very good (or very bad!) example of what happens when people do not pay attention to the firsthand, historical reports of Jesus' life, ministry, and death. All we know about Jesus comes from those New Testament records, and if a person ignores them, he or she no longer does history. One substitutes speculation for history and the results are of no value whatsoever.

Suppose we were to do the same thing with other historical figures. A fine biblical theologian of the 19th century, Richard Whately—who had a great sense of humor—wrote a book titled, *Historic Doubts relative to Napoleon Buonaparte*. Skeptics had said that you couldn't believe the New Testament accounts of Jesus because everyone was prejudiced—either they loved Jesus or they hated him. Whately used their own argument to show (as a joke) that Napoleon had never existed—since everyone writing about him either loved him or hated him! This shows that if you use bad reasoning about Jesus, you'll mess up history in general!

But How Good Are the Gospel Records?

Suppose we compare the New Testament books with other writings of the ancient world. What do we find?

In the case of the New Testament, the existing manuscripts are far closer in time to their authors than in the case of *any other books of the Greco-Roman world*. Two among numerous examples: Caesar's *Gallic Wars* and Tacitus' *Annals*: 1,000 years between their composition and our first complete copies. When I was at university, I spent a semester studying the Latin poetry of Catullus. We have that poetry in only three manuscripts, and they are *1,600 years later than the original writings!* But for the New Testament, we have thousands of manuscripts, including ones that go back to less than a century after the events described. Two virtually complete texts of the Gospels exist from as early as the 4th century (*Codex Sinaiticus* and *Codex Vaticanus*). There is a fragment of the Gospel of John that must be dated before John's death—around A.D. 95. Because the biblical books were regarded as sacred, they were copied with the greatest of care and we can be sure that what we have today is substantially what the Apostolic writers or their associates actually wrote.

When some years ago I successfully debated a philosophy professor on the subject at the University of British Columbia, I showed that if you throw out the New Testament, you must at the same time discard virtually your entire knowledge of the classical world. My opponent then said (but no one believed him): "All right. I shall throw out my knowledge of the classical world." A classics professor in the audience jumped up and cried, "Good Lord! Not *that*."

And How Reliable Are the Gospel Witnesses?

Of course, good documents could convey bad testimony. How good are the witnesses to the life, death, and resurrection of Christ?

As a lawyer, I am to assume that witnesses, just like the person or persons on trial, are innocent until proven guilty. Therefore, the "burden of proof"—the responsibility for proving that the testimony is unreliable and the witnesses are not to be trusted—must fall on the critic. Can critics of the life of Christ show that the witnesses—Matthew, Mark, Luke, John, Paul, etc.—should not be trusted?

Absolutely not.

One technique employed by lawyers to see if a witness is reliable or not is to look first at the witness and then at what he or she says. The witness and what the witness says are considered from the standpoint of their basic nature and in terms of what might have influenced them.

If we do this with the Gospel writers, what do we find? In terms of character, they had no criminal records or psychological problems, and so cannot be dismissed as unreliable. They were clearly not influenced by their Jewish society to present Jesus as the Son of God (since the Jewish leadership did not believe that Jesus was the promised Messiah).

As for their writings, they have, as translator J. B. Phillips nicely put it, "the ring of truth." A New Testament Gospel does not always present the same information as another Gospel, but they do not contradict, but instead complement, each other. A lawyer just loves to have two opposing witnesses say *exactly* the same thing: he knows that they have "colluded" with each other and cannot be trusted.

Not so with the New Testament materials.

And archaeology backs up what the Gospel witnesses declare. For example, we have an inscription dated about A.D. 30 that confirms what the Gospels say about Pontius Pilate—that he was prefect (governor) of Judaea at the time of Jesus' trial and death.

I am also a certified International Fraud Examiner. Fraud examination generally tried to determine whether the three standard characteristics of alleged fraud are present: opportunity, motive, and low moral character.

The Gospel writers and the authors of the other New Testament books did not display those marks of fraud. They had no motive to lie about Jesus—quite the opposite—since the religious leadership of the country was dead set against the idea that Jesus was the God of the Old Testament, come to earth as Messiah and King of the Jews. Indeed, most of them died for their beliefs in Jesus' divinity.

They had been taught by Jesus that lying was of the devil (John 8: 44-45), so they would not have lied even on his behalf.

And, had they attempted to do so, they would not have been able to get away with it anyway, since hostile witnesses were present throughout Jesus' ministry—the Jewish religious leaders—and they would have blown the whistle had the Gospel witnesses given false testimony concerning him. If they were willing to crucify Jesus, they certainly would have had the means, the motive, and the opportunity to show that the New Testament writers were presenting false testimony. They did not do so—because they could not.

The Miracles Issue

But what is the real source of arguments against the resurrection of Jesus? How can the critics ignore his appearances to a host of people—and not just believers—over a forty day period before he publicly ascended to heaven? How can anyone deny this, when we know that over 500 people saw the risen Christ (I Corinthians 15)? The answer is that many people simply refuse to believe that miracles ever happen.

How, logically, could anyone maintain that miracles never occur? You would have to look under every rock in the universe—past, present, and future—to make sure there wasn't a miracle going on there! No one can do that.

If we want to be scientific, we need to check out the evidence for or against any miracle claim. Of course, there will be "miracles" for which the evidence is so poor or non-existent that we shall reject the supposed event. But if the evidence is good, we have no choice but to go with it. We don't know the universe so well that we can say that this or that event is impossible.

However, isn't a resurrection so strange that we would need to have an infinite amount of evidence in favour of it? Hardly. A celebrated 18th-century pastor to lawyers in England (Thomas Sherlock) pointed out that a resurrection is simply someone dead now and alive later. We have plenty of information about the reverse: people alive now, and dead later. But the evidence needed in both instances is *exactly the same*: being able to distinguish dead people from live people! Those living at the time of Christ were just as able to do this as we are. If they (or we) couldn't tell the difference between the live ones and the dead ones, we would be burying the wrong people!

Go into a funeral parlor and offer someone present a McDonald's fish burger. If he eats it, he is alive. After the resurrection, Jesus ate with his disciples (Luke 24).

Can't We Just Substitute a "Spiritual" Resurrection?

But why not avoid all this by believing in a "spiritual" resurrection of Jesus, not a physical, bodily one? Wouldn't that keep us from having to defend a real miracle? Maybe, but at much too high a cost.

There is no evidence for a "spiritual" resurrection. Remember: after Easter morning, Jesus eats with the disciples. And doubting Thomas touches the nail prints in the resurrected Jesus' hands and thrusts his hand into the wound in his side made by the soldiers who crucified him (John 20). And if Jesus had risen only "spiritually," there would be no assurance that believers in him would (as he promised) be raised physically at the Last Judgment.

In this regard, a wee philosophical point is worth mentioning. Evidence is possible for a physical event—but what evidence could ever exist for something purely "spiritual"? The people who go for naked spirituality are talking about things that no one could ever show to be true. Look at all the cults and isms that maintain (mutually contradictory) "spiritual truths." Christianity must not fall into that pit. Christian faith begins with a physical virgin birth, attests to physical—historical—fulfillments of prophecies and actual miracles, and sees its Lord physically ascend into heaven with the promise of returning in the same manner at the end of time (Acts 1:11). Let's not change Christianity from fact to some kind of unprovable mysticism.

A Final Word About the Importance of All This

But why is all this important? Answer: because salvation depends on it. Jesus himself said: "I am the Way, the Truth, and the Life; no one comes to the Father but by me" (John 14:6). And the Apostle Paul, writing under divine inspiration, told us specifically the nature of the saving gospel (1 Corinthians 15):

> Now, brothers and sisters, I want to remind you of the gospel I preached to you, which you received and on which you have taken your stand. By this gospel you are saved, if you hold firmly to the word I preached to you. Otherwise, you have believed in vain.

For what I received I passed on to you as of first importance: that Christ died for our sins according to the Scriptures, that he was buried, that he was raised on the third day according to the Scriptures, and that he appeared to Cephas, and then to the Twelve. After that, he appeared to more than five hundred of the brothers and sisters at the same time, most of whom are still living, though some have fallen asleep. Then he appeared to James, then to all the apostles, and last of all he appeared to me also.

Thus, the physical resurrection of our Lord is essential to eternal life. It is the foundation of our life after death with Christ and a central pillar of Christian faith. To deny it is to deny the truth of Christianity—and to cut us off personally from the wondrous gift that that resurrection provides to everyone who believes in the One whom God raised from the dead for our salvation.

10. Chronological Contradictions in the Gospels?

Is It Important?

Secularists have rightly argued that if the New Testament accounts of the life of Christ represent confused chronology, this raises serious doubts as to the historical value of those narratives. Religious liberals have naïvely thought that they were answering this by admitting contradictions, but arguing that they represent different "faith perspectives" and literary differences on the part of early Christian communities and thus that the biblical materials should not be taken as narrative history.

However, in the face of Nicodemus' difficulty in understanding and accepting spiritual new birth (John 3:12), Jesus responded: "If I have told you earthly things, and you do not believe, how then will you believe if I speak of heavenly things?" If the Bible cannot manage a consistent chronological narrative of earthly events, why would we trust it theologically, as when it prophetically speaks of the future—of Christ's second coming at the end of time, for example?

How To Resolve Apparent Chronological Contradictions?

The most common technique is to point out that a writer (*any* writer, not just the Gospel authors) does not have to maintain a strict chronological sequence in what he or she writes. One can arrange material topically rather than chronologically, and one can, without prejudice, move back and forth from a chronological to a topical organization of one's subject matter—and *vice versa.*

This approach is very helpful, but it hardly solves all potential problems. Thus, even if one argues that Luke's Gospel is likely to be the most chronologically-orientated of the four Gospels (see Luke's specific assertion to this effect in the preface to his Gospel—Luke 1:1-4), the topical will still have to be justifiably distinguished from the chronological where both appear to be employed. And one will still have to reconcile Luke's narrative with what is contained in the other Synoptic Gospels and in the Fourth Gospel.[1]

In this short paper, we shall employ a different approach—one that by no means denies topicality but which endeavors to solve some of the most intractable difficulties whilst assuming that the biblical writers are seriously trying to present an accurate chronology of the events in our Lord's earthly life and ministry. We suggest (to use legal terminology) that the burden of proof falls on the interpreter who wishes to depart from a chronological treatment of the Gospel materials. In a sense, this approach is little more than an application of the fundamental hermeneutic rule that narrative texts should be understood in their natural, historical sense unless the text itself shows that the author is moving to another literary style. Worth noting also is Luther's caution that in interpreting the Bible, "metaphor is the devil's tool." Our salvation has to be grounded in a genuine historical incarnation, and we need to be able to depend on the biblical texts for a historical Christ, not a literary creation.[2]

Our Approach

We shall consider five examples of alleged contradiction and argue that in each instance the contradiction evaporates if one supposes that *both of the conflicting narratives are correct, since they recount an event that happened more than once in our Lord's ministry.* This methodology assumes, to be sure, the fundamental logical axiom of non-contradiction, that A cannot be non-A at the same time under the same conditions. It is never a contradiction when one writer leaves out material that another writer includes. Contradiction is present only when one writer says A and another writer asserts non-A.

Moreover, our approach takes into account the extent of Jesus' three-year ministry and the fact, stated expressly in John's Gospel, that "there are also many other things which Jesus did, the which, if they should be written every one, I suppose that even the world itself could not contain the books" (John 21:25). Thus, one should expect that many of our Lord's miracles would have been repeated and many teachings presented again and again to different audiences. Doublets, therefore, would be natural in

---

[1] A. T. Robertson's classic harmony of the Gospels is based on the assumption of Lucan chronological priority. The just-published *Jésus: l'encyclopédie*, ed. Joseph Doré (Paris: Albin Michel, 2017) does likewise: "Notre choix: suivre le récit de Luc" (p. 21).

[2] See the essays in Montgomery, *Defending the Gospel in Legal Style* (Bonn, Germany: Verlag für Kultur und Wissenschaft, 2017).

10. Chronological Contradictions in the Gospels?

the recounting of the three-year ministry. It is sheer liberal fundamentalism to assume that a teaching or event in Jesus's earthly career recounted in the Gospels could not have taken place on several occasions.

Here is a table of five alleged chronological contradictions in the Gospel record:

Event	Synoptics versus	Gospel of John
Cleansing of the Temple	Occurs at the *end* of Jesus' earthly ministry	Occurs at the *beginning* of Jesus' earthly ministry
Jesus before Pilate	Occurs as first event in the trial of Christ	Occurs after soldiers' mocking (John 19)
Disciples at the crucifixion	Disciples positioned far from the cross	Disciples right at the cross

Event	Matthew, Mark, John	Luke
Meeting of the disciples with the resurrected Christ	Occurs in Galilee	Occurs in Jerusalem

Event	Matthew	Luke
Disciples pluck grain	Occurs right *after* healing of centurion's servant	Occurs *before* healing of centurion's servant

In every one of these five instances, there is every reason to suppose that the event happened *twice*, thus taking it out of the realm of chronological contradiction. Specifically:

- Jesus' cleansed the Temple *both* at the beginning *and* at the end of his ministry. Considering the condition of the Temple, one might have expected Jesus to do this even more than twice!
- There is no reason to limit Jesus's interrogations before Pilate to a single instance. The extralegal procedure employed against Jesus by the Jewish religious leaders and the political machinations involved are entirely consistent with two interrogations.

- The crucifixion occurred in an open area, not in a confined space. Therefore, it is only natural that the disciples moved about and were sometimes at a distance from the cross, sometimes near to it.
- The resurrected Christ met the disciples *both* in Jerusalem *and* in Galilee. A contradiction would be present only if one of the narrators had said that the contact occurred *only* in Jerusalem or *only* in Galilee.
- Is there any metaphysical reason why grain cannot be plucked on more than one occasion?

An Analogy

We can diagram the above five problems using a spiral, the "A" and the "B" on the circumference representing two different chronologies of the events, one later and one earlier:

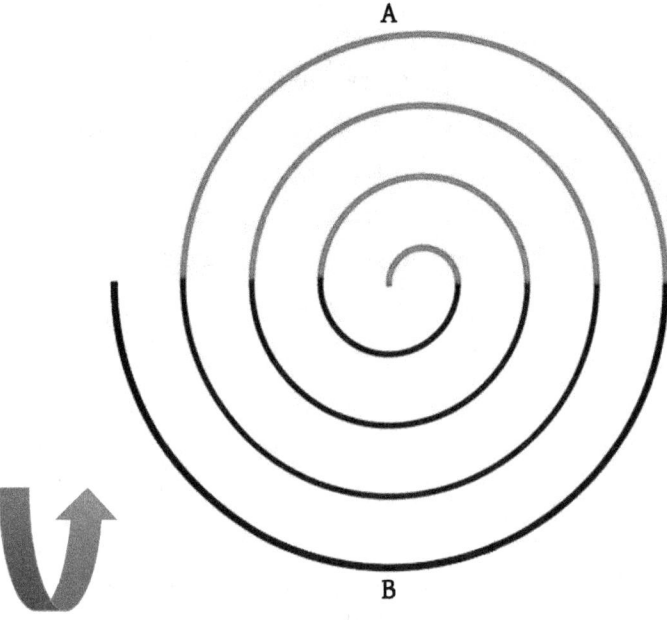

A	B
Synoptics	Jn
Mt, Mk, Jn	Lk
Mt	Lk

10. Chronological Contradictions in the Gospels? 83

Now, as an analogy, let us think of our spiral as a racetrack representing the "24 Hours of Le Mans"—that world-famous auto competition. Journalists come to report the race from all over the world. One paper states that the Peugeot blew a tire (or had carburetor problems or needed a driver replacement) during the first lap of the race. Another paper says that this happened during a later lap of the race. Contradiction? Not by any logical necessity. Considering the nature of the Le Mans races, it is perfectly possible (indeed, likely) that the unfortunate event may have occurred at least *twice* during the race, once in the first lap and again in a later lap.

We normally give the benefit of the doubt to accounts such as this, rather than regarding one account as the result of negligence or ignorance or perversity on the writer's part.

Can we not be at least as generous in our treatment of the Gospel writers' efforts to set forth an accurate account of the activities and teachings of God almighty, come to earth to die for the sins of the world? Surely, the Divine author, standing behind the human authors, deserves no less.

11. A More Consistent Application of Literary "Higher Criticism"

With appreciation to Archbishop Richard Whately for his classic, *Historic Doubts relative to Napoleon Buonaparte*

The Higher Critical Approach

The merits of the so-called Higher Criticism are taken for granted in liberal theological circles, in the mainline theological seminaries and in most university religion departments. Even in public libraries, the *Interpreter's Bible*, though manifesting badly out-of-date higher critical content, is considered a standard reference tool.

The essence of the Higher Critical methodology is to view the New Testament documents (and a good deal of the Old Testament) as literary endeavors to set forth religious and moral teaching, not as historical narratives.

How is such an approach justified—particularly in the face of the considerable efforts on the part of the biblical authors to assert the factuality of their material (e.g., Luke 1), plus the difficulty of denying historicity in light of the presence of hostile witnesses to the life and ministry of Jesus (who would surely have reveled in its non-factuality had that been the case)? All this is downplayed by an appeal to the ancient Jewish *Midrash* practice of creating quasi-historical stories that often build on or expand existing scriptural material, the purpose being to provide religious or moral lessons. In short, *the literary style of extrinsic writings is allowed to trump the solid historical claims of the material itself.*

For clarity, let us take a typical example of *Midrashim*. In Rabbinical literature (see the 1906 *Jewish Encyclopedia*), the giant Og—Deut. 3: 11. 13; Num. 21: 33, Joshua 13: 31—

> was not destroyed at the time of the Flood (Niddah 61a), for ... the waters reached only to his ankles (Midr. Peṭirat Mosheh, i. 128, in Jellinek, "B. H." ii.). ... It was Og who brought the news to Abraham of the captivity of Lot. This he did, however, with an evil motive, for he thought that Abraham would seek to release Lot and would be killed in battle with the great kings, and that he, Og, would be able to marry the beautiful Sarah (Gen. R. xlii. 12). A long lease of life was granted him as a reward for informing Abraham, but

because of his sinister motive he was destined to be killed by the descendants of Abraham. Og was present at the banquet which Abraham gave on the day Isaac was weaned (comp. Gen. xxi. 8). As Og had always declared that Abraham would beget no children, the guests teasingly asked him what he had to say now that Abraham had begotten Isaac, whereupon Og answered that Isaac was no true descendant since he could kill Isaac with one finger. It was in punishment for this remark that he was condemned to live to see a hundred thousand descendants of Abraham and to be killed in battle against them. (Gen. R. liii. 14). When Jacob went to Pharaoh and blessed him (Gen. xlvii. 7), Og was present, and the king said to him: "The grandson of Abraham, who, according to thy words, was to have no descendants, is now here with seventy of them." As Og cast an evil eye upon the children of Israel, God foretold that he would fall into their hands (Deut. R. i. 22).

During the battle of Edrei (Num. xxi. 33) Og sat on the city wall, his legs, which were eighteen ells long, reaching down to the ground; Moses did not know what monster he had before him until God told him that it was Og. Og hurled an entire mountain against the Israelites, but Moses intercepted it (Deut. R. *l.c.*).... Og uprooted a mountain three miles long, intending to destroy all Israel at once by hurling it upon their camp, which was also three miles in length; but while he was carrying it upon his head a swarm of locusts burrowed through it, so that it fell round his neck. When he attempted to throw off this unwieldy necklace long teeth grew from both sides of his mouth and kept the mountain in place. Thereupon Moses, who was himself ten ells tall, took an ax of equal length, jumped upward ten ells, so that he could reach Og's ankles, and thus killed him (Ber. 54b).

The Higher Critical argument is that if this sort of thing occurred in extrabiblical Jewish materials, it is legitimate to assume that it occurred in the Bible as well—particularly when one encounters stories containing miracles or other unusual events.

Even in Evangelical circles, such literary criticism is not entirely ruled out. Thus, Robert Gundry, emeritus professor at Westmont College, Santa Barbara, California, was removed—with difficulty—from membership in the Evangelical Theological Society (committed to biblical inerrancy) because he maintained that the Magi in Matthew's narrative of our Lord's birth were not historical figures but literary creations—to show that even gentiles could come to the truth of the gospel.

A Consistent Expansion of the Higher Critical Methodology

It is our contention that the practitioners of literary Higher Criticism have not seen the importance and value of a wider application of their hermeneutic. They have limited it to biblical materials, neglecting its obvious importance to modern allegedly historical events and writings.

We illustrate with a single example: *formgeschichtliche Methode* critic Rudolf Bultmann. Our contention is that this individual did not in fact live at all: he is a mythological figure doubtless created by the community of radical European New Testament scholars to move that field in the direction of an existential reading of Scripture and the non-necessity of any apologetic for the historicity of the biblical narratives concerning Jesus Christ. We may suppose that the circle of so-called "post-Bultmannians" (Fuchs, Ebeling, Conzelmann, Käsemann, and their ilk) developed the Bultmann story to further their theological views.

Absurd, you say? Do we not have birth and death dates for Bultmann (1884-1976)? his professorship at Marburg and contact with, e.g., philosopher Martin Heidegger there? Yes, but just as in the case of the New Testament documents, it was vital to include ostensible historical data (Cesar Augustus, the Herods, Caiaphas, *et al.*) in the narrative to give it a patina of factuality.

Arguing as the Higher Critics do, far more important than the mention of actual historical figures and events in the documents is the literary atmosphere within which the biblical (or Bultmannian) narratives appeared—in the latter case, the Europe of the mid-to-late 19th century. Consider but two illustrations of how, in that 19th-century culture, purely literary events were portrayed as *de facto* history.[1]

First, *Alice in Wonderland*, by mathematician Charles Dodgson, writing pseudonymously as Lewis Carroll. "Alice" was a real person: Alice Liddell; the "Dodo" was doubtless Dodgson himself, with his mild stutter—he would pronounce his name as "Dod-Dodgson." The setting is the Oxford of the writer's day. There are even characters in the story that have been identified as Disraeli and Gladstone. But these historical details hide the kind of non-historical myth that in fact comprises the narrative:

---

[1] More recent but less literary examples would include Martin Marty's theologian Franz Bibfeldt and Alexander McCall Smith's Professor Dr Moritz-Maria von Igelfeld.

CHAPTER VII. A Mad Tea-Party

There was a table set out under a tree in front of the house, and the March Hare and the Hatter were having tea at it: a Dormouse was sitting between them, fast asleep, and the other two were using it as a cushion, resting their elbows on it, and talking over its head. 'Very uncomfortable for the Dormouse,' thought Alice; 'only, as it's asleep, I suppose it doesn't mind.'

The table was a large one, but the three were all crowded together at one corner of it: 'No room! No room!' they cried out when they saw Alice coming. 'There's *plenty* of room!' said Alice indignantly, and she sat down in a large arm-chair at one end of the table.

'Have some wine,' the March Hare said in an encouraging tone.

Alice looked all round the table, but there was nothing on it but tea. 'I don't see any wine,' she remarked.

'There isn't any,' said the March Hare.

'Then it wasn't very civil of you to offer it,' said Alice angrily.

'It wasn't very civil of you to sit down without being invited,' said the March Hare.

'I didn't know it was *your* table,' said Alice; 'it's laid for a great many more than three.'

'Your hair wants cutting,' said the Hatter. He had been looking at Alice for some time with great curiosity, and this was his first speech.

'You should learn not to make personal remarks,' Alice said with some severity; 'it's very rude.'

The Hatter opened his eyes very wide on hearing this; but all he *said* was, 'Why is a raven like a writing-desk?'

'Come, we shall have some fun now!' thought Alice. 'I'm glad they've begun asking riddles.—I believe I can guess that,' she added aloud.

'Do you mean that you think you can find out the answer to it?' said the March Hare.

'Exactly so,' said Alice.

'Then you should say what you mean,' the March Hare went on.

'I do,' Alice hastily replied; 'at least—at least I mean what I say—that's the same thing, you know.'

'Not the same thing a bit!' said the Hatter. 'You might just as well say that "I see what I eat" is the same thing as "I eat what I see"!'

'You might just as well say,' added the March Hare, 'that "I like what I get" is the same thing as "I get what I like"!'

'You might just as well say,' added the Dormouse, who seemed to be talking in his sleep, 'that "I breathe when I sleep" is the same thing as "I sleep when I breathe"!'

What we have here is a mythopoeic tale—a story presented as history but not history at all.

11. A More Consistent Application of Literary "Higher Criticism"

A second—and even more telling—illustration: the Baron Münchhausen. His story was published in 1785 but its great popularity came in the 19th century, and we quote a typical passage from Thomas Seccombe's 1895 edition of a Kearsley text:

THE SURPRISING ADVENTURES OF BARON MUNCHAUSEN [1785]

by Rudolf Erich Raspe

CHAPTER XVI

This is a very short chapter, but contains a fact for which the Baron's memory ought to be dear to every Englishman, especially those who may hereafter have the misfortune of being made prisoners of war.

On my return from Gibraltar I travelled by way of France to England. Being a foreigner, this was not attended with any inconvenience to me. I found, in the harbour of Calais, a ship just arrived with a number of English sailors as prisoners of war. I immediately conceived an idea of giving these brave fellows their liberty, which I accomplished as follows:—After forming a pair of large wings, each of them forty yards long, and fourteen wide, and annexing them to myself, I mounted at break of day, when every creature, even the watch upon deck, was fast asleep. As I hovered over the ship I fastened three grappling irons to the tops of the three masts with my sling, and fairly lifted her several yards out of the water, and then proceeded across to Dover, where I arrived in half an hour! Having no further occasion for these wings, I made them a present to the governor of Dover Castle, where they are now exhibited to the curious.

As to the prisoners, and the Frenchmen who guarded them, they did not awake till they had been near two hours on Dover Pier. The moment the English understood their situation they changed places with their guard, and took back what they had been plundered of, but no more, for they were too generous to retaliate and plunder them in return.

The Baron was in fact an historical personage (Hieronymus Karl Friedrich, Freiherr von Münchhausen, 1720–1797), who had a dangerous habit of telling remarkable stories about himself; he was appalled when one Rudolf Erich Raspe published *Baron Munchausen's Narrative of his Marvellous Travels and Campaigns in Russia*, first in German and then in English and soon translated into many other languages. Indeed, not far from our home in the Alsace is the town of Munchhausen; it claims the Baron as its own. But the interesting aspect for our argument here is that the book seems on the surface to be an historical account, whereas in fact it is pure fiction, betrayed by its inclusion of the strangest of events.

We must therefore recognize that the principles of literary Higher Criticism are applicable not just to biblical material of early times but also to subsequent historiography and the hermeneutic understanding of texts.

Rudolf Bultmann is thus just one of many potential victims of a rigorous application of the Higher Criticism to historical material in general.

Conclusion

To be sure, there is another possible approach. It is to see the fallibility of judging historical materials by the standard of contemporary literature. Instead of allowing extrinsic materials to govern the interpretation of a given document, would it not be more sensible to allow the document to speak for itself and act as its own interpreter—at least in those cases where there is solid reason to take its material as factual history? Such an approach would have the considerable advantage of inductively starting and finishing with the work to be understood, instead of forcing it (in spite of its claims to historicity) to conform to materials written by others and for other purposes.

Should the reader of the present essay be interested in this alternative solution, may we recommend this author's *Tractatus Logico-Theologicus* and *Defending the Gospel in Legal Style*—where, by way of numerous theological examples, the unscholarly nature of the Higher Criticism is examined in detail?

If, however, that alternative is rejected in favour of regarding biblical narratives as non-historical, we plead for greater consistency in the application of literary Higher Criticism beyond the sacred texts. Note that doing so can result in the de-historicizing of virtually anything—perhaps including, eventually, one's very own existence.

12. A Short and Easie Method with Postmodernists

Abstract

Among the major secular opponents of the claim that there is "no other name by which we must be saved" than that of Jesus Christ is the philosophy of Postmodernism.

We contend that the often prolix contemporary theological attempts to refute Postmodernism have generally produced more heat than light. The proper approach is hardly that of John G. Stackhouse, Jr. (*Humble Apologetics*), who makes unnecessary concessions to the Postmodernist mentality, and, in doing so, weakens the classic case for Christianity. Rather, we need to recognise that Postmodernism is epistemologically flawed from the outset and that even its advocates cannot consistently live by its worldview.

This paper therefore treats (1) the nature and origins of Postmodernism, (2) the law of non-contradiction, illustrated by an interesting computer program in the Pascal language, and (3) the objection that "religious" claims should not be subjected to the same rigorous epistemological criteria as claims in everyday life.

Introduction

Our title is derived from a celebrated and often reprinted 18th-century work of apologetics: Charles Leslie's *A Short and Easie Method with the Deists: Wherein the Certainty of the Christian Religion Is Demonstrated*.[1] It is our contention that the detailed and often prolix contemporary attempts to refute Postmodernism have generally produced more heat than light. We also believe that the proper approach is hardly that of John G. Stackhouse, Jr. (*Humble Apologetics*), where unnecessary concessions to the Postmodernist mentality weaken the classic case for Christianity.[2] The right method to follow is not that of the aphorism, "If you can't beat 'em, join 'em," but a

---

[1] 8th ed., London: J. Applebee, 1723.
[2] See the trenchant review by Canadian judge Dallas Miller in 4/3 *Global Journal of Classical Theology*, October, 2004 (www.phc.edu).

realisation that Postmodernism is epistemologically flawed from the outset and that even its advocates cannot consistently live by its worldview.

The Nature of Postmodernism

Postmodernism, admittedly, is an amorphous phenomenon—rather like the New Age mentality: exceedingly difficult to pin down owing to the fact that its adherents and fellow travellers do not maintain a single credo. But one of the most helpful analyses of the phenomenon has been provided by D. E. Polkinghorne, who identifies four basic themes: (1) foundationlessness, (2) fragmentariness, (3) constructivism, and (4) neo-pragmatism.

> The tacit assumptions of this epistemology of practice are: (a) there is no epistemological ground on which the indubitable truth of knowledge statements can be established; (b) a body of knowledge consists of fragments of understanding, not a system of logically integrated statements; (c) knowledge is a construction built out of cognitive schemes and embodied interactions with the environment; and (d) the test of a knowledge statement is its pragmatic usefulness in accomplishing a task, not its derivation from an approved set of methodological rules.[3]

The Postmodernist, in maintaining that no concrete epistemic foundation exists, focuses on the immediate and the local, not on any general truths (since there are none); for him or her, the only reality is the product of one's personal constructs and the question is never whether *x* is true but whether by accepting *x* one will arrive at a satisfactory outcome. Advocates of this viewpoint include American psychologists George A. Kelly (creator of "PCT"—Personal Construct Theory)[4] and Kenneth J. Gergen.[5] Postmodernism has impacted not only psychological counselling, but also the wider spheres of law, literature, philosophy, theology, and the media.[6]

---

[3] D. E. Polkinghorne, "Postmodern Epistemology of Practice," in S. Kvale (ed.), *Psychology and Postmodernism* (London: Sage, 1992), pp. 146-47.
[4] George A. Kelly, *The Psychology of Personal Constructs* (New York: Norton, 1955).
[5] K. J. Gergen, "Toward a Postmodern Psychology," in Kvale, *op. cit.*, pp. 17-30. On Postmodernism in general, see Christopher Butler, *Postmodernism; A Brief Insight* (New York and London: Sterling, 2002).
[6] Cf. Montgomery, "Speculation vs. Factuality: An Analysis of Modern Unbelief," in his *Christ As Centre and Circumference* (Bonn, Germany: Verlag für Kultur und Wissenschaft, 2012), sec. 1.

Historical Excursus

How did such a viewpoint come about? And how could it have gained influence in a western world that prides itself on scientific objectivity? The answer lies in Luther's profound insight that the history of our fallen race is that of a drunk reeling from one wall to the other.

In the 18th century European thought, especially in Germany, jettisoned the Christocentric insights of the Protestant Reformation for so-called "Enlightenment" rationalism.[7] By the 19th century, philosophers—the most influential being Hegel and the post-Hegelians—had convinced themselves that they could arrive at the very "essence" of universal truth by unaided human reason.

In reaction, Danish lay theologian Søren Kierkegaard saw such efforts as *hubris*. He recognized that it is a chimerical dream to think that one can arrive at the essence of the universe by human reason. Because mankind's finite condition is characterized by *Angst* and estrangement, it is impossible to get beyond *"Existenz"*—one's own subjective condition. The only solution is to find Christ, the source of salvation, at the heart of one's personal existence.

But the existential movement originating with Kierkegaard developed chiefly along atheistic lines in the writings of 20th century philosophers Heidegger and Sartre. Kierkegaard's remedy ('truth is subjectivity") for the disease of rational idealism turned out to be as bad as the disease itself, for it spawned a subjectivistic perspective that has impacted almost every aspect of modern society.[8]

Consider a few prominent examples. In philosophy of science: the Kuhn thesis (progress in science is the result of changes in philosophical perspective, not the consequence of newer or better objective evidence). In law: the Critical Legal Studies movement ("CLS"), holding that legal texts

---

[7] See Montgomery, "From Enlightenment to Extermination," *Christianity Today*, 11 October 1974; reprinted in Montgomery, *The Shaping of America* (Minneapolis: Bethany, 1981) and in *Christians in the Public Square* (Calgary, Alberta: Canadian Institute for Law, Theology and Public Policy, 1996).

[8] The proper solution is to recognize that, although we cannot by unaided human reason arrive at the meaning of the universe as a whole, we do indeed have the ability to investigate particular facts (in science, history, etc.)—facts such as the historicity, character and resurrection of Jesus Christ. One thereby encounters *special revelation*—biblical truth—which provides by God's grace and not by human rationality an objective grounding for subjective salvation and insight into ultimate issues. I have developed this in my many apologetics writings.

have no inherent, objective meaning; we are thus to employ them politically so as to achieve our personal, subjective ideals of justice.[9] Literature: the "hermeneutical circle," which asserts that the meaning of a text can never be established apart from the subjective stance of the interpreter (cf. James Joyce's *Ulysses*). Music: the atonal (Schoenberg). Art: post-impressionism, Dada, and their successors (Marcel Duchamp's "Nude Descending a Staircase").[10]

In such a subjective cultural context, the appearance of Postmodernism seems entirely comprehensible—perhaps even inevitable.

Story-telling

One of the most common (and frustrating) aspects of discussion with a Postmodernist is his or her insistence on "telling one's own story." You are allowed—indeed, encouraged—to tell your story: let us say, the story of your conversion, based on your solid conviction of the factual truth of the Christian gospel. This is then followed by the Postmodernist's story, which, needless to say, is incompatible with the position you have just set forth.

This incompatibility, however, does not bother the Postmodernist to any observable degree. Why? Because for him or her there is no single, objective truth. Each of us constructs reality as he or she sees fit, and the issue is simply the pragmatic effects of those constructs in one's experience.

One is reminded of existentialist Jean-Paul Sartre's account of his encounter with a young resistant during the German occupation of France in World War II. The young man very much wanted to escape through Spain to join de Gaulle and the Free French in London, but his mother was dependent on him. What should he do? Sartre's response was: "Decide! There are no omens in the world, and, if there were, we would give them their meaning."[11] We are not told the young man's reaction to these words; we expect he went away mumbling: "That's the last time I go to an existentialist for advice!"

The fundamental problem here lies in the fact that (to paraphrase George Orwell), although all stories are equal, some are more equal than others. That is to say, there are sublime (and true) stories, and there are

---

[9] Montgomery, *Christ Our Advocate* (Bonn, Germany: Verlag für Kultur und Wissenschaft, 2002), pp. 32–33.
[10] Cf. Montgomery, *The Suicide of Christian Theology* (Minneapolis: Bethany, 1970).
[11] J.-P. Sartre, *Existentialism and Human Emotions* (New York: Philosophical Library, 2000).

horrific (and damnable) stories. Would we really be willing to accept Hitler's story as set out in *Mein Kampf* and treat it as having the same validity as the story of Jesus' loving sacrifice of himself on the Cross for the sins of the world? Surely, there are objective ethical values that cannot be ignored. Descriptively, the world is full of stories; normatively, they must be distinguished on the basis of the moral quality and truth-value (if any) they represent.

A trenchant critic of Postmodernist therapy writes—and the very same point applies *mutatis mutandis* in the theological realm:

> How can a person be encouraged to acknowledge truly unpleasant truths, especially those sordid, unflattering facts which may lack the compensation of a tragic dimension, if one assumes that there is no distinction between truth and mere fiction—but only stories about stories about stories? And what is to prevent psychotherapy from turning into an elaborate workshop for rationalization, a place for spinning self-justificatory fantasies and fostering all the subtle complacencies of narcissistic entitlement and self-satisfaction?[12]

And beyond the realm of "self-justificatory fantasies" rises the spectre of political power. Those who have the power are in a position to choose the story that is heard and prevails. Where there is no objective standard for distinguishing true from false stories, those with power will make the choice—excluding, imprisoning, killing those who disagree.

The Law of Non-contradiction

The Postmodern error cuts far deeper than psychological and ethical considerations. The Postmodernist's refusal to reject stories in contradiction with other stories betrays a solipsist epistemology: there is no objective world; only worlds constructed by the storytellers exist, and these pose no problem even when in mutual contradiction.

The difficulty with such an approach is that no one can consistently live that way—and, as Francis Schaeffer was wont to say, a philosophy that even its adherents cannot live by cannot possibly be true. The Eastern mystic may declare that the material world is *maya*—illusion—but will still treat it as real and employ a map to find a Chinese restaurant. The adherent of the cult of Christian Science may declare pain to be unreal but will

---

[12] Louis A. Sass, "The Epic of Disbelief: The Postmodernist Turn in Contemporary Psychoanalysis," in Kvale, *op. cit.*, p. 177.

still scream when stuck with a pin—declaring (at minimum) that "the illusion of pain was almost as bad as the pain would have been."

The Postmodernist, whilst declaring that mutually self-contradictory stories can all be true, nonetheless assumes the law of non-contradiction. He or she hardly believes—to take an obvious example—that the story being told at the moment can simultaneously be true *and* false. If told that he or she just said non-*x* when *x* had been in fact declared, the Postmodernist would certainly attempt to correct the listener.[13]

Let us consider a practical illustration both of the ethical point raised in the previous section of this paper and of the logical point just made. A Teetotalers Club and a Drinkers Club have mutually exclusive membership requirements. There is, however, suspicion that the same individual or individuals may have joined *both* societies. A computer programme is therefore developed to determine if this is the case:[14]

program Hypocrite (OUTPUT, First, Second);

{Identifies persons who have hypocritically joined both a Drinkers} {Club and a Teetotalers Club, and demonstrates the absolute} {necessity of the law of non-contradiction in all areas of life,} {practical as well as theoretical, i.e., the principle at the root} {of all formal logic that A cannot = ~A at the same time under the} {same conditions. The programme will name the first common entry} {appearing on the two membership lists; only after deleting that} {name from the lists and rerunning the programme will a second} {hypocrite be identified—and so on. When all common names have} {been removed, the programme will show no result; this will} {likewise be the case should no hypocritical common member of the} {two organisations exist. *Membership pledge of the Drinkers Club:*} {"I promise in the name of St Paul to imbibe an alcoholic drink} {each day—a fine French wine if possible." *Teetotalers' pledge:*} {"I promise in the name of Carry Nation never to drink an} {alcoholic beverage, even for my stomach's sake."}

---

[13] Cf. the discussion of multiple logics in Montgomery, *Tractatus Logico-theologicus* (4th ed.; Bonn, Germany: Verlag für Kultur und Wissenschaft, 2009), proposition 2.2.

[14] The following programme is set out in the standard Pascal language—as are programmes on the author's website: www.jwm.christendom.co.uk To run this programme, one must employ a Pascal compiler; we suggest THINK Pascal 4.5 (available free on the web). It is worth noting that all computer operations (not just this one) rely on the law of non-contradiction: "The entire computer concept is founded on the law of non-contradiction: in binary computer language you must choose 'yes' or 'no'—a 'dialectic answer' is no answer at all. There are no neo-orthodox computers" (Montgomery, *Computers, Cultural Change, and the Christ* [Wayne, NJ: Christian Research Institute, 1969], p. 15).

12. A Short and Easie Method with Postmodernists

var

First, Second: TEXT;

Name1, Name2: string;

begin

WRITELN('Object: to identify at least one hypocrite who has joined both the Drinkers and the Teetotalers Club.');

RESET(First, 'drinkersfile');

RESET(Second, 'temperancefile');

READLN(First, Name1);

READLN(Second, Name2);

repeat

if Name1 < Name2 then

begin

READLN(First, Name1);

end;

if Name2 < Name1 then

begin

READLN(Second, Name2);

end;

until Name1 = Name2;

WRITE('A hypocrite, whose name appears on both lists, is: ', Name1, '!');

end.

The membership lists of the two clubs are as follows; they are fed into the above programme as text files:

Drinkers Club Membership List
Gangee (Sam)
Johnson (Samuel)
Luther (Martin)
Montgomery (John)
Schlonk (Alphonso)
Twist (Oliver)
Xavier (Rodney)

Teetotalers Club Membership List
Falwell (Jerry)
Heartacre (Silvia)
Loopy (David)
McAgony (Alister)
Perfect (Wholesome)
Schlonk (Alphonso)
Ziltch (Methusula)

The programme "Hypocrite" is then run and the result is as follows:

Output Result of Running the "Hypocrite" Programme:

Object: to identify at least one hypocrite on the member lists of the Drinkers Club and the Teetotalers Club.

A hypocrite, whose name appears on both lists, is:

Schlonk (Alphonso)!

It is our contention that the Postmodernist, no more than the anti-Postmodernist, would be satisfied with Schlonk's conduct and would insist that he cease to be a member of at least one of the two societies.

But Aren't We Dealing with "Religion"?

The objector may well retort that our examples appear compelling, but they operate in the non-religious area—and in matters of religion it may well be proper to allow a multiplicity of diverse (even contradictory) viewpoints, since religious assertions are metaphysical in nature.

Our ethical example (Hitler's story) shows, however, the interlocking of ordinary life with absolute moral values. Indeed, there is no bright line separating religion from other spheres of life. All knowledge is interlocked. Our divisions of the pie of knowledge are arbitrary—to facilitate study and because no one can master all areas of thought. Physics slides into chemistry, chemistry into the biological sciences, biology into psychology, psychology into sociology, sociology into history, history into literature; etc., etc.

And where the Christian religion is concerned, earth and heaven conjoin. God reveals himself in ordinary human history and human experience—through prophets and apostles and principally through the incarnation of His Son for the salvation of the human race. Thus the same law of non-contradiction that informs ordinary life will apply equally to ultimate questions of religious truth.

As C. S. Lewis put it, the Christ-symbol Aslan and the false god Tash cannot be blended into a "Tashlan."[15] There is one and only one proper foundation: "Other foundation can no man lay than that is laid, which is Jesus Christ" (1 Corinthians 3:11). There is only one saving story, namely the gospel story. As Jesus said expressly: "I am the way, the truth, and the life: no one comes unto the Father but by me" (John 14:6). And thus, from the days of the Apostles, the church has always proclaimed: "Neither is there salvation in any other: for there is none other name under heaven given among men, whereby we must be saved" (Acts 4:12).

---

[15] In *The Last Battle,* the concluding volume of the Chronicles of Narnia.

PART TWO: THEOLOGY, THE FUTURE, AND THE OCCULT

1. Law & Morality: Friends or Foes?

An Inaugural Lecture

The immediate occasion for this lecture was my advancement, on 4 June 1993, to a personal Professorship. Was this a moral act? Since the man who serves as his own lawyer has a fool for a client, I am not the one to answer that question. Instead, I wish to express my deepest thanks to Vice-Chancellor A. J. Wood, who nominated me for the chair, and to the Conferment Panel, especially its external members, Professors P. Hirst of Cambridge University and K. Goulding of Middlesex University, for their votes of confidence.

My Professorship is in Law and Humanities, attesting my conviction that the dry, technical field of the law (as it is generally perceived by non-lawyers) cannot be separated from the value-laden domain of the liberal arts. The very "idea of a university", as John Henry Newman declared in his great work of that title, requires the integration of learned disciplines: a *universitas* that will encompass science and art, law and human values.

Newman was also at pains to show that no such integration can occur without an all-embracing, integrative principle, and therefore that a university without the religious dimension is a contradiction in terms. If he was right, my employment of theological categories later in this lecture will be fully justified. If not, I shall at minimum have demonstrated that English universities, unlike their American counterparts, do not suffer from the kind of "political correctness" that excludes religion from academic discussion for fear of offending someone. I tend toward the view, in any case, that a lecture incapable of offending anyone is probably too bland for public presentation.

Our subject is law and morals, and the connection, if any, between them. Do they operate in air-tight compartments? If not, what is their relationship? Are they friends or enemies?

This is a topic, to be sure, which has attracted considerable attention among English academics and the general public for well over a generation, ever since the famous Hart-Devlin debate commencing with Lord Devlin's 1959 British Academy Maccabaean Lecture in Jurisprudence entitled, The *Enforcement of Morals*.[1] That lecture produced a tempest, and the

---

[1] Sir Patrick Devlin, *The Enforcement of Morals* (London: Oxford University Press for the British Academy, 1959), and frequently reprinted.

waves from it continue to batter the shores of academe. Professor H. L. A. Hart and others were intensely disturbed by such passages as Devlin's concluding remarks:

> A man who concedes that morality is necessary to society must support the use of those instruments without which morality cannot be maintained. The two instruments are those of teaching, which is doctrine, and of enforcement, which is the law. If morals could be taught simply on the basis that they are necessary to society, there would be no social need for religion; it could be left as a purely personal affair. But morality cannot be taught in that way. Loyalty is not taught in that way either. No society has yet solved the problem of how to teach morality without religion. So the law must base itself on Christian morals and to the limit of its ability enforce them, not simply because they are the morals of most of us, nor simply because they are the morals which are taught by the established Church—on these points the Law recognizes the right to dissent—but for the compelling reason that without the help of Christian teaching the law will fail.

Our task is not to replay the Hart-Devlin arguments—others have done that—but to attempt to analyse, at the most fundamental level, whether law and morals do in fact have an essential interrelationship, and, if they do, whence moral values can justifiably be derived and the implications of a non-relativistic value system for a pluralistic society. We shall begin with the arguments for *not* connecting law and morals, proceed to the case *for* connecting them, then endeavor to establish a *justifiable source* for moral principles, and finally offer guidelines for *applying* those moral values in a pluralistic legal milieu.[2]

Law Versus Morals

In the popular mind—for the man or woman on the Clapham omnibus—ethics and the law (or, at least, lawyers) are at opposite poles. American columnist and television commentator Andy Rooney tells the following personal story:

> When I was at MGM years ago, I worked for a producer named Voldemar Vetluguin. I was in his office one day when his assistant came in.

---

[2] We do not attempt a formal definition of "morality," but employ the term in the ordinary-language sense of "normative ethical values." For a more rigorous definitional analysis, see, *inter alia*, François Prevet, *La loi morale et l'évolution des idées* (Paris: Sirey, n.d.) and G. Wallace and A. D. M. Walker (eds.), *The Definition of Morality* (London: Methuen, 1970).

"You got an angry letter from the American Bar Association," the assistant said. "They've been keeping records and they say that in the last 179 movies in which lawyers were portrayed, they were shown as dishonest 151 times. What should I say to them?"

Vetluguin sat there thinking a minute; then he turned to his assistant and said, "Tell them if those figures are right, the lawyers got a break."[3]

The lawyers themselves have not helped the common perception of their ethical standards. When William Kuntsler says, "Screw the law—you get the guy off any way you can,"[4] one may perhaps discount it on the basis of Kuntsler's neo-Marxist radicalism; but what about F. Lee Bailey's declaration, "Prosecuting or defending a case is nothing more than getting to those people who will talk for your side, who will say what you want said"[5]? Of some twenty thousand lawyers who attended the San Francisco convention of the American Bar Association in 1987, twelve turned up for the session on how to provide better legal access to the public.[6] Perhaps the classical writers have not been far wrong:

Here malice, rapine, accident conspire,
And now a rabble rages, now a fire;
Their ambush here relentless ruffians lay,
And here the fell attorney prowls for prey.
-*Samuel Johnson*

God works wonders now and then;
Behold! a lawyer and an honest man.
-*Ben Franklin*

He saw a lawyer killing a viper
On a dunghill hard by his own stable
And the Devil smiled, for it put him in mind
Of Cain and his brother Abel.
-*Samuel Coleridge*

---

[3] Andrew Roth and Jonathan Roth, *Devil's Advocates: The Unnatural History of Lawyers* (Berkeley, California: Nolo Press, 1989), p. 142.
[4] Jonathan Roth and Andrew Roth (eds.), *Poetic Justice* (Berkeley, California: Nolo Press, 1988), p. 43.
[5] Roth, *Devil's Advocates* (*op. cit.*), p. 147.
[6] *Ibid.*, p. 159. It may be of interest that I was one of a significant number of American attorneys who several years ago resigned from the American Bar Association (a voluntary organisation, not a licensing body) when it officially identified itself with the pro-choice stance on the issue of abortion.

But the morals (or absence thereof) among those practising the law does not prove that there is or is not a logical connection between the field of ethics and the field of law. What arguments have been presented to show a necessary disjunction between law and morals per se?

The classic philosophical attempt to sever law and morals was that of Immanuel Kant. In his *Groundwork of the Metaphysic of Morals*, he argues:

> The essence of things does not vary with their external relations; and where there is something which, without regard to such relations, constitutes by itself the absolute worth of man, it is by this that man must also be judged by everyone whatsoever—even by the Supreme Being. Thus morality lies in the relation of actions to the autonomy of the will—that is, to a possible making of universal law by means of its maxims.[7]

In this (typically dense) passage,[8] Kant is distinguishing between morality, which is a function of the "autonomy of the will" and has to do purely with inner motivation, and the law, which focuses on "external relations"—conformity to external standards. For morality, only motive or intention is important; the moral man will act with an inner consciousness of duty, and whether that motivation conforms or does not conform to external legal standards is of no consequence to the inherent morality of his inner being. Law, in diametric contrast to morality, concerns itself only with externals—whether a legal act is performed or not—without regard to the motives behind it.

The naïveté of Kant's position will be immediately apparent to the legally trained. Fundamental to the definition of a crime are the dual concepts of *actus reus* and *mens rea*—the "guilty act" and the "guilty intent"—concepts which, according to Lord Denning, go back at least to St. Augustine in the 5th century.[9] Except for a very limited number of statutory crimes, guilt can only be established when the accused has not simply done an illegal act but has in fact done it with the appropriate general or specific criminal intent. Indeed, as Del Vecchio has well said, "If Kant had been a

---

[7] Immanuel Kant, *The Moral Law, or Kant's Groundwork of the Metaphysic of Morals*, ed. and trans. H. J. Paton (3d ed.; London: Hutchinson's University Library, 1956), p. 107 (para. 85).

[8] Macaulay is supposed to have remarked, after attempting to comprehend Kant's *Critique of Pure Reason*, "It is remarkable in this day and age that one intelligent man cannot write so that another intelligent man can understand him."

[9] Sir Alfred Denning, *The Changing Law* (London: Stevens, 1953), p. 112. From Augustine the *mens rea* "found its place in the laws of Henry I. . . . That has been the rule of English law from that time to this. In order that an act should be punishable, it must be morally blameworthy. It must be a sin."

jurist, he would have understood how important is the consideration of the *animus* in every branch of Law."[10] Trendelenburg goes even further in refuting Kant when he points out, in his *Naturrecht auf dem Grunde der Ethik*, that Kant's separation of the legal from the moral in this fashion "leads to the external formal legality of the Pharisees."[11]

But it is not only philosophers who have endeavored to drive a wedge between law and morals. Juridical scholars themselves have also made the attempt, albeit on different grounds.

Sheriff Gordon, in his standard work, *The Criminal Law of Scotland*, maintains that legal responsibility is in principle amoral: the idea at root is not to provide infallible moral results in particular cases but to maintain a general concept of legal responsibility in society. He illustrates by the teacher who, before going out of the classroom, singles out a boy and says, "I shall hold you responsible for any noise." The issue here is not the boy's ability to prevent the noise; responsibility is imputed to achieve desired social ends. For Gordon, law entails authority, and rules issued by that authority; whether the rules are ethical or not and whether they achieve moral ends in each particular case are secondary questions.[12]

The position of Sheriff Gordon derives, of course, from the legal philosophy of Positivism or Realism, as set forth by John Austin and Jeremy Bentham in the 19th century. For the Positivists, "law is the command of the sovereign" and the introduction of moral issues into the definition of the law partakes of "nonsense on stilts," to use Bentham's epithet for Blackstone's Natural Law ideals. In our century, the strongest form of Legal Positivism has been that of the so-called Scandinavian Legal Realists (Hägerström, Olivecrona, Alf Ross), who have argued, along the lines of the Vienna Circle of Logical Positivists and the first edition of A.J. Ayer's *Language, Truth and Logic*, that ethical ideas are analytically meaningless and technically nonsensical: law must be defined entirely without reference to moral values. A milder form of Legal Positivism is that of the American Legal Realists (O. W. Holmes, Jr, Karl Llewellyn), who, while agreeing with the Scandinavians that moral considerations must not enter into the definition of law, are willing (and often eager) to discuss moral and policy questions as separate and distinct (non-legal) issues.

---

[10] Giorgio del Vecchio, *The Philosophy of Law*, trans. T.O. Martin (Georgetown: Catholic University of America Press, 1953), pp. 110–11.

[11] Adolf Trendelenburg, *Naturrecht auf dem Grunde der Ethik* (2d ed., 1868), p. 21.

[12] G. H. Gordon, *The Criminal Law of Scotland* (Edinburgh: Green, 1967), p. 45. For a critique, see W. D. Lamont, *Law and the Moral Order* (Aberdeen: Aberdeen University Press, 1981), especially pp. 110–13.

Legal Positivism, whether in its original English form or in its Scandinavian and American variations, has been subjected to intense criticism in recent years.[13] Perhaps the most damning argument against it has been the amoral legal systems of 20th century totalitarianism (Nazi Germany, Vichy France, Stalinist Russia), which have epitomised legal power without moral restraint.[14]

Returning to Sheriff Gordon's illustration: Would we want to live in a society where any person (perhaps a Jew or a Black) could—by arbitrary fiat—be held accountable at law for wrongs committed by others? Granted, some law is better than no law, since anarchy is the closest to hell we can get on this earth. But just this side of total anarchy on the scale of infernalities is the immoral legal system.

The Interdependence of Law and Morals

Over against Kant and the Legal Positivists, we argue for the connection of law and morals. To demonstrate this, we shall maintain (1) that moral law is a direct source of positive law, (2) that law can and does influence morals, and, finally (3), that morality deeply affects the content of the positive law.

Morals as a source of law. When one turns from the philosophers of law and the textbook writers to the most distinguished common law judges of modern times, one finds strong reason to believe that morality has a central influence on the very creation of the positive law. In America, Judge Dillon, writing semi-autobiographically in his immensely influential work, *The Law and Jurisprudence of England and America*, declared:

> Law is not ethics, it is true; but except so far as laws are arbitrary or conventional regulations, or are mere usages and customs not having a moral quality,—if there be any such,—they have an ethical foundation....
>
> Law in its nature is therefore opposed to all that is fitful, capricious, unjust, partial, or destructive....

---

[13] See John Warwick Montgomery, *The Law Above the Law* (Minneapolis: Bethany, 1975); the leading essay of this book has also been published in *Law & Justice*, No. 112/113 (Hilary/Easter, 1992). Cf. also M. J. Detmold, *The Unity of Law and Morality: A Refutation of Legal Positivism* (London: Routledge & Kegan Paul, 1984); and, in general, the critical entries in chaps. 16 ("Positivism. British Theories"), 17 ("The Pure Theory"), and 21 ("Modem Realism") in R. W. M. Dias, *A Bibliography of Jurisprudence* (3d ed.; London: Butterworths, 1979).

[14] Cf. Dominique Rémy (ed.), *Les Lois de Vichy* (Paris : Editions Romillat, 1992).

1. Law & Morality: Friends or Foes?

Kant's philosophy is to me, I am sorry to confess (for it may be my fault), in general unprofitable enough in practical results; but there is one noble passage of his that made on me an impression that years have never effaced or dimmed: "There are two things which, the more I contemplate them, the more they fill my mind with admiration,—the starry heavens above me, and the moral law within me."

Not less wondrous than the revelations of the starry heavens, and much more important, and to no class of men more so than to lawyers, is the "moral law" which Kant found within himself, and which is likewise found within and is consciously recognised by every man. This moral law holds its dominion by divine ordination over us all, from which escape or evasion is impossible. This moral law is the eternal and indestructible sense of justice and of right written by God on the living tablets of the human heart, and revealed in His Holy Word. It is considerations of justice and right that make up the web and woof and form the staple of a lawyer's life and vocation. The lawyer's work and business are, it is true, with human laws; but Let me repeat, the lawyer makes a grievous mistake who supposes law to be the mere equivalent of written enactments or judicial decisions.... If unblamed I may advert to my own experience, I always felt in the exercise of the judicial office irresistibly drawn to the intrinsic justice of the case, with the inclination, and if possible the determination, to rest the judgment upon the very right of the matter. In the practice of the profession I always feel an abiding confidence that if my case is morally right and just it will succeed, whatever technical difficulties may appear to stand in the way; and the result usually justifies the confidence.[15]

Such comments inevitably remind one of Lord Denning on the English judicial scene. After examining Denning's early judgments and a number of his extra-judicial writings, F. E. Dowrick provides an evaluation that even Denning's critics would not contest: "As a judge of first instance in 1947 in the High Trees House case he startled the profession by the use of a moral proposition as an integral part of his reasoning in such a way as to appear to challenge a deep-rooted legal principle, and he has continued to use moral criteria liberally in the process of restating the law in the Court of Appeal."[16] Dowrick analyses Denning's use of moral categories in the following terms:

---

[15] John Dillon, *The Laws and Jurisprudence of England and America* (Boston: Little, Brown, 1894), pp. 14 ff.
[16] F. E. Dowrick, *Justice According to the English Common Lawyers* (London: Butterworths, 1961), p. 88.

In his judicial technique the notion may be discerned operating in two ways. In some cases he overtly relies on some moral principle, the validity of which is assumed *a priori*, and which he applies casuistically to the facts before the court. In others he concentrates upon the facts before the court, setting them out not only in the narrow form disclosed in the pleadings but in their wider social context, and then, relying on an intuitive sense of right and wrong, pronounces a moral judgment *ad hoc*.[17]

Whether or not we agree with Denning's apparent willingness to subordinate precedent to the personal morality of the judge, we are compelled to see in his work—which unquestionably constitutes the single most influential judicial activity in England in this generation—clear evidence of morality providing a concrete and powerful source of legal development.

Law as an influence on morals. A. L. Goodhart, in his *English Law and the Moral Law*, has provided important illustrations of the fact that the relation between law and morality is not a one-way street. In certain instances, public morality has dragged its feet and only the pressures of enlightened legislation or judicial decision have been successful in raising the moral tone of society. The criminal law against duelling is a striking example. "Today a man who becomes engaged in a duel would be regarded as a moral wrongdoer: two centuries ago a man who refused to accept a challenge might well have been regarded as a social outcast."[18] This general change of moral perception was squarely due to the conscientious judicial application of anti-duelling statutes.

The various Married Women's Property Acts offer another illustration. For centuries, society at large was not troubled by the fact that the *feme covert*—like the infant or the imbecile—suffered severe impediments to property ownership in her own right. It was only due to enlightened legislation and its implementation by the courts that the married woman's merger of civil existence in that of her husband came to be recognised as morally reprehensible. To the extent that the modern married woman has

---

[17] *Ibid.*, p. 89. On Denning's judicial philosophy and practice, see: Peter Robson and Paul Watchman (eds.), *Justice, Lord Denning and the Constitution* (Aldershot, Hants : Gower, 1981) [highly critical of Denning's moral style and influence]; J.L. Jowell and J.P.W.B. McAuslan (eds.), *Lord Denning: the Judge and the Law* (London: Sweet & Maxwell, 1984) [a well-balanced festschrift]; Edmund Heward, *Lord Denning: A Biography* (London: Weidenfeld and Nicolson, 1990; Iris Freeman, *Lord Denning: A Life* (London: Hutchinson, 1993); and the several annual numbers of *The Denning Law Journal* (University of Buckingham, 1986 to date).

[18] A. L. Goodhart, *English Law and the Moral Law* (London : Stevens, 1953), pp. 147–49.

attained economic independence, she owes the public approval of her liberated status very largely to the work of legislators and judges.

On the basis of such examples Goodhart argues in conclusion:

> The civil law has played an important part in shaping the moral law of this country. This is hardly surprising because both of them are essential and interrelated parts of our civilisation. Any attempt to separate them in action is to cut "the seamless web" of English law, as Maitland has called it, because the law is seamless not only in its history but also in the forces which give it its life.

The influence of morals on the content of the law. The interrelationship between law and morals is perhaps best symbolised by the chemical sign for a reversible reaction, the double-arrow ($\rightleftarrows$), indicating that each factor works simultaneously on the other. Law influences morality; at the same time, morality is in the continuous process of influencing law. Since this latter aspect of the equation is less readily appreciated in legal circles, we shall spend considerably more time in the discussion of it.

Whether one examines the civil or the criminal law, one encounters a multitude of illustrations of the direct impact of morality on legal doctrine.

In the sphere of the criminal law, consider the fundamental historical distinction between *mala in se* and *mala prohibita*: crimes that are evil or heinous in themselves as contrasted with crimes that are such only because they are prohibited by statute. The practical significance of this distinction lies in the fact that if one commits a mere *malum prohibitum* and then seeks within that framework to have the court rectify an injustice one has suffered, the court will generally do so; but in the case of a *malum in se*, the court will refuse and simply leave the parties where they are.

Thus, if you engage voluntarily in a fight with someone, committing the *in se* crimes of battery or affray, and then attempt to sue your adversary civilly in tort for injuring you, you will get nowhere under common law. Except where statute has changed the common law (as it has in many jurisdictions), the courts will not assist you in recovering a gambling debt. Should you visit a house of prostitution and pay by cheque, and the cheque is dishonoured, the Chicken Ranch will not be able to sue you on the cheque.

Why does the common law take this position? Simply because it intuitively recognises the tremendous moral gulf dividing, on the one hand, wrongs that are not inherently evil but are criminalized for social purposes, and, on the other, wrongs that in fact represent inherent immorality. The *malum in se*/*malum prohibitum* distinction presupposes a moral standard capable of distinguishing genuine evil from merely conventional wrongdoing.

Moving on to the civil law, we can readily see the direct influence of morality in the major areas of contract, wills and trusts, and tort.

The modern law of *contract* would be unrecognisable apart from the fundamental notion of *good faith*. The Uniform Commercial Code (UCC), which has codified the common law throughout the United Status and has such international influence that it has been translated in its entirety into French, declares: "Every contract or duty within this code imposes an obligation of good faith in its performance or enforcement" (Art. 1–203), and good faith is defined as "honesty in fact in the conduct or transaction concerned" (Art. 1–201 [19]).

Where did this concept of good faith come from? The rather vague notion of *bona fides* in Roman law was early christianised by way of the biblical understanding of good conscience and the theological claim that Christian revelation provided "an absolute moral standard." By the end of the Middle Ages, "good faith was perceived, in philosophical thinking, as a universal ethical principle." As a result, good faith came to be "applied in both the civil and the common law, the two major legal traditions in the modern world."[19]

Professor A. W. B. Simpson concludes his discussion of *consideration* in the common law of contract with the following significant judgment:

> The view that the law of contract is the handmaid of commerce seems to me to be mistaken if it is opposed to the view that the law of contract expresses, in a form thought appropriate (bearing in mind the practicalities of litigation), moral ideas. For commerce, like other areas of life, must be conducted morally if the general good is to be furthered, and there is no special set of principles of commercial morality. The doctrine of consideration is indeed intensely moralistic, and we may disagree with some of its judgments; what is mistaken is to fail to see that a good law of contract has as its function in relation to the commercial world the imposition of decent moral standards.[20]

---

[19] J. F. O'Connor, *Good Faith in International Law* (Aldershot, Hants : Dartmouth, 1991), pp. 25, 30.

[20] A. W. B. Simpson, *A History of the Common Law of Contract* (Oxford: Clarendon Press, 1987), p. 488. The formal rejection of Lord Mansfield's doctrine of moral consideration in the common law of contract in no way militates against the argument just presented. In point of fact, the major applications of Mansfield's doctrine (to hold as binding the promise to pay a debt discharged through bankruptcy, the promise to pay a debt barred by a limitation period, and the promise after majority to pay

I. Law & Morality: Friends or Foes?

The branch of contract law known as *quasi-contract* offers particularly powerful evidence of the impact of morality on law. Originally based on the notion of a fictional contract, the modern law of quasi-contract is in reality a device by which unjust, i.e., immoral, enrichment can be avoided. Wrote Sir Henry Maine in his classic, *Ancient Law*:

> A quasi-contract is not a contract at all. The commonest sample of the class is the relation subsisting between two persons, one of whom has paid money to the other through mistake. The law, consulting the interests of morality, imposes an obligation on the receiver to refund.[21]

Closely related to the quasi-contractual abhorrence of unjust enrichment is the doctrine of the *constructive trust*. A constructive trust is a trust relationship imposed by law in the interests of justice. Dean Ames uses the following simple illustration:

> A man kills his daughter in order to inherit her real estate. Under the statute the land descends to him as her heir. May he keep it? It seems clear that equity should compel him to surrender the property. As it is impossible to make specific reparation to the deceased, he should be treated as a constructive trustee for those who represent her, that is, her heirs, the murderer being counted out in determining who are the heirs.[22]

Here, the murderer is definitively an heir of his victim and should therefore take an appropriate portion of her estate under the laws of intestate succession. To avoid this immoral result (legally profiting from one's own crime), the law of trusts artificially makes the murderer a trustee of what he would normally receive: a trustee who holds mere naked legal title to the estate for the entire benefit of the other heirs, who become the holders of the equitable title and thus the sole beneficiaries of the estate. The result, in strict accord with the moralities of the case, is that the murderer benefits not at all from his crime.

---

a debt incurred during infancy) have been sustained in most common law jurisdictions as exceptions to the requirement of legal consideration. In effect, the moral exceptions swallow the rule!

[21] Sir Henry Maine, *Ancient Law*, ed. Sir Frederick Pollock (London: Murray, 1930), pp. 365–66. Cf. Sir P. H. Winfield, *The Law of Quasi-Contracts* (London: Sweet & Maxwell, 1952), *passim*.

[22] James Barr Ames, "Law and Morals," in: *Jurisprudence in Action*, foreword by Hon. Robert H. Jackson (New York: Baker, Voorhis, 1953), p. 22. Ames's essay was an effort specifically to counteract the separation of law and morals in O. W. Holmes, Jr's address, "The Path of the Law."

Another example of the application of moral principle to the law of *estates* is provided by J. Farwell, in the Chancery case of *Stevens v King* ([1904] 2 Ch. Div. 30, 33):

> The doctrine that a legacy lapses by the death of the legatee in the testator's lifetime means, I take it, that the whole object of the testator in giving the legacy has failed by reason of the legatee's death. But that must depend on the question what the testator's object was. I think that the cases of Williamson v. Naylor [3 Y. & C. Ex. 208], Philips v Philips, [3 Hare, 281; 64 R. R. 296] and In re Sowerby's Trust [2 K. & J. 630] have established the rule that, if the Court finds, upon the construction of the will, that the testator clearly intended not to give a mere bounty to the legatee, but to discharge what he regarded as a moral obligation, whether it were legally binding or not, and if that obligation still exists at the testator's death, there is no necessary failure of the testator's object merely because the legatee dies in his lifetime; and therefore death in such a case does not cause a lapse.

Tue legal area of *tort*, or what the civil lawyers call "delict," is a fruitful source of moral illustration. Tort covers legally recognised injuries which do not arise from breach of contract (negligence, misrepresentation and fraud, nuisance, defamation, etc.). As early as 1789, the court (Lord Kenyon, C J) was faced with a case in which the defendant encouraged the plaintiff to sell goods to X on credit, knowing full well that X was uncreditworthy: *Pasley v Freeman* (King's Bench: 3 T.R. 51). The defence was that no privity of contract existed between plaintiff and defendant. The court treated the case as sounding in tortious deceit. Kenyon:

> All laws stand on the best and broadest basis which go to enforce moral and social duties. Though, indeed, it is not every moral and social duty the neglect of which is the ground of an action. For there are, which are called in the civil law, duties of imperfect obligation, for the enforcing of which no action lies. There are many cases where the pure effusion of a good mind may induce the performance of particular duties, which yet cannot be enforced by municipal laws. But there are certain duties, the non-performance of which the jurisprudence of this country has made the subject of a civil action. And I find it laid down by the Lord Ch. B. Comyns (Com. Dig. Tit. Action upon the Case for a Deceit, A. 1), that "an action upon the case for a deceit lies when a man does any deceit to the damage of another." . . .
>
> There are many situations in life, and particularly in the commercial world, where a man cannot by any diligence inform himself of the degree of credit which ought to be given to the persons with whom he deals; in which cases he must apply to those whose sources of intelligence enables them to give that information. The law of prudence leads him to apply to them; and

1. Law & Morality: Friends or Foes? 115

> the law of morality ought to induce them to give the information required....
>
> It is admitted that the defendant's conduct was highly immoral and detrimental to society. And I am of opinion that the action is maintainable on the grounds of deceit in the defendant, and injury and loss to the plaintiffs.

The modern law of *negligence* takes its rise from the ethically-grounded "neighbour principle" set forth by Lord Atkin in the leading case of *Donoghue v Stevenson* (H L [1932] L. R., A. C. 562). This was the famous snail-in-the-ginger-beer case (an American parallel involved, characteristically, a mouse in a Coca Cola bottle!).

Could the consumer successfully sue the manufacturer of the ginger beer? Observe Lord Atkin's reasoning:

> The liability for negligence, whether you style it such or treat it as in other systems as a species of "culpa," is no doubt based upon a general public sentiment of moral wrongdoing for which the offender must pay. But acts or omissions which any moral code would censure cannot in a practical world be treated so as to give a right to every person injured by them to demand relief. In this way rules of law arise which limit the range of complainants and the extent of their remedy. The rule that you are to love your neighbour becomes in law, you must not injure you neighbour; and the lawyer's question, Who is my neighbour? receives a restricted reply. You must take reasonable care to avoid acts or omissions which you can reasonably foresee would be likely to injure your neighbour. Who, then, in law is my neighbour? The answer seems to be—persons who are so closely and directly affected by my act that I ought reasonably to have them in contemplation as being so affected when I am directing my mind to the acts or omissions which are called in question.

Fascinatingly, we learn from Atkin's eldest grandson, who was seventeen at the time, that the neighbour principle had its origin in an ecclesiastical context.

> During the summer holidays of 1931 I was staying at Craig-y-don with other members of the family. In those days the family went to Matins at the Aberdovey Church every Sunday morning and there was a large family lunch with Aunts and cousins presided over by my Grandfather, who took much pride in his carving of the joint. He often used the carving time and the carving weapons to conduct a discussion. I remember on several occasions that the post-church discussion about the snail and the ginger beer bottle case—

who is my neighbour?—was an easily understandable theme immediately after church.²³

The ecclesiastical connection should not seem strange when we recall that Lord Atkin's negligence principle is simply a more narrowly focused version of Luke 10: 25–37.

***

Whether one examines the judicial sources of law or looks at the specific interlocking relationships of morality and law as illustrated by the major legal disciplines, one is forced to the conclusion that law and morals are not merely acquaintances, but friends.²⁴ So powerful is the symbiotic connection between them that two University of Sheffield legal philosophers have titled their jurisprudential opus, *Law As Moral Judgment*. They argue—though on neo-Kantian grounds which we shall soon discover to be inadequate—the truth that "a Legal Order is a Moral Order." They go so far as to define a law as "a rule which there is a moral right to posit for attempted enforcement."²⁵ For them—and their position is fully supported by the facts which we have adduced here—"the concept of law is not morally neutral."²⁶

---

[23] Quoted in Geoffrey Lewis, *Lord Atkin* (London: Butterworths, 1983), p. 57.

[24] It should be emphasised that the legal fields from which we have drawn illustrations above are by no means the only ones providing examples of the inherent connection of law and morality. Thus in the field of conflict of laws (private international law), Morris points out how the older, political doctrine of cornity has been largely replaced by the moral doctrine of duty or obligation: see J. H. C. Morris, *The Conflict of Laws*, ed. David McClean (4th ed.; London : Sweet & Maxwell, 1993), pp. 104–105.

[25] Deryck Beyleveld and Roger Brownsword, *Law As Moral Judgment* (London: Sweet & Maxwell, 1986), pp. 159-60.

[26] *Ibid.*, p. 33. These authors attempt a formal justification of their viewpoint in their recent essay, "The Dialectically Necessary Foundation of Natural Law," in Alan Norrie (ed.), *Closure or Critique: New Directions in Legal Theory* (Edinburgh: Edinburgh University Press, 1993), pp. 22–44. Cf. also David Lyons, *Moral Aspects of Legal Theory* (Cambridge: Cambridge University Press, 1993), especially chap. i ("The Internal Morality of Law," critiquing Lon Fuller) and chap. 4 (focusing especially on Ronald Dworkin).

The Source of Moral Values

If morality and law are necessarily intertwined, and if moral principles are essential to the proper functioning of the law, we cannot avoid the most vexing question of all: Where are proper moral principles to be discovered? Here legal discussion turns a philosophical (and theological) corner.

The primitive Legal Positivism of Austin and Bentham focused solely upon the command-element in law, relegating moral considerations (Austin's Unitarian ethic, Bentham's Utilitarianism) to the realm of the extralegal. H. L. A. Hart, in our century, raised Positivism to a new level of sophistication by distinguishing between the Austinian "primary rules" and higher-level "secondary rules" allegedly justifying them. Ronald Dworkin, Hart's successor at Oxford, argues that even the secondary rules are not enough: one must move beyond these to the realm of *principle* in order properly to understand legal operations. And how can the principles of a legal system, including its moral principles, be validated? Here, Dworkin leaves us at sea, without an epistemological compass of any kind:

> We could not devise any formula for testing how much and what kind of institutional support is necessary to make a principle a legal principle, still less to fix its weight at a particular order of magnitude. We argue for a particular principle by grappling with a whole set of shifting, developing and interacting standards (themselves principles rather than rules) about institutional responsibility, statutory interpretation, the persuasive force of various sorts of precedent, the relation of all these to contemporary moral practices, and hosts of other such standards.[27]

To be sure, Dworkin's dilemma is entirely understandable and elicits considerable sympathy. A legal system requires principled underpinnings. These will either be transcendent and absolute, or imminent and relativistic. As an inheritor of modern American cultural pluralism, Dworkin opts for the latter, leaving him in the amorphous realm of "contemporary moral standards."

But can such standards fill the bill? In point of fact, contemporary moral standards are the inevitable reflection and expression of current values, and these have no more necessary moral force than past values. Fifty million Frenchmen can be wrong. Deriving moral principles by counting noses or by doing opinion surveys is an egregious instance of G. E. Moore's naturalistic (or sociologist's) fallacy: it endeavors to derive the *ought* (the normative) from the *is* (the descriptive). Eighteenth-century

---

[27] Ronald Dworkin, *Taking Rights Seriously* (London: Duckworth, 1977), pp. 40–41.

secular Natural Law theory suffered from this very same failing; it naively believed that a consensus of moral opinion would necessarily yield the moral absolutes (the "inalienable rights") law and society required for their proper functioning.

Recently, neo-Kantian efforts have been made by such distinguished political theorists as Rawls, Nozick, and Gewirth to solve the dilemma. Gewirth well illustrates the blind alley to which all these endeavors lead. He seeks to demonstrate that Kant's categorical imperative is indeed a necessary principle of practical reason ("so act as if your maxims had to serve at the same time as a universal law"). How? By arguing that no human being can rationally reject the fundamental moral principle—guaranteeing respect for each individual's moral rights—that "I have rights to freedom and well-being because I am a prospective purposive agent." If I deserve freedom and well-being simply because of my humanity, I must accord them to all others because they also are human. No-one, according to Gewirth, can rationally claim that rights depend on anything less—on one's intelligence, on one's race, on "being named 'Wordsworth Donisthorpe,'" or the like.[28]

However, need we point out that the rejection of moral imperatives by the Ghengis Khans, the Hitlers, and the Stalins of this world has *always* been based on their conviction (rational to them!) that their uniqueness justified operating apart from ordinary moral standards? Nietzsche will always be able to rationalise the "transvaluation of values" and a life "beyond good and evil" on the part of the self-proclaimed *Übermensch*.

As Wittgenstein demonstrated in the *Tractatus* (propositions 6.41–6.421), "The sense of the world must lie outside the world. ... Ethics in transcendental." The fundamental moral principles required for a proper legal system cannot arise from within the system itself or from the society which it serves. Morals must not be confused with mores. And water cannot rise above its own level. Ethics is transcendental, and thus the moral imperatives of the legal system must have a transcendental source.[29]

But in the face of competing transcendental claims, what choice do we make? Religious options are hardly a matter of indifference, as the cultic

---

[28] Alan Gewirth, "The Epistemology of Human Rights," in *Human Rights*, ed. E. F. Paul, J. Paul, and F. D. Miller, Jr. (Oxford: Blackwell, 1984), pp. 14–17.

[29] See my *Law Above the Law* (op. cit. in note 13 above). Cf. also Detmold, *op. cit.* (in note 13 above), pp. 259–64.

horrors of Jonestown, Guyana, and Waco, Texas, amply demonstrate. Having addressed this question in several of my previous works,[30] I shall not treat it systematically here, but merely offer a parabolic answer—which, as a matter of fact, represents an actual historical incident.

At the time of the French Revolution, efforts were made by many Deists and *philosophes* to create substitute religions for Christianity. One such attempt was "Theophilanthropy," a deification of man, invented by David Williams, an English Deist. In France, Louis Marie de La Revellière-Lépeaux took up the torch and endeavored to spread the faith. On delivering a tedious paper promoting this system of worship, he received the following comment from Talleyrand: "For my part, I have only one observation to make. Jesus Christ, in order to found His religion, was crucified and rose again—you should have tried to do as much."[31]

May we suggest that the proper test of a transcendental claim is its historical facticity: not merely that it asserts its divine truth but more especially that it offers concrete, verifiable evidence that God has indeed come into our midst. In the case of historic Christianity, this test is amply fulfilled and we are thereby provided with a revelational source (the Bible) whose transcendental character is attested by the Incarnate and Resurrected Christ himself.[32]

Concretely, what does such a transcendental source of morality offer the legal system? In the first place, it delivers us not only from the subjectivism of contextual and situational ethics,[33] but also from the vagaries of Dworkin's "shifting, developing and interacting standards." The Bible provides three kinds of moral norms: *specific ethical rules*, such as the Decalogue[34]; *more general principles*, e.g., the declaration (1 Timothy 5:8) that he

---

[30] John Warwick Montgomery, *History and Christianity* (Minneapolis: Bethany, 1965); *Christianity for the Toughminded* (Minneapolis: Bethany, 1973); *Faith Founded on Fact* (Nashville: Thomas Nelson, 1978); *Evidence for Faith: Deciding the God Question* (Richardson, Texas: Probe, 1991); etc.

[31] On this incident, see Duff Cooper, *Talleyrand* (London: Jonathan Cape, 1935), pp. 95-96, and Jean Orieux, *Talleyrand*, trans. Patricia Wolf (New York: Alfred A. Knopf, 1974), p. 160.

[32] Cf. Luke 24:36-48. On the question of form- and redaction-criticism of the New Testament documents, see Montgomery, 3/12 *Ecclesiastical Law Journal* 45-46 (January, 1993) and 60/4 *New Oxford Review* 20-22 (May, 1993).

[33] See Joseph Fletcher and John Warwick Montgomery, *Situation Ethics: True or False* (Minneapolis: Bethany, 1972).

[34] "In one of his early works Gladstone summarized the four authorities for human action as follows: it is written, it is natural, it is expedient, it is customary. If we apply these categories to law, we may say that the first of them, 'it is written',

who neglects his own family is "worse than an infidel", providing a transcendental basis for the common law doctrine of quasi-contractual liability for one's spouse's necessaries; and *overall descriptions of and judgments upon man's nature and fallen state*, such as the evidence in Genesis 3:12–13 that human beings have a powerful tendency to shift the blame for their reprehensible acts to others—a fact that justifies, *inter alia*, the M'Naghten rule limiting the insanity defence to those situations where the accused did not understand the nature and quality of his act or was unable to appreciate its wrongfulness.

Moreover, biblical revelation goes well beyond such identifications of what objectively constitutes a wrongful act in the civil or criminal spheres (the *actus reus*). Unlike other scriptures, the Bible also speaks directly to the central issue of the *mens rea*: subjective, wrongful intent. Why is this so important? Maitre Nicolas Jacob gives us the answer when he writes:

> Il faut conclure que la morale est, avant tout, un problème de formation personnelle; elle doit rendre l'homme capable d'agir de telle façon qu'il se réalise pleinement et c'est certainement une erreur de réduire la morale à un catalogue d'actes a faire et à ne pas faire. La morale est l'art d'être homme et non pas un code qui ne peut conduire qu'à l'éternelle histoire du pharisien et du publicain.[35]

The Bible recognises that evil proceeds "out of the heart" (Matthew 15:18–20; Mark 7:20–23), and that the only ultimate remedy for illegality and the flouting of the standards of the law is a change of heart: conversion, possible because the same God who revealed the true moral path for his creatures was willing, in his love, even to die for them when they wilfully departed from it, thereby providing the opportunity for restoration and a changed life.[36]

---

derives the authority of law from Divine institution. The Mosaic law, and in particular the Ten Commandments, have been regarded as possessing an authority of this kind, being written with the finger of God."—Sir Thomas Murray Taylor, *The Discipline of Virtue: Reflections on Law and Liberty* ("University of Durham. Riddell Memorial Lectures," 26; London: Oxford University Press, 1954), p. 23. See also H. B. Clark, *Biblical Law* (2d ed.; Portland, Oregon: Binfords & Mort, 1944).

[35] N. Jacob, et al., *Pratique du droit et conscience chrétienne* (Paris: Éditions du Cerf, 1962), p. 165.

[36] For a detailed discussion of this theme in the context of human rights, see John Warwick Montgomery, *Human Rights and Human Dignity* (2d ed.; Edmonton, Alberta, Canada: Canadian Institute for Law, Theology and Public Policy, 1995), especially chaps. 7 and 8.

Transcendental Morality in a Secular Legal Context

But—one may well object—what makes us think that a moral standard derived from an alleged transcendental revelation will be of practical use? Moreover, if the human being suffers so much from finitude that he cannot arrive unaided at moral absolutes, is it not unlikely that he would properly understand or apply revelational truths should they be given to him?

Several points can be raised in answer to these entirely legitimate objections. First, it is an empirical fact that biblical morality has been well enough understood and effectively enough applied to constitute perhaps the most important single influence on modern Western legal systems (the European civil law system and the Anglo-American common law).

Earlier we noted the introduction of the fundamental concept of the *mens rea* into Western law from the theology of St. Augustine. Maître Troplong of the Institute, after a minute study of the positive influence of Christianity on Roman civil law by way of the Justinian Code, concluded that Christian truth "alimente la racine de notre droit, et nous vivons plus encore par elle que par les idées échappées à la ruine du monde grec et du monde romain."[37] Professor Patrick Nerhot has recently demonstrated that early Christian techniques of biblical interpretation permanently influenced all subsequent styles of Western legal hermeneutics.[38]

The impact of generations of ecclesiastical chancellors on the development of the Courts of Chancery and on the doctrines of equity is well known to any serious student of the common law. And, in our own time, the most influential judges on the English bench—one thinks immediately of Denning, Diplock, and Hailsham—have consciously employed their Christian moral beliefs in the writing of what Ronald Dworkin has felicitously termed the "serial novel" of the law.

To the objection that a supposed transcendent revelation carries no guarantee of absolute comprehensibility or effectiveness of application, one may also reply by way of Basil Mitchell's parable:

> Supposing a stranger comes into a Kingdom with whose laws and institutions he is unfamiliar. He asks an inhabitant, "Why do you do things in this way?" The inhabitant replies, "Because this is the way the King commands; moreover, our institutions have the following practical advantages," which

---

[37] M. Troplong, *De l'influence du Christianisme sur le droit civil des Romains* (Paris: Charles Hingray, 1843), p. 364. Cf. the Preface to the same author's *Le droit civil expliqué. De la vente*, I (3d ed.; Paris: Charles Hingray, 1837).

[38] Patrick Nerhot, *Law, Writing, Meaning: An Essay in Legal Hermeneutics*, trans. Ian Fraser (Edinburgh: Edinburgh University Press, 1992), especially chap. 14.

he then proceeds to enumerate. The stranger objects. "Your argument," he says, "is two-pronged; you justify your institutions by reference to the King's authority and also by considerations derived from social science. This procedure is fatal to the King's authority: for it either makes the King a social scientist or it deprives his authority of any relevance to your affairs." It is not difficult to see how the inhabitant will answer this. "We have reason to believe," he will say, "that our King is very wise and that is why we accept his authority. Our independent investigations in social science lend support to this belief of ours, in so far as we are able to rely upon them, although we do not make the mistake of supposing that our social scientists are omnicompetent. We have need, of course, to interpret the King's commands, so as to apply them intelligently to the changing problems of our society and we find it a useful rule to interpret them in such a way that they make sense. In doing this we receive valuable help from the King himself."

There is no need to stress the limitations of the parable, but it does, I think, fairly make the essential point, which is that the insights of theology are not to be regarded as prescriptions to be applied unreflectively to a world with which they have no affinity. If Christianity is true it should illuminate precisely those human needs which men are found in experience to have, and this not by accident but because the God of revelation is also the God of nature.[39]

Finally, to the line of reasoning set forth in this lecture the objector may pose the particularly worrisome question: If one does accept a transcendent, revelational morality as the absolute foundation of law, will that not inevitably lead to intolerance—the forcing of Christian ethical principles upon those in a secular society who are not themselves believers?

An impolitic (though not unreasonable) response might be that, if the revelation in question is indeed what it claims to be, the "enforced morality" would be of equal benefit to all those living under the rule of law, whatever their personal beliefs—and, furthermore, for English subjects at least, the establishment of "the Reformed part of the Holy Catholic Church in this Kingdom" makes Christian morality normative constitutionally.[40]

But such an answer is too facile. As I have maintained elsewhere,[41] the Christian in a modern pluralistic, heavily secularised society must be espe-

---

[39] Basil Mitchell, *Law, Morality, and Religion in a Secular Society* (London: Oxford University Press, 1967), pp. 117–18.
[40] For countries practising the so-called "separation of church and state" (such as the United States), this latter consideration is, of course, not applicable. See Montgomery, *The Shaping of America* (corrected ed.; Minneapolis: Bethany, 1981), *passim*.
[41] *Ibid.*, pp. 152–58.

cially careful not to imperil the spread of the biblical gospel by insensitively ramming Christian morality down the throats of unbelievers. We must have no reduplications of the Puritan Commonwealth, in which the populace is forced to act externally like believers whether they are such or not. The sad result of these efforts is always the institutionalisation of hypocrisy and the loss of respect for genuine Christian values.

In concrete terms, the Christian believer will recognise that there are two types of moral command in Scripture, as represented by the First and the Second Tables of the Decalogue. The First Table is concerned with one's relationship with God ("vertical" morality: against polytheism, profanity, sabbath-breaking, etc.); the Second has to do with one's relationship to one's fellow man ("horizontal" morality: thou shalt not murder, steal, commit adultery, defame, etc.). The former must never be forced on unbelievers even if Christians are in the majority and could manage such legislation by vote of Parliament, for the proper relationship with God can only come about by volitional, personal decision and commitment.

Where "horizontal" morality is at issue, however, believers ought indeed to use the democratic process to build a more ethical society and legal system. Second Table moral principles can be defended by what Mitchell calls "independent investigations in social science" and even unbelievers can be persuaded to support them for the sake of creating and maintaining an honourable rule of law and a society which one can be proud to pass on to one's children. The boundaries of horizontal morality are not always fully clear biblically, but there is little difficulty in showing that they embrace the right-to-life, the preservation of marriage and the nuclear family, unqualified condemnation of hard-core and child pornography, and opposition to homosexual practices. Where right-to-life is concerned, so fundamental is the biblical theme of protecting the helpless child that it may be necessary for Christians even to suffer the wrath of pro-choicers and a reduction in secular openness to evangelical witness for the sake of legislating greater protection for the lives of the unborn.[42]

However we decide these most controversial of moral issues and whatever the nature of future legislation and court decisions in respect to them, the general conclusion is plain: law cannot avoid morality and the best law will be infused by the best morality. The need for transcendent moral foundations today is apparent on all sides, both within and without the legal

---

[42] John Warwick Montgomery, *Slaughter of the Innocents* (Westchester, Illinois: Crossway, 1981). For my critique of Professor Dworkin's approach to the abortion issue, as set out in his new book, *Life's Dominion*, see my article, "New Light on the Abortion Controversy?," 60/7 *New Oxford Review* 24–26 (September, 1993).

professions. Sir Henry Slesser, one of Her Majesty's Lords Justices of Appeal, put the matter squarely a generation ago; we end with his words—or, more accurately, with Psalm 127:1, with which he concludes:

> The modern world lacks the sense of the supernatural effect of wrong-doing, the offence against God, which alone, as the ancient Hebrews proclaimed, can give final vitality and endurance to law, criminal or civil.
>
> Without a prevailing moral sanction, no number of laws, police, judges or prisons will save society from disruption, and such sanction, to command general consent, must be based upon generally accepted transcendent belief. "Unless the Lord keep the city, the watchman waketh but in vain."[43]

---

[43] Sir Henry Slesser, *The Art of Judgment*, foreword by Lord Denning (London: Stevens, 1962), pp. 147–48.

2. Millennium

Millennium mə-len´ē-əm [Lat. *mille*-'thousand' plus *annus*-'year']

A time of penultimate divine triumph over the forces of evil on earth before God's final conquest of all His enemies and the establishment of everlasting righteousness. The corresponding Greek expression in Rev. 20:4-7, *chília étē*, gives rise to the term "chiliasm," properly a synonym for "millennialism" but sometimes used in a pejorative sense to designate especially gross and sensual conceptions of bliss on earth.

I. In Ancient Religious Literature

A. Canonical Picture

Much stress is placed in the canonical OT on a future condition of earthly blessedness for the Jewish nation (Isa. 9:6; 11:1–12:6; 40:9–11; 52:7–12; Jer. 33:17–22; Ezk. 37:25; Hos. 3:4f.; Joel 3:20 [MT 4:20]; Am. 9:14f.; Zec. 9:9f.; etc.). But this period is not temporally limited and so, though compatible with a time of millennial bliss, does not expressly require it. The eternity of the messianic kingdom as delineated in such key prophetic books of the OT as Daniel (2:44; 7:27) leads millennial interpreters to extend the history of Israel's restoration across the millennial age into the ultimate eschaton when "God shall be all in all" (cf. Culver; W. M. Smith, *World Crisis and the Prophetic Scriptures* [1951], pp. 179–237; *Israeli/Arab. Conflict and the Bible* [1967]; Saarnivaara, pp. 24–37). Thus, in spite of attempts, represented by W. E. Biederwolf's *Millennium Bible* (1924), to find chiliastic teaching clearly set forth in the OT, the biblical foundation of the doctrine cannot be located there.

As for the NT, 1 Cor. 15:22ff. is regarded, even by those who oppose millennial views, as providing through its "doctrine of a limited reign of Christ . . . a foothold in the Church for chiliastic expectations" (E. Bratke, in Sch.-Herz. [repr. 1950], VII, 375). Other NT passages to which millennial interpreters occasionally appeal are Mt. 19:28; 25:31–46; Lk. 14:14; 1 Thess. 4:13–18. But it is almost universally admitted, by both opponents and advocates of millennialism, that the case for the doctrine rests squarely on the exegesis of Rev. 20. According to this text, after Messiah's victory over the beast, the false prophet, and all their followers, Satan will be confined in a bottomless pit for one thousand years. During this period Christ will reign with His martyred saints, who have been brought to life in the "first resurrection" at the outset of the millennial period. At the end of the thousand years Satan will be loosed for a little time, the ultimate battle between God and His adversaries will occur, and the last judgment will take place, followed by "second death" of all evil forces and the establishment of everlasting righteousness. The disputed questions relative to this passage are whether the text is to be taken literally (millennialism) or figuratively (amillennialism) and, assuming a millennial interpretation, whether the second coming of the Lord is to precede (premillennialism) or follow (postmillennialism) the time of chiliastic victory. To these questions we shall return later (see III below).

B. Apocrypha and Pseudepigrapha

Noncanonical Jewish literature of the biblical era offers several instances of temporally delimited periods of divine rule. The four most important examples, in chronological order, are: (1) 1 En. 91:12–17 and ch. 93; (2) 2 En. 32:3–33:1; (3) 2 Esd. 5:1–7:35; and (4) 2 Baruch.

(1) The 1 Enoch passages are in the section known as the "Apocalypse of Weeks," considered by R. H. Charles (*Book of Enoch* [1917], p. xiv) "the oldest pre-Maccabaean" portion of the book. The seer has Enoch predict the future in terms of ten unequal "weeks." During the final three apocalyptic weeks judgment will take place against oppressors (eighth week), the whole godless earth (ninth week), and the evil angels (tenth week). Although only at the end of time, following the tenth week, does perfection come about ("the first heaven shall depart and pass away, and a new heaven shall appear, . . . and all shall be in goodness and righteousness, and sin shall no more be mentioned for ever"), the eighth week constitutes a kind of millennial interlude, since "at its close they [the righteous] shall acquire houses through their righteousness, and a house [the temple] shall be built for the Great King in glory for evermore, and all mankind shall look to the path of uprightness" (Charles, pp. 132–34). No personal Messiah, however, plays a role in these predictions.

(2) An analogous picture is offered by 2 En. 32:3–33: 1. In this apocalypse, "written by an Alexandrian Jew during the first fifty years of our era" (R. H. Pfeiffer), the world exists for a total of seven days of a thousand years each, and the Lord decrees that the seventh constitutes a penultimate sabbath, to be followed by the endless eighth day of eternal bliss. No Messiah is integrated into this millennial picture, but the implicit use of the canonical theme that "a thousand years in thy sight are but as yesterday" (Ps. 90:4; 2 Pet. 3:8), with the consequent specification of a future era of explicitly millennial dimensions, is noteworthy.

(3) 2 Esd. 5:1–7:35 presents a vision of the end time almost certainly written before the end of the 1st cent. A.D. "The details include the promise that God's Messiah will reign in his kingdom four hundred years; after this he and all humankind will die, and primeval silence will prevail for seven days; finally will come the Resurrection and the Day of Judgment" (B. M. Metzger, *Intro. to the Apocrypha* [1957], p. 26). The sharp contrasts between this prediction and canonical teaching should be noted—contrasts in no way blunted by the reference to "Jesus" in 7:28, which derives from the Latin text only and "is due to a Christian corrector" (Oesterley). The four-hundred-year figure is explained in the Talmud (T.B. *Sanhedrin* 99a; Midr. *Tanhuma, Ekeb* 7) as deriving from Israel's period of captivity in Egypt (cf. Gen. 15:13; Ps. 90:15; Mic. 7:15). Other talmudic estimates of the length of Messiah's kingdom were 40 years (equaling the period in the wilderness), 70 years, 100 years, 365 years, 600 years, 1000 years, 2000 years, and 7000 years. The logic behind such figures was often the assumption of symmetry (history consisted of 2000 years before the giving of the Law and 2000 years under it, so Messiah's reign would be of this same length) or the symbolism of joy contained in the numbers 1000 and 7000 (see F. Weber, *Jüdische Theologie auf Grund des Talmud* [1897], pp. 371–73).

(4) 2 Baruch, "written about the same time as II (IV) Esdras (ca. A.D. 90)" (Pfeiffer, HNTT, p. 86), portrays a messianic kingdom as the successor to four world kingdoms, the last of which is Rome (chs. 39–40). In chs. 29 and 73 the messianic reign is depicted in terms quite obviously recapitulating the Edenic paradise and annulling the curse placed upon our first parents: childbearing will occur painlessly (cf. Gen. 3:16), and the soil will become so fertile (cf. Gen. 3: 17–19) that each vine will have a thousand branches, each branch a thousand clusters, each cluster a thousand grapes! Papias later applied this description to the Christian millennium.

What is the bearing of these pseudepigraphical and apocryphal millennialisms on the NT conception as set out in Rev. 20? If any influence exists at all, it is of the most indirect kind, not extending beyond the general idea of a future divine interregnum. Neither 1 Enoch nor 2 Enoch connects a personal Messiah with penultimate bliss; the Messiah of 2 Esdras reigns only four hundred years and then dies; and the technicolor portrait of chiliastic blessings in 2 Baruch (almost certainly composed too late to have influenced Revelation in any case) has no parallel in the NT. Even the thousand-year span of time in Rev. 20 need not be derived from 2 Enoch, since the apostle John was able to rely, no less than the author of 2 Enoch, on Ps. 90:4 for the 1 day = 1000 years formula.

C. Question of Persian Origin

Some have made efforts to locate in ancient Persian religious literature an extra-canonical source for the Bible's millennial teaching. Zoroastrianism conceived of the last times as consisting of three millennia, each with its particular savior. "The later Parsi legends distinguish three great prophets who will appear before the end of the world. . . . They will be commissioned to check the influence of the devil, which increases at the time when this world is verging toward its end" (M. Haug, *Essays on the Sacred Language, Writings, and Religion of the Parsis* [1878], p. 314). Only with the appearance of the third and greatest savior—Sosyosh, a supernatural offspring of Zoroaster himself—will the world be permanently transformed; then "the devil will disappear" and "all the world will remain for eternity in a state of righteousness" (Yt. 19:89f.; quoted in Haug, p. 217). We are told that "these ideas exerted strong influence upon the apocalyptic expectations of late Judaism" (*Encyclopedia of the Lutheran Church*, II [1965], s.v. [K. Hutten]), and this opinion is supported by F. Cumont (RHR [1931]. 29–96) and M. Eliade (*Myth of the Eternal Return* [1954], pp. 124–27). On the other hand, W. Adams Brown warned, "Our sources for the Persian eschatology are so late (the Bundahis, in their present form, dating not earlier than the 7th cent. A. D. . . .) that we must use great caution in drawing conclusions" (HDB, III, s.v.). Factors such as the lateness of the Mazdean sources and the radical difference between their trimillennial view and the unitary messianic kingdom in the Judeo-Christian tradition have led to a rejection of the Persian-influence theory by N. Söderblom (*La Vie future d'après le mazdéisme* [1901], pp. 270–320), and, more recently, P. Vulliaud (p. 33); and with this judgment we concur. One must be especially careful, even when some genuine similarities exist between two religious positions, not to assume that one must have influenced the other. The unique characteristics of the millennial eschatology in Rev. 20 warrant the closest examination on their own ground.

II. In Church History

A. Patristic Period

Those who regard millennialism as an alien import into the Christian faith have been much embarrassed by its early and widespread acceptance in the patristic Church. Salmond, for example, who considered millennial conceptions totally foreign to Christ's teachings, had to admit that "the dogma of a Millennium . . . took possession of Christian thought at so early a date and with so strong a grasp that it has sometimes been reckoned an integral part of the primitive Christian faith" (p. 312).

Papias, who had personal contact with those taught by Christ and His apostles and may well have been a disciple of the apostle John, asserted that "the Lord used to teach concerning those [end] times" that "there will be a period of a thousand years after the resurrection of the dead and the kingdom of Christ will be set up in material form on this very earth" (cited in Eusebius *HE* iii.39.12; Irenaeus *Adv. haer.* v.33.3f.). Though Papias fleshed out his millennial reference with details from 2 Baruch (see above), his account is a weighty testimony to primitive Christian eschatological beliefs.

The author of the Epistle of Barnabas (no later than A. D. 138) "is a follower of chiliasm. The six days of creation mean a period of six thousand years because a thousand years are like one day in the eyes of God. In six days, that is in six thousand years, everything will be completed, after which the present evil time will be destroyed and the Son of God will come again and judge the godless and change the sun and the moon and the stars and he will truly rest on the seventh day. Then will dawn the sabbath of the millennial kingdom (15,1–9)" (Quasten, I, 89).

Justin Martyr, "the most important of the Greek apologists of the second century" (Quasten, I, 196), while granting that "many who belong to the pure and pious faith and are true Christians think otherwise" than he on the millennial issue, explicitly declared: "I and others are right-minded Christians in all points and are assured that there will be a resurrection of the dead and a thousand years in Jerusalem, which will then be built, adorned and enlarged" (*Dial.* 80f.; cf. J. Daniélou, VC, 2 [1948], 1–16).

Other important patristic millennialists were Irenaeus (see below, the final quotation in this article); Hippolytus of Rome and Julius "Africanus" (see Froom, I, 268–282, and note his helpful tabular summary of patristic views, pp. 458f.); Victorinus of Pettau, the chiliasm of whose commentary on Revelation was edited out by amillennialist Jerome (see Quasten, II, 411–13; Froom, I, 337–344); and the Africans Tertullian (*Adv. Marc.* iii.24; *Apol.* 48; cf. Quasten, II, 318, 339f.), Cyprian (see Froom, I, 331–36), and Lactantius (whose detailed picture of millennial bliss in *Divine Institutes* vii.14, 24, 26 by no means presupposes Zoroastrian influence—Eliade notwithstanding). In taking a millennial viewpoint, these fathers ranged themselves on the side of orthodoxy in two particulars: they supported the apostolicity and canonicity of Revelation (against those who combined a denial of its authenticity with amillennialism, e.g., Dionysius of Alexandria, as cited in Eusebius *HE* vii.14.1–3; 24.6–8); and they opposed both the Gnostics, whose dualistic spiritualizing of Christian doctrine completely wiped out eschatological hope, and Christian Platonists such as Origen (*De prin.* ii.11.2), whose rejection of a literal millennium stemmed from an idealistic depreciation of matter and a highly dangerous allegorical hermeneutic (A. C. McGiffert, *History of Christian Thought*, I [1932], 227f.).

It is a moot point whether the Clementine epistles, the Shepherd of Hermas, the Didache, the Apocalypse of Peter, Melito of Sardis, the letters of the Lyons martyrs, Methodius of Tyre, and Commodian show traces of millennialism. Polycarp of Smyrna and Ignatius of Antioch certainly do not—but little can be derived one way or the other from arguments from silence. Active opposition to chiliastic views arose (1) as a result of Origen's influence (thus Eusebius's later shift to amillennialism, *HE* iii.39, with his false attribution of chiliastic origins to the heretic Cerinthus, *HE* iii.28); (2) in reaction to Montanist excesses, e.g., their prophetess's claim that "Christ came to me in the form of a woman . . . and revealed to me that this place [the insignificant village of Pepuza] is holy and that here Jerusalem will come down from heaven" (Epiphanius xlix.1; cf. McGiffert, I, 171); and (3) as a defense against attempts to calculate the end time (a practice that has consistently brought discredit, through guilt-by-association, to millennialism in every age: e.g., cf. Vulliaud, pp. 75–85; Toulmin and Goodfield, *Discovery of Time* [1965], pp. 55–73; H. J. Forman, *Story of Prophecy* [1940]; R. Lewinsohn, *Science, Prophecy and Prediction* [1961]; L. Festinger, *et al.*, *When Prophecy Fails* [1956]; T. C. Graebner, *Prophecy and the War* [1918]; *War in the Light of Prophecy* [1941]; and finally, as an especially gross modern example, O. J. Smith, *Is the Antichrist at Hand? What of Mussolini* [1927]).

B. Middle Ages and Reformation

No theologian of the ancient Church had a greater influence on its history during the medieval period than Augustine. Once a chiliast himself but driven away from that position by the "immoderate, carnal" extremism of some of its advocates (*Civ. Dei* xx.7), he followed the symbolical-mystical hermeneutic system of the fourth-century donatist Tyconius in arguing that the thousand years of Rev. 20 actually designated the interval "from the first coming of Christ to the end of the world, when He shall come the second time" (xx.8). Thus was "a new era in prophetic interpretation" introduced, wherein Augustine's conception of the millennium as "spiritualized into a present politico-religious fact, fastens itself upon the church for about thirteen long centuries" (Froom, I, 479, with tabular summary of medieval views, 896f.; see also R. C. Petry, *Christian Eschatology and Social Thought: A Historical Essay on the Social Implications of Some Selected Aspects in Christian Eschatology to A.D. 1500* [1956], pp. 312–336). Millennialism did not die, but under the pressure of the "medieval synthesis" it tended to assume

2. Millennium

aberrational forms, particularly after the year 1000 when the Augustinian chronology (if literalized) ran out. Thus, as is frequently the case, polar extremes developed: mystical, spiritualistic chiliasms presupposing the end of the church-age, as represented by Joachim of Fiore's "third age of the Spirit," and by Cathari, Spiritual Franciscans, and Waldenses; and grossly materialistic chiliasms bound up with the crusading enterprise, as illustrated by Urban II's speech at Clermont: "As the times of Antichrist are approaching and as the East, and especially Jerusalem, will be the central point of attack, there must be Christians there to resist." (On both varieties of medieval chiliasm, see J. J. von Döllinger, *The Prophetic Spirit and the Prophecies of the Christian Era*, published with his *Fables Respecting the Popes* [1872]; A. Vasilev, *Byzantion* [1942/43], pp. 462–502; R. A. Knox, *Enthusiasm* [1950], pp. 110–13; and esp. N. Cohn, *Pursuit of the Millennium ... in Europe from the 11th to the 16th Century* [1961].)

Though both Renaissance and Reformation stood against the world view of medieval scholasticism, they did not oppose the accepted Augustinian amillennialism. The Renaissance was too favourable toward Neoplatonic modes of thought to be chiliastic, and the Reformers were so (legitimately) preoccupied with correcting the Church's soteriological errors that they could not give high priority to eschatology. But from the pre-Reformers Wyclif and Hus to Luther, Calvin, and the doctrinal affirmations of Protestant Orthodoxy, the papacy was identified with the antichrist. This conviction led many Reformation Protestants to believe that the end of the world was at hand (T. F. Torrance, *SJT*, Occasional Papers 2, pp. 36–62; Vulliaud, pp. 127f.). Had it not been for the outbreak of chiliasm in a particularly offensive form at Münster (1534), early Church teaching on the millennium might have been recovered along with other doctrines obscured in the medieval synthesis. The speculations of radicals, however, as concretized in Münzer's "Zion," were so offensive to all that this was rendered impossible. The Augsburg Confession, art. 17 (Lutheran) and the Helvetic Confession, art. 11 (Reformed) expressly rejected such "Jewish opinions" (but, let it be noted, did not reject millennialism per se—cf. Peters, *Theocratic Kingdom*, I, 531–34; M. Reu, *Lutheran Dogmatics* [1951], pp. 483–87; and Saarnivaara, pp. 94f.).

Virtually all the Reformation commentators on Rev. 20 followed the Augustinian line, even when other aspects of their eschatology seemed to cry out for a millennial interpretation of the passage (cf. tabulation of views in Froom, II [1948], 530f.). The same was true even of Anabaptists: "except for Melchior Hofmann, only a few fringe figures of the Anabaptist movement were chiliastic" (*Mennonite Encyclopedia*, I, 557). The oft-heard claim that theosophical mystic Jakob Böhme was a millennialist is repudiated by his own writings (cf. J. J. Stoudt, *Sunrise to Eternity* [1957], pp. 127f.). In contrast, many of the seventeenth-century divines of the Westminster Assembly, e.g., Thomas Goodwin, were decidedly premillennial in their theology (cf. P. Schaff, *Creeds of Christendom*, I, 727–756); and "Cambridge Platonist" Henry More believed in a chiliastic future when "all the goodly Inventions of nice Theologers shall cease ... and the Gospel shall be exalted" (see A. Lichtenstein, *Henry More* [1962], pp. 101f.).

C. Modern Times

New England Puritanism, continental Pietism, and the evangelical revivals of the 18th cent. came long enough after the events of the Reformation that perspective on the Reformers' limitations became possible. Among the results were increased missionary outreach and more careful eschatological study. Chiliasm revived, and it was generally of the premillennial variety (cf. the tabular summary of seventeenth- and eighteenth-century interpretations of Rev. 20 in Froom, II, 786f.). Except for Jonathan Edwards, who was postmillennial (J. P. Martin, *The Last Judgment ... from Orthodoxy to Ritschl* [1963], pp. 71f.), virtually all the Christian leaders of colonial America maintained premillennialism: John Davenport, Samuel Increase, and Cotton Mather; Samuel Sewall; Timothy Dwight (tabulation of views in Froom, III, 252f.; see also G. H. Williams, *Wilderness and Paradise in Christian Thought* [1962]). Spener, Halle Pietist and hymnwriter Joachim Lange, and distinguished NT scholar J. A. Bengel held millennial views. John Wesley's hymns attest his early premillennarian belief, though later he embraced Bengel's concept of a future double millennium (first on earth, with Satan bound; second in heaven, representing the saints' rule with Christ).

In sum, it can hardly be maintained, as is commonly alleged, that chiliastic belief did not have serious influence in Christendom before the rise of Adventist sects and J. N. Darby's Plymouth Brethren in the 19th cent., and the appearance of the Scofield Reference Bible and the Fundamentalist movement early in the 20th cent. (cf. W. H. Rutgers, *Premillennialism in America* [1930]; L. Gaspar, *The Fundamentalist Movement* [1963], pp. 7f., 53f., 157). Certainly Darby and the Scofield editors introduced the Church to dispensationalism (at least as a formal theology), and premillennialism was an essential element in that hermeneutical schema; but a premillennarian view of Rev. 20 did not logically require dispensational commitment and had in fact existed independently of it since the early days of the Church.

D. Utopian Dream

Secular utopianism is a theme in the history of ideas correlative with the millennial hope, and it is instructive to note that where Christian millennial expectation has been absent or downplayed its utopian counterpart has entered the breach. Greco-Roman civilization conceived of history cyclically, with the "golden age" as a future hope (cf. Vergil's 4th Eclogue). During the amillennial Middle Ages the legend of an idealistic kingdom in the East, under the rule of Christian "Prester John," captured the imagination and directly influenced the mythology of exploration (Ponce de Leon's search for the fountain of youth, Pizarro's quest for a city of gold). The Renaissance, similarly unsympathetic to chiliasm, marked the beginning of literary utopianism with the work of Thomas More. The rise of the modern secular era during the deistic "Enlightenment" offered a secular alternative to the Christian millennium in what Carl Becker perceptively termed "the heavenly city of the 18th-century philosophers." The Marxist goal of a "classless society," the Nazi dream of the "thousand-year Reich," and aspects of the capitalist-materialist "American way of life" are inversions of the millennial hope. E. Voegelin (*Order and History* [1956]) has rightly seen them as illustrations of "metastatic gnosis," the idolatrous effort of man to create a millennial kingdom for himself without God. It would appear that the loss of theocentric chiliasm leaves a vacuum into which rush the monstrosities of anthropocentric utopianism. At the same time, perennial utopian dreams (and extrabiblical religious chiliasms, as in the Parsi faith—see I.C above) can be viewed as the groping of the human soul, individual and collective, for the truth embodied in Christian eschatology. (See, e.g., S. Baring-Gould, *Curious Myths of the Middle Ages* [1866–1868]; K. Mannheim, *Ideology and Utopia* [1936]; E. Sanceau, *The Land of Prester John* [1944]; F. R. White, ed., *Famous Utopias of the Renaissance* [1946]; K. Amis, *New Maps of Hell* [1960]; S. B. Liljegren, *Studies on the Origin and Early Tradition of English Utopian Fiction* [1961]; J. P. Roux, *Les Explorateurs au moyen âge* [1961]; R. Thévenin, *Les Pays légendaires* [1961]; C. Walsh, *From Utopia to Nightmare* [1962]; G. Kateb, *Utopia and Its Enemies* [1963]; *Daedalus*, Spring, 1965; L. Gallagher, *More's "Utopia" and Its Critics* [1964]; E. L. Tuveson, *Millennium and Utopia* [1964]; H. B. Franklin, *Future Perfect* [1966]; M. R. Hillegas, *The Future as Nightmare* [1967]; T. Molnar, *Utopia, the Perennial Heresy* [1972]; J. W. Montgomery, *Where Is History Going?* [1969].)

III. Contrasting Millennialisms

A. Amillennial Allegory

Since chiliasm is bound directly to the interpretation of Rev. 20, consideration must be given to the diverse ways in which this passage has been exegeted. Amillennialists are unconvinced that the chapter should compel belief in a literal period of penultimate divine triumph, either before or after the Parousia. Liberal theology takes this viewpoint because of its objection to the miraculous character of predictive prophecy and because of its reductionistic approach to biblical inspiration; the book of Revelation loses force because of its alleged disunity, lack of authenticity, or factual unreliability (see, e.g., A. Harnack, *Enc.Brit.* [11th ed. 1910–1911], XVIII, 461–63; R. H. Charles, *Studies in the Apocalypse* [1913]; comm. on Revelation [2 vols., ICC, 1920]; *Lectures on the Apocalypse* [1922]; G. R. Berry, *Premillennialism and OT Prediction* (1929); and R. W. McEwen's "Factors in the Modern Survival of Millennialism" [Diss., University of Chicago, 1933]). "Conservative" amillennialism holds to a symbolical interpretation of Rev. 20, either in the Augustinian manner or along the lines of W. W. Milligan (*Expos.B.*): "The saints reign for a thousand years; that is, they are introduced into a state of perfect and glorious victory." Important orthodox proponents of amillennialism include G. Vos, *Teaching of Jesus Concerning the Kingdom of God and the Church* (1903; repr. 1951); W. Masselink, *Why Thousand Years?* (1930); F. E. Hamilton, *Basis of Millennial Faith* (1942); P. Mauro, *The Seventy Weeks* (1944); O. T. Allis, *Prophecy and the Church* (1945); G. L. Murray, *Millennial Studies* (1948); A. Pieters, *Seed of Abraham* (1950); L. Berkhof, *Kingdom of God* (1951); *Second Coming of Christ* (1953); J. Wilmot, *Inspired Principles of Prophetic Interpretation* (1967). The difficulty all amillennialisms face is the textual weight of Rev. 20. The admission of liberal amillennialist Salmond concerning this passage is noteworthy: "The figurative interpretation, it must be owned, cannot be made exegetically good even in its most plausible applications. ... This remarkable paragraph in John's Apocalypse speaks of a real millennial reign of Christ on earth together with certain of His saints, which comes in between a first resurrection and the final judgment" (pp. 441f.).

B. Postmillennial Progress

Postmillennialism of both a "conservative" and a "liberal" type is likewise to be found in the Church. Orthodox advocates of this position (among the best: P. Fairbaim, *Interpretation of Prophecy* [1865]; Hodge, Shedd, and

Strong, in their systematic theologies; B. B. Warfield, *Biblical Doctrines* [1929]; J. M. Kik, *Revelation Twenty* [1955]; L. Boettner, *The Millennium* [1958]) interpret Rev. 20 less symbolically than do the amillennialists (a period of divinely ordained blessedness will in fact precede the end), but nonliteral force is given to the details of the chapter (no de facto resurrection of martyrs or physical presence of Christ on earth is anticipated during the millennial period). Rather, God's immanent power will be more fully manifest over His enemies as the time of Christ's return draws closer. Boettner argues, "We do not understand how anyone can take a long range view of history and deny that across the centuries there has been and continues to be great progress, and that the trend is definitely toward a better world" (p. 136).

This is precisely the opinion of "liberal" postmillennialists—but their confidence stems from a different quarter: the eighteenth-century optimistic view of man as basically good and the nineteenth-century "myth of progress." Thus the old modernism found premillennialism abhorrent because "the world is found to be growing constantly better" (S. J. Case, *The Millennial Hope* [1918], p. 238) and "the clear vision of present-day prophets . . . in religion, in philosophy, and in business, revels in a growing future of blessedness for mankind" (G. P. Mains, *Premillennialism* [1920], p. 107). Unchastened by two world wars, the new secular theology endeavors to revivify nineteenth-century motifs along much the same lines, e.g., with its view of an immanent Christ more and more fully manifested in the social movements of our day. (For critique see J. W. Montgomery, *Suicide of Christian Theology* [1970].) Protestant "process theology" (J. B. Cobb, Jr., S. Ogden, N. Pittenger) sees man dynamically growing into God. Roman Catholic evolutionary theologian Teilhard de Chardin glimpses God "up ahead" where human history will be fully divinized at a Christic "Omega point" (cf. Schillebeeckx, *God the Future of Man* [1968]; J. W. Montgomery, *Ecumenicity, Evangelicals and Rome* [1969]). Moltmann's "theology of hope," in part dependent on Ernst Bloch's dialectic humanism, has similar affinities with postmillennial confidence in the future of the human drama.

Critics of postmillennialism, whether of the conservative or of the liberal variety, argue that neither the Bible nor human history offers ground for assuming that the human situation is in process of continual amelioration; indeed, because of humanity's sinful condition, the reverse would appear to be the case. And "if world history is not a movement of progress but rather tends to an increasing concentration of anti-christian power, then the second advent of Jesus for which the Church is praying is not a direct continuation and completion of world history but an event that comes from an entirely different dimension, that suddenly breaks off the preceding development and throws the whole constitution of the present world off its hinges" (K. Heim, *Jesus the World's Perfecter* [1961], p. 189).

C. Premillennial Philosophy of History

Premillennialism endeavors to offer as literal an interpretation of Rev. 20 as possible (Christ will physically return to a world under the sway of the antichrist, defeat him, and with the resurrected saints rule on earth a thousand years; the ultimate destruction of Satanic power will then occur and "God shall be all in all"). Naturally, such an eschatology is anathema to the liberal theological community, so premillennialism is a phenomenon to be observed today only among those holding a strong doctrine of biblical inspiration. The major differences among contemporary premillennialists do not touch the above points, but have to do with whether the millennium ought to be integrated into a dispensational view of Scripture, and whether the "lifting up" of the Church spoken of in 1 Thess. 4:17 occurs before, during, or after the great antichristic tribulation ("pretribulation rapture," as supported by E. S. English, *Re-Thinking the Rapture* [1954], v. "midtribulation rapture," as argued by N. B. Harrison, *The End* [1941]. v. "posttribulation rapture," as maintained by N. S. McPherson, *Triumph Through Tribulation* [1944]). Without any attempt to classify according to these differences, we can list the most important modern supporters of the premillennial position: F. Godet, *Studies on the NT* (1873); E. R. Craven, comm. on Revelation (Lange, 1874); N. West, *The Thousand Years* (1880); Peters; S. P. Tregelles, *Hope of Christ's Second Coming* (1886); J. A. Seiss, *The Last Times* (1878); *Lectures on the Apocalypse* (1900); W. E. Blackstone, *Jesus is Coming* (1908); A. Reese, *Approaching Advent of Christ* (1917); T. Zahn, *Intro. to the NT* (1909); comm. on Revelation (*KEK*, 1926); A. C. Gaebelein, *Return of the Lord* (1925); H. A. Ironside, *Lamp of Prophecy* (1940); L. S. Chafer, *Systematic Theology* (1948); G. E. Ladd, *Crucial Questions about the Kingdom of God* (1952); *The Blessed Hope* (1956); C. C. Ryrie, *Basis of Premillennial Faith* (1953); Culver; C. L. Feinberg, *Premillennialism or Amillennialism?* (1954); J. D. Pentecost, *Things to Come* (1958); J. F. Walvoord, *Millennial Kingdom* (1959): M. C. Tenney, "Importance and Exegesis of Rev. 20:1-8," in J. F. Walvoord, ed., *Truth for Today* (1963).

The arguments for premillennialism are generally of two types: exegetical and doctrinal. Exegetically, the claim is made that only a literal interpretation of Rev. 20 fulfills the basic hermeneutic rule that a passage of Scripture must be taken in its natural sense unless contextual considerations force a nonliteral rendering. (The burden of proof thus falls upon the opponent of premillennialism to show that such considerations do in fact exist.) Doctrinally, the premillennialist argues that the vindication of God's ways to humanity entails Christ's victory and reign in the very sphere in which Satanic power has so long been manifest. For God's will to be done "on earth as it is in heaven" demands what T. A. Kantonen has so effectively termed "the harvest of history" (*The Christian Hope* [1954], pp. 65-70; cf. Peters, III, 427-442; and A. J. McClain, *Greatness of the Kingdom* [1959], pp. 527-531). A. Saphir asked, "Is earth simply a failure, abandoned by God to the power of the enemy, the scene of divine judgment, and not the scene of the vindication and triumph of righteousness?" (*Lectures on the Lord's Prayer* [1870]). Perhaps the best statement of the case remains that of Irenaeus (*Adv. haer.* v.32.1) at the end of the 2nd cent.: "It behooves the righteous first to receive the promise of the inheritance which God promised to the fathers, and to reign in it when they rise again to behold God in this creation which is renovated, and that the judgment should take place afterwards. For it is just that in that very creation in which they toiled or were afflicted, being proved in every way by suffering, they should receive the reward of their suffering; and that in the creation in which they were slain because of their love to God, in that they should be revived again; and that in the creation in which they endured servitude, in that they should reign. For God is rich in all things and all things are his. It is fitting, therefore, that the creation itself, being restored to its primeval condition, should be without restraint under the dominion of the righteous" (*ANF* translation).

Bibliography.—Two encyclopedic general works are H. Corredi, *Kritische Geschichte des Chiliasmus* (4 vols., 1794); L. F. Froom, *Prophetic Faith of our Fathers* (4 vols., 1946-1954). Bibliographical sources are best represented by A. D. Ehlert, *Bibliographic History of Dispensationalism* (1965); for utopianism, G. Neglcy, ed., catalog of the Utopia Collection of Duke University Library (1965). Other significant works and those cited twice or more in the article are: R. D. Culver, *Daniel and the Latter Days*; W. S. LaSor, *The Truth about Armageddon* (1982); J. B. Payne, *Encyclopedia of Biblical Prophecy* (1980); G. N. H. Peters, *Theocratic Kingdom* (3 vols., 1884; repr. 1952); J. Quasten, *Patrology* (3 vols., 1950); U. Saarnivaara, *Armageddon* (1966); S. D. F. Salmond, *Christian Doctrine of Immortality* (2nd ed. 1896); P. Vulliaud, *La Fin du monde* (1952).

3. Demon Possession: A Brief Commentary

Commentary on Mark Crooks's Essay, "On the Psychology of Demon Possession: The Occult Personality"

The present short commentary on Crooks's essay focuses on Crooks's methodological distinction between proper empirical, scientific method and the so-called "religion of science." It argues that only when this distinction is maintained can one avoid a metaphysical positivism that makes impossible any scholarly evaluation of occult phenomena.

I am neither a psychologist nor a psychiatrist, but, on the basis of my books *Principalities and Powers: The World of the Occult* and *Demon Possession,* cited by Mark Crooks in his article under discussion, I have been asked to provide a brief comment concerning it. As a philosopher and professor of law, my remarks will necessarily focus on epistemology and standards of evidence, especially as applied to occult and allegedly supernatural phenomena.

In my view, the most important single contribution of Crooks's article lies in his preference for factual evidence over metaphysical opinion. He rightly holds that—at least since the eighteenth-century so-called Enlightenment—naturalistic worldviews have become a new orthodoxy. To admit anything beyond the naturalistically "normal" identifies one as a naïve obscurantist, deserving of ostracism from the scientific community. To accept any explanations beyond the naturalistic is a mark of political incorrectness and the kiss of academic death.

Crooks, on the other hand, understands the vital distinction between scientific method—relying on empirical, factual evidence no matter the consequences—and what has been termed "the religion of science": the metaphysical commitment to naturalistic explanations, even when the evidence does not offer sufficient support for them. Crooks is a serious empiricist. If the data require, or even favour, non-naturalistic explanations of occult phenomena, he prefers to go with the evidence rather than forcing the data to fit a preconceived naturalistic universe.

Examples abound throughout the Crooks essay. His critiques of McNamara's "positive possession" and the views of Davies, of Randi, and of Carl Sagan are particularly telling. Let me reinforce the Sagan analysis by material from my most recent work, *Defending the Gospel in Legal Style.*[1]

I deal with Sagan's adage, "Extraordinary claims require extraordinary proof"—an assertion which, if correct, would justify limiting the analysis of occult phenomena such as demon possession to reductionistic naturalism regardless of the weight of the evidence for a non-naturalistic explanation of such occurrences. (In the following lengthy quotation, read "occult" for "religious" or "theological," and "veridical occult phenomenon" for "miracle.")

> When one passes into the realm of religious commitment, does one not face insuperable problems not to be found in the legal realm—since religious decisions are of an eternal dimension? Can the unbeliever not argue that it is simply impossible in principle for evidence—any evidence—to justify religious commitment?
>
> Historically, this style of argument has been presented in different guises. Going back to late classical times is the axiom, "the finite is not capable of the infinite":[2] the world is incapable of the presence of the absolute, so no amount of evidence could ever demonstrate the presence of the infinite in our finite world. The fallacy of this argument (applicable not only to a divine Incarnation and an infallible Bible, but also to the real presence of Christ in the Holy Eucharist) is simply that, *qua* human beings, we have no idea what God is or is not capable of, so we have no business ruling out events *a priori*. It may well be that the reverse of the aphorism is true: *infinitum capax finiti*! Only a factual investigation of the world to see if God has entered it will ever answer the question.
>
> Then there is Lessing's "ditch": the claim that the accidental facts of history can never attain or justify the absolute truths of reason. Here, a serious category mistake has been made. If the "absolute truths of reason" are purely formal, lacking entirely in content, then they have nothing to do with Christian religious claims at all. If, however, they are factual in nature, then only factual investigation and probability reasoning could justify them. But this is exactly what historical proof consists of: probable evidence for historical occurrences. If, for example, God became man in Jesus Christ, that contention is as capable of historical investigation as are any other purported occurrences.
>
> David Hume argued that no miracle could ever be demonstrated, since (on the basis of "uniform experience") it would always be more miraculous

---

[1] J. W. Montgomery (2017). *Defending the gospel in legal style* (pp. 26–30). Bonn: Verlag für Kultur und Wissenschaft.

[2] Cf. Peter Bruns (1999). Finitum non capax infiniti: Ein antiochenisches Axiom in der Inkarnationslehre Babais des Grossen (nach 628). *Oriens Christianus, 83,* 46–71.

that one claiming a miracle or providing evidence for it were not deceiving or deceived than that the miracle actually happened. Miracle arguments (such as the case for the resurrection of Christ) are therefore impossible from the outset. But Hume's position has been thoroughly refuted—and not just by Christian philosophers.[3] The intractable problem with the Humean argument is that it is perfectly circular: to be sure, if nature is completely uniform (i.e., if natural laws are never broken), miracles do not occur. *But that is precisely the question requiring an answer!* And the only way properly to respond is by engaging in serious factual investigation of given miracle claims. One cannot short-circuit the miracles issue by *a priori* pontifications about the nature of the universe. Indeed, ... in an Einsteinian, relativistic universe, no event can be excluded on principle: everything is subject to empirical investigation.

But the most influential current argument against the effectiveness of religious claims based on historical evidence is that represented by the adage, "Extraordinary claims require extraordinary proof"—a saying popularized by the late Carl Sagan but which apparently originated with sociologist Marcello Truzzi.[4] Does not this declaration constitute an obvious truth militating against all miracle claims—and in particular the resurrection of Christ? Since a miracle is maximally "extraordinary," would not the evidence required to demonstrate it have to be maximally extraordinary as well?

In a word, the answer is No! Why? In line with what we have noted above, the Truzzi-Sagan tag would have meaning if, and only if, one knew the fabric of the universe—its cosmic laws and what therefore can and cannot happen; but in Einsteinian, relativistic terms, no one has such knowledge, so no one can rationally determine the probabilities for or against a given event: only factual investigation permits one to conclude that event *x* did or event *y* did not occur....

But what about the very concept of a "miracle"? Is not the notion in itself so extraordinary that no amount of evidence could properly count to prove it? Here we must distinguish *mechanism* from *factuality*. The mechanism of a miracle is indeed beyond our ken—but that is irrelevant to whether or not such an event occurs. As long ago as the 18th century, Thomas Sherlock, Master of London's Temple Church and pastor to barristers, noted that the case for the resurrection of Jesus Christ does not depend on our comprehension of how resurrections occur but squarely on whether there is sufficient evidence that Jesus died on the Cross and that following his death he showed

---

[3] J. Earman (2000). *Hume's abject failure: The argument against miracles.* New York: Oxford University Press.

[4] See J. W. Montgomery (2011). Apologetics insights from the thought of I. J. Good. *Philosophia Christi, 13,* 203–212; reprinted in Montgomery, *Defending the gospel in legal style* (cited in note 1 above), pp. 161–69.

himself physically alive to sound witnesses.[5] There is thus nothing "extraordinary" about determining that Jesus rose from the dead: one need only show (a) that he died and (b) that later he was physically alive — determinations which we make every day (though in reverse order).

Are we saying that miracle evidence should be accepted as readily as non-miracle evidence? The visions of Fatima and the appearance of the Angel Moroni to Joseph Smith on the same basis as Lincoln's assassination and Hitler's *Anschluss*? We are saying simply that the standard of proof does not depend on the frequency of the event (since all historical events are unique) nor on the characterisation of the event as "miraculous" or "non-miraculous." The standard of proof depends, in all instances, on the quality of the evidence in behalf of the claimed event—that and nothing more; that and nothing less. If one were to claim that a peach can be miraculously turned into a cumquat, he or she would have to show, by ordinary scientific means, that there is a peach present at the outset, and, then, afterwards, a cumquat. For a resurrection from the dead: the same kind of testimony is required as for any other historical event—in this instance, that the object of the miracle was in fact dead and then, afterwards, physically alive. The issue of proof is not in any way metaphysical: one relies on sound historical investigation of the testimony to miracle claims of past events (or sound contemporary scientific investigation, in the case of the peach). The nature of the claim determines the method of proof, and the standard will be that appropriate to parallel determinations in the same realm.

But let us conclude with the essence of Crooks's argument, in his own words:

> Realize that a worldview, positivist or otherwise, by its nature cannot be logically entailed by empirical data as such. There is also the complementary suggestion that otherwise successful naturalistic explanations do not receive such validation from their embedding worldview. Thus the post-Enlightenment interpretive paradigm, as such, that did away with "explanatory gremlins" (e.g., demons) has never been experimentally or theoretically established. The only reason it seems to have been so is that the success of naturalistic explanations in the physical sciences seems to necessitate a monopolistic reductionist scheme.

If psychologists, parapsychologists, psychiatrists, and historians of ideas were to pay just a modicum of attention to Crooks's seminal essay, those fields of scientific investigation would have the perspective essential for a

---

[5] T. Sherlock (1729). *Tryal of the witnesses of the resurrection of Jesus*. London: J. Roberts. Sherlock's book is photolithographically reproduced in the revised edition of J. W. Montgomery (1980). *Jurisprudence: A Book of Readings*. Strasbourg: International Scholarly Publishers.

return to a genuine empirical examination of reality. The result would be a wondrous turnabout, not merely in the investigation of occult phenomena and of the personalities of those suffering such deleterious experiences, but across the entire gamut of scientific endeavor.

4. The World View of Johann Valentin Andreae

Laudemus sed Caveamur

We begin with a word of praise and a word of warning. It would be difficult to overstate the value of this symposium in celebration of the four-hundredth birthday of J.V. Andreae. Few names in the history of western thought have less deserved the relative oblivion to which that 'Phoenix of the theologians' has been relegated. Andreae was an *uomo universale* in the best sense of that Renaissance expression: not only was he a leading figure in the Rosicrucian mystification and a creator of one of the greatest literary utopias of all time (the *Christianopolis*), but his scientific interests tied him to important advances being made by his Lutheran co-religionists in early 17th-century Tübingen (Schickhardt and the calculating machine; the mathematical-astronomical labors of Maestlin and Kepler); his creative writing (the *Chymical Wedding*) was to influence no less important productions than Goethe's *Faust*; his herculean expenditure of himself as pastor literally saved from annihilation two Black Forest towns sacked in the Thirty Years War; his efforts to establish Christian tradesmen's gilds and societies of believers to promote intellectual, charitable, and spiritual activity have continuing direct influence today (his long shadow even touches the English Royal Society); his vigorous promotion of ecumenical discussion was and is in the best tradition of theological cooperation without compromise; and his general impact on the church life of Württemberg, and through it on German Protestantism in general, was such that Stuttgart historian Dr. Gerhard Schäfer has not hesitated to assert that Andreae was the single most important influence on the church history of the Württemberg territory for over two hundred years. When, therefore, the Bibliotheca Philosophica Hermetica, its founder Joseph R. Ritman, and its director Dr. F.A. Janssen, honour the memory of Johann Valentin Andreae through the creation both of an Andreae exhibition and of an international symposium devoted to his life and thought, they place the entire scholarly world in their debt.

But a powerful warning must accompany the laudation. Andreae must be celebrated for the right reasons. To remember him for the wrong reasons would be worse than not to remember him at all. The descriptive brochure of the Bibliotheca Philosophica Hermetica rightly relates 'the great cultural stream of Gnosticism' to alchemy and Rosicrucianism, and goes on to assert: 'The objective pursued by 17th-century Rosicrucians was a reformation whereby Hermetism, alchemy and mysticism would be integrated. Their writings, brought forward by the circle around Johann Valentin Andreae, started a new wave in the Hermetic tradition.' But was this in fact Andreae's objective? Was Andreae a hermeticist? If not, to make him one would be singular disservice to his memory, even if carried out with the best of intentions.

Another example: At the close of an influential essay on Andreae, Professor Martin Brecht points up the failure of Andreae's reforming efforts and compares him to Hemingway's hero in *The Old Man and the Sea* who, having battled a giant fish, ultimately brings back only its skeleton.[1] Was Andreae Hemingway's Santiago—that Promethean writer's own alter ego, endeavoring (like Melville's Captain Ahab) to dominate Nature and achieve a superhuman goal in an imperfect world? Professor Brecht would certainly not carry the analogy in this direction, but many—perhaps the majority—of contemporary writers on Andreae would feel quite comfortable with such an interpretation. What kind of a man was Andreae, after all? If we do not answer this fundamental question accurately, it makes little difference what else we do in order to preserve Andreae's name from lethean waters.

The plan of the present essay is first to identify who Johann Valentin Andreae was *not*, and then to see who he actually *was*. In carrying out this task, I unapologetically rely upon my two-volume work, *Cross and Crucible*, published in 1973 in Nijhoff's monographic series, the 'International Archives of the History of Ideas', and based upon my Strasbourg dissertation defended in 1964.[2] It might seem redundant to employ arguments already in circulation for so many years. However, to my amazement and consternation, this work—in spite of universally laudatory reviews[3]—has been ignored by a good number of those subsequently treating Andreae's life and labors,[4] and in certain cases has been cited by those who manifestly have

---

[1] Martin Brecht, 'Johann Valentin Andreae', in Martin Greschat (ed.), *Orthodoxie und Pietismus* (Stuttgart 1982), p. 134. The reference is to Ernest Hemingway, *The Old Man and the Sea* (New York 1952).

[2] John Warwick Montgomery, *Cross and Crucible. Johann Valentin Andreae (1586-1654), Phoenix of the Theologians* (The Hague 1973), 2 vols. (Hereafter cited as *Cross and crucible*.)

[3] E.g. Roland Edighoffer, 'Andreana', in: *Études germaniques*, 34 (1979), p. 287-88.

[4] Unfortunate enough is the unpublished Cologne doctoral dissertation, *Alchemie und Mystik in Johann Valentin Andreaes 'Chymischer Hochzeit Christiani Rosencreütz'*

not read it or come to terms with the evidence it sets forth. This is not to say that *Cross and Crucible* has had no effect, particularly where documentation rather than speculation characterizes an author's approach,[5] but the fact is that the predominant understanding of Andreae's world-view today remains much what it was before the appearance of *Cross and Crucible*. In the apostolic phrase: 'Brethren, these things ought not to be'—and the Bibliotheca Philosophica Hermetica symposium offers a valuable opportunity to do something about it!

The Myth of a Rosicrucian Andreae

In surveying scholarly opinion prior to the 1970's on Andreae's relation to the Rose Cross, I observed that, in one way or another, the leading 20th century writers on the subject (Kienast, Peuckert, Schick, and Scholtz) all viewed Andreae as a Rosicrucian occultist. Indeed, 'Peuckert, the influential editor of the *Zeitschrift für Deutsche Philologie*, has especially weighed the teutonic scales, for his view of Andreae as "nature philosopher", "pansophist" (in Peuckert's special sense of Paracelsian esoterist), and "white magician" has been reinforced by the second edition of Pansophie (1956)'.[6] And the picture has not appreciably changed since 1970: witness Heiner Höfener's 1981 reprint edition of Andreae's *Christianopolis*, in his 'Klassiker

---

(1966) by Bernhard Kossmann; though defended a full two years after my dissertation at Strasbourg, the thesis shows no acquaintance whatever with its predecessor. Far more inexcusable is Wolfgang Biesterfeld's widely used German edition of Andreae's *Christianopolis* (Stuttgart 1975), which displays no knowledge of *Cross and crucible*, and repeats as 'received wisdom': 'Man nimmt heute als sicher an, daß Andreae der Verfasser dreier anonymer Schriften gewesen ist, die gewissermaßen als Gründungsurkunden jener Bewegung, die häufig mit der Freimaurerei in Verbindung gebracht wird, gelten können' (p. 155).

[5] A fine example is Inge Mager's meticulously researched essay, 'Die Beziehung Herzog Augusts von Braunschweig-Wolfenbüttel zu den Theologen Georg Calixt und Johann Valentin Andreae', in: Martin Brecht (ed.), *Pietismus und Neuzeit. Ein Jahrbuch zur Geschichte des neueren Protestantismus*, Bd. VI (Göttingen 1980), p. 76–98. Cf. the valuable continuation of pure Andreae bibliographical scholarship as illustrated by Wolf-Dieter Otte, 'Eine Briefsammlung aus dem Umkreis von Johann Valentin Andreae und seinem Sohn Gottlieb', in: Paul Raabe (ed.), *Wolffenbüttler Beiträge. Aus den Schätzen der Herzog August Bibliothek*, Bd. V (Frankfurt am Main 1982), p. 155–61.

[6] *Cross and crucible*, I, p. 160-61. It is of interest that Kienast's *Johann Valentin Andreae und die vier echten Rosenkreutzer-Schriften* (1926) was reissued photolithographically in 1970 by Johnson in New York.

der Utopischen Literatur' series, where—without so much as a mention of the evidence marshalled in *Cross and Crucible*—Höfener declares:

> Der Initiator und Verfasser der Rosenkreuzer-Schriften, der Adept des 'Wahren Christentums' von Johann Arndt, der chiliastische Reformator stellt sich als utopisierender Lustspiel-Autor vor? Doch Andreae bedurfte keiner Schutzbehauptung, zumal seine *Christianopolis* im Jahre 1619 anonym erschien. Auch war er von der Rosenkreuzer-Idee, die er als Student im Tübinger Freundeskreis ausbrütete, später selber nicht mehr angetan [...] 1619, in jenem Jahr, da auch *Christianopolis* erschien, gab Andreae seine Abrechnung mit der Rosenkreuzer-Bruderschaft [...].[7]

Let us examine briefly five contemporary variants on the persistent stereotype of Andreae as Rosicrucian, and then endeavor to reach more solid ground.

(1) Frances A. Yates. Dr. Yates, an influential English historian of ideas, does not attribute the authorship of the Rosicrucian manifestos to Andreae: indeed, for her, the true origins of the Rose Cross must be found in the thought of Giordano Bruno, in the mystical and alchemical impact of peripatetic English occultists John Dee and Edward Kelley at the court of Emperor Rudolf II in Prague and elsewhere in the German lands, and, finally, in the English chivalric-theatrical influence on the ducal court in Württemberg (the heraldic coat-of-arms of St. George is emblazoned with roses and a red cross; Friedrich of Württemberg was inducted into the Order of the Garter in 1603). But for Yates Andreae was himself deeply touched by these ideological and theatrical currents, and his world-view (at least as a young man) was in a large measure reflective of the Rosicrucian mindset:

> The *[Chymical] Wedding* is but another version of the allegories of the *Fama* and the *Confessio*. In the manifestos, Christian Rosencreutz was associated with an order of benevolent brethren; in the wedding, he is associated with an order of chivalry. The R. C. Brothers were spiritual alchemists; so are the Knights of the Golden Stone. The activities of the R. C. Brothers were symbolized through the treasures in their vault; similar activities are symbolized through the treasures in the castle. In fact, the theme of a vault containing a tomb actually occurs in the *Wedding*, surely an allusion to the famous vault of the *Fama*; and the *Wedding* opens with a personification of Fame, sounding her trumpet call.

---

[7] Heiner Höfener (ed.), *Johann Valentin Andreae. Christianopolis* (Hildesheim 1981), p. III-IV.

4. The World View of Johann Valentin Andreae

Though *Fama* and *Confessio* may not be written by the same hand as the *Wedding*, the plan of the allegories in all three works bears the stamp of minds working in concert, bent on sending out into the world their myth of Christian Rosencreutz, a benevolent figure, centre of brotherhoods and orders.[8]

Although this passage appeared a year before the publication of *Cross and Crucible* (1973), it could have been corrected by consulting the dissertation underlying it, which had been available since 1964. Remarkably, in her later work, *Astraea. The imperial theme in the sixteenth century* (1975), Dr. Yates, while stating that 'this book ends where my last book, *The Rosicrucian Enlightenment* began, in the years immediately preceding the outbreak of the Thirty Years' War', and expressly referring again to the Rosicrucian theme, in no way alters the views she previously set forth.[9] What are the problems with these views? As Roland Edighoffer has rightly observed, Yates' English explanation of Rosicrucian origins may 'séduire le lecteur' but nevertheless remains only an hypothesis.[10] Specifically, Yates seems unaware both of Andreae's unequivocal repudiation of occult soteriology and his firm adherence to Reformation Lutheranism. Moreover, she is misled into thinking that because the Rosicrucian manifestos on the one hand and Andreae's *Chymical Wedding* on the other often employ the same symbolic motifs, they do so for the same reason; in point of fact, Andreae uses occult motifs to present a Christian corrective to occultism.[11]

(2) Richard van Dülmen. Van Dülmen's longstanding interest in J. V. Andreae is reflected in his German editions of the *Christianopolis*, the *Theophilus*, and the *Chymical Wedding* (together with the Rosicrucian manifestos), issued as volumes 4, 5, and 6 of the monographic series, 'Quellen und Forschungen zur Württembergischen Kirchengeschichte' (general editors: Martin Brecht and Gerhard Schäfer). In Van Dülmen's 1973 Preface to his texts of the *Fama*, *Confessio*, and *Chymische Hochzeit* (this Preface remains unaltered in the third edition of 1981),we are informed that 'Auf jeden Fall war er [Andreae] der Hauptinitiator des Mythos von der Bruderschaft des

---

[8] Frances A. Yates, *The Rosicrucian Enlightenment* [London 1972], p. 65.
[9] Frances A. Yates, *Astraea. The imperial theme in the sixteenth century* (London 1975), p. 213–14.
[10] Edighoffer, op. cit., p. 286. Edighoffer incorporates this same criticism into his *Rose-Croix et société idéale selon Johann Valentin Andreae*, I (Neuilly s/Seine 1982), p. 220–22.
[11] *Cross and crucible*, II, p. 264–83, and the commentary following.

Rosenkreuzes'.[12] The nuances of Van Dülmen's position on Rosicrucian origins and Andreae's world-view are to be found in his work, *Die Utopie einer christlichen Gesellschaft: Johann Valentin Andreae* (1978):[13] Andreae is the author of the *Fama*, but not of the *Confessio* (a newly discovered marginal note in Andreae's friend Besold's copy of the *Fama* convinces Van Dülmen that Andreae wrote the *Fama*); Andreae's consistent life-orientation was to promote a new reformation by which Christian intellectuals would substitute an enlightened Christian humanism for the dead orthodoxy of Lutheran ecclesiasticism.

As with Yates, so with Van Dülmen: *Cross and Crucible* could have prevented serious misinterpretations of Andreae's activity and message—if (in Van Dülmen's case) it had not only been cited but also been allowed to interact in depth with his own researches. Thus, the series of thematic oppositions between the *Fama* and the *Chymical Wedding*, set forth in tabular form in *Cross and Crucible*,[14] makes any argument for common authorship exceedingly difficult, particularly when combined with Kienast's philological examination of the dialect differences between the 'pure Swabian' *Hochzeit* and the but vaguely Swabian Rosicrucian manifestos.[15]

The only new item of evidence Van Dülmen brings to bear on the question is Christoph Besold's marginal note in his copy of the *Fama*, and this is indeed worth examining. The note reads: 'Auctorem suspicor J.V.A. Et est et Andreanorum avitum insigne, crux et rosae—qualis certe crux depingitur in der Chymischen Hochzeit'.[16] Observe that here Besold claims no personal knowledge whatever of the origin of the *Fama* or of Andreae's authorship of it. He merely 'conjectures' (*suspicor*)—as so many others have done across the centuries—on the basis of the rose and cross in the Andreae family coat-of-arms (derived, in fact, from Luther's own coat-of-

---

[12] Richard van Dülmen (ed.), *Johann Valentin Andreae. Fama Fraternitatis (1614), Confessio Fraternitatis (1615), Chymische Hochzeit [...]* (Stuttgart 1981³), p. 9.

[13] Richard van Dülmen, *Die Utopie einer christlichen Gesellschaft. Johann Valentin Andreae*, I (Stuttgart-Bad Cannstatt 1978). Readers should be warned not to rely uncritically on the inadequately researched bibliography of Andreae's writings on p. 279–94.

[14] *Cross and crucible*, I, p. 226–28.

[15] Cf. ibid., p. 189–90.

[16] Van Dülmen, *Die Utopie [...]*, p. 76. Incredibly, in his note to this marginalium (p. 223), Van Dülmen appears to give credence to the hoary attempt to find Andreae identified in the first letters of the concluding line of the *Fama*: J[ohann] V[alentin] A[ndreae] S[tipendiarius] T[ubingensis]. I have analogized this to the subjectivistic cryptographic claims in support of Baconian authorship for Shakespeare's plays (*Cross and crucible*, I, p. 191–92).

4. The World View of Johann Valentin Andreae

arms).[17] In reality, this manuscript note constitutes a powerful argument against either Andreae or any close member of his circle of friends (such as Tobias Hess) having been responsible for the *Fama*: for surely Besold, as a member of that circle,[18] would then have known about it and would not have had to conjecture about the question of authorship!

As for Van Dülmen's view that Andreae distanced himself from Reformation Lutheranism—an argument contradicted by the evidence marshalled on virtually every page of *Cross and Crucible!*—Roland Edighoffer has well observed:

> Le désir de présenter Andreae essentiellement comme un humaniste chrétien aboutit parfois dans l'ouvrage de Richard van Dülmen à une distorsion des réalités ainsi qu'à une dépréciation des valeurs luthériennes. Il est discutable d'écrire qu'Andreae se détachait de la compréhension réformée du monde dans la mesure où il cherchait à y étendre l'influence chrétienne, ou que son optimisme apostolique était uniquement fondé sur la connaissance, et non sur la certitude de la grâce rédimante. On ne saurait davantage affirmer qu'il minimisait l'importance du mal et du péché, notamment dans la *curiositas*, source de tant d'errements chez les humains. En vérité, Andreae demeure, par son engagement dans le monde, par son souci de l'action constructive, par son zèle apostolique et par les méthodes qu'il emploie pour y parvenir, un disciple de Luther, et Richard van Dülmen le reconnaît parfois. Son interprétation un peu trop intellectualiste et 'eclairée' aurait sans doute pu être tempérée par des références plus nombreuses aux deux *Invitationes Fraternitatis Christi* et à la *Veri christianismi solidaeque philosophiae Libertas*.[19]

(3) Martin Brecht. Professor Brecht of Münster has distinguished himself as a specialist in the history of Württemberg in general and in the history of the Tübinger Stift in particular (indeed, he served for several years as its director); since Andreae had been one of the *stipendiarii*,[20] it was quite natural for Professor Brecht to devote special attention to that important figure of Württemberg church history. In a major work on Andreae published in 1977,[21] and in subsequent essays in 1981 and 1982, Brecht has followed *Cross and Crucible* in one important respect and deviated from it on another, equally fundamental question. The point of agreement has to do

---

[17] Ibid., p. 194-95 and figure 12A-B.
[18] Ibid., p. 34-35, p. 201.
[19] Edighoffer, 'Andreana' (op. cit. in note 3 above), p. 290.
[20] *Cross and crucible*, I, p. 47-52.
[21] Martin Brecht, 'Johann Valentin Andreae. Weg und Programm eines Reformers zwischen Reformation und Moderne', in: Id. (ed.), *Theologen und Theologie an der Universität Tübingen* (Tübingen 1977), p. 270-343.

with Andreae's matured world-view: Brecht sees the Andreae of the post-Rosicrucian phase as thoroughly imbued with Luther's christology, theology of the Word, and realistic understanding of the impossibility of creating a perfect utopian society in a sinful, fallen world; Andreae thus offers a most attractive picture of solid Reformation orthodoxy leavened by Protestant pietism. Neither a mystic nor an occultist, the mature Andreae exemplifies the Lutheran believer, in the world but not of it, giving himself as a 'little Christ' to his neighbor.[22]

Where Brecht parts company with *Cross and Crucible* is in his conviction that the young Andreae did in fact write the *Fama* and the *Confessio*[23] while a devoted member of an occult (but also pietistic Christian) circle at Tübingen between 1608 and 1610 which centered on Andreae's friend Dr. Tobias Hess. Subsequently, both Hess and Andreae renounced their youthful folly. 'Sie brachte Andreae einerseits von dem phantastischen Rosenkreuzerprojekt ab und formulierte andererseits ein konkretes neues Ideal'[24]—an ideal in full accord with the Reformation Lutheran view of the believer as *simul justus et peccator*, impacting society by his living faith.

Unhappily, Brecht places himself in a cruel and unnecessary dilemma. Since Andreae categorically denied his having written the Rosicrucian manifestos (a denial fully supported by powerful internal and external evidence), as well as his having ever been involved in the mystification they represented, Brecht has a liar on his hands if his supposition as to Rosicrucian origins is correct. But an Andreae who prevaricates, letting the end justify the means, is hardly the orthodox, christocentric theologian (much less the pietist) Brecht rightly makes out Andreae to be.

(4) Otto Borst. Borst is a popular Swabian historian who published essays on Andreae in 1980 and 1981. The first constitutes a chapter in his book, *Die heimlichen Rebellen. Schwabenköpfe aus fünf Jahrhunderten*; there Andreae is presented as 'Archetypus' of 'schwäbisch-pietistischen Religiosität', yet at the same time as 'founder' of the Rosicrucian Brotherhood and 'definitively the author of two of the four original Rosicrucian writings'.[25] For these claims, Borst offers no evidence whatever; indeed, his essay is entirely without documentation. The same is true of his 1981 publication, whose subtitle clearly indicates its thrust: *Württemberg als Christia-*

---

[22] Cf. *Cross and crucible*, I, p. 112-57.
[23] '[...] weisen heute alle Indizien auf Andreae als Verfasser der Rosenkreuzerschriften hin': Brecht, 'Johann Valentin Andreae' (op. cit. in note 1 above), p. 124.
[24] Martin Brecht, 'Kritik und Reform der Wissenschaften bei Johann Valentin Andreae', in: Friedrich Seck (ed.), *Wissenschaftsgeschichte um Wilhelm Schickhard* (Tübingen 1981), p. 129.
[25] Otto Borst, *Die heimlichen Rebellen* (Stuttgart 1980), p. 26-27.

4. The World View of Johann Valentin Andreae

nopolis? Johann Valentin Andreae und die Genese der württembergisch-schwäbischen Eigenart.[26] Borst's view of Andreae might not inaccurately be regarded as a less scholarly variation on Brecht's, with a stronger dose of regionalism; and the same dilemma applies to the former as to the latter: Would an archetypical Swabian pietist, for expediency's sake, lie about his involvement in Rosicrucianism? The evidence of history does not support such a characterization of Andreae, however much the traditional stereotype of him may push in that direction.

(5) Gerhard Wehr. This semi-popular writer brings us full circle back to the 'occult Andreae' of mystical literature. In 1980, Wehr edited the Rosicrucian manifestos together with Goethe's fragment 'Die Geheimnisse'.[27] The following year he delineated Andreae's supposed connection with the Rose Cross in a book titled, *Profile christlicher Spiritualität*; the (undocumented) essay on Andreae included therein is captioned simply: 'Johann Valentin Andreae—Autor der rosenkreuzerischen Manifeste'.[28] What Wehr means by 'Christian spirituality' is painfully evident from companion chapters which put Andreae in the same bed with Paracelsus, Jakob Böhme, and Novalis. A further barometer to Wehr's understanding of spirituality is provided by his earlier (1980) publication, *Alle Weisheit ist von Gott. Gestalten und Wirkungen christlicher Theosophie*.[29] Any resemblance to the Andreae of history is purely coincidental.

The Real Andreae

Toward Solid Ground

The preceding survey reveals that, in at least some respects, current Andreae scholarship at its best (Van Dülmen, and more especially Brecht) is moving to a greater level of sophistication. Instead of asking just one question, namely, Was Andreae an occultist?, contemporary students of Andreae tend to pose two questions: (a) What was Andreae's *Weltanschauung*? and (b) Was he implicated in the Rosicrucian mystification (as author of the manifestos or otherwise)? Moreover, the answers now being given to the question of Andreae's world-view are not uniformly of the stereotyped

---

[26] Otto Borst, *Württemberg als Christianopolis?* (Stuttgart 1981).
[27] Gerhard Wehr (ed.), *Rosenkreuzerische Manifeste. Die Grundschriften der Rosenkreuzer und Goethes Fragment 'Die Geheimnisse'* (Schaffhausen [Switzerland] 1980).
[28] Gerhard Wehr, *Profile christlicher Spiritualität* (Schaffhausen [Switzerland] 1982), p. 109-134.
[29] Gerhard Wehr, *Alle Weisheit ist von Gott* (Gütersloh 1980).

pansophist variety: Van Dülmen presents Andreae as a Christian humanist; Brecht sees him, at least in his maturity, as a Reformation Lutheran in the best sense of the term.

But Andreae is still regarded as having written one or more of the manifestos and thus to have been the key to Rosicrucian origins. One would suppose that as the force of Andreae's Christian perspective becomes clearer to his interpreters, there would be correspondingly greater discomfort in identifying him with the Rosicrucian phenomenon—or, at minimum, more nuanced (tortured?) explanations of his connection with that mystification. That such is indeed the case is illustrated by the important recent work of Roland Edighoffer on Andreae and the Rose Cross.

Professor Edighoffer of the Sorbonne has contributed a number of valuable papers on the subject to the journal *Études germaniques* and written a helpful German-language article on the state of Andreae scholarship and his own position in relation to it.[30] That position is most fully developed to date in volume one (1982) of Edighoffer's two-volume work, *Rose-Croix et Société idéale selon Johann Valentin Andreae*. (Infuriatingly, readers have had to wait more than four years for volume two to identify or verify any and every bibliographical citation in volume one—since all notes to the first volume, plus bibliography and index, were left for volume two!) But even without documentation, the book advances Andreae scholarship considerably, especially in the French-speaking world, where Paul Arnold's *Histoire des Rose-Croix et les origines de la Franc-Maçonnerie* (1955) was previously the most comprehensive (and at the same time grossly misleading) treatment of Andreae's world-view.[31]

In a word, Edighoffer is fully cognizant of the centrality of Reformation Lutheran theology to Andreae's life and thought. 'Le véritable Andreae,' he writes, 'celui dont la présente étude a tenté de tracer le portrait, n'était ni un occultiste, ni un utopiste.'[32] Rather,

> Héritier d'une des plus illustres dynasties théologiques et pastorales du Wurtemberg, il ne songeait nullement à renier la pureté doctrinale qu'avaient défendue ses aïeux: dans son oeuvre, il ne cesse de rappeler son attachement à la *Confession d'Augsbourg* et à la *Formule de Concorde*, il cite souvent, à côté de Luther, les noms des 'Hercules chrétiens' qu'ont été, selon lui, Melanchthon, Brenz, Johann Gerhard et, bien sûr, son grand-père Jakob An-

---

[30] Roland Edighoffer, 'Johann Valentin Andreae. Vom Rosenkreuz zur Pantopie', in: *Daphnis* 10 (1981), p. 211–39.
[31] See *Cross and crucible*, II, p. 268–70, p. 512.
[32] Edighoffer, *Rose-Croix et société idéale* (op. cit. in note 10 above), p. 456.

dreae [...] Son action constante et multiple en faveur d'un christianisme authentiquement vécu lui apparut toujours comme parfaitement orthodoxe: il aimait à rappeler que le meilleur exemple d'une harmonie totale entre la vie et la doctrine avait été précisément Luther.[33]

Edighoffer agrees with *Cross and Crucible* that the *Chymical Wedding* was written to counteract and to christianize the hermeticism of the Rosicrucian manifestos (specifically, the *Fama*, impregnated as it was with Paracelsian nature mysticism).[34] Indeed, he strengthens this argument by maintaining that Andreae's *Theca gladii spiritus* (1616) performed a parallel function as against the *Confessio Fraternitatis*,[35] with its apocalypticism à la Joachim of Flora.[36]

Such a perspective, one might well imagine, would have led Edighoffer to place Andreae outside the circle of those who created the Rosicrucian mystification. Certainly his argumentation does not permit him to attribute the authorship of the manifestos to Andreae. Nonetheless, Edighoffer is not convinced by the detailed arguments in *Cross and Crucible* that the content of the *Fama* and the *Confessio* was known as early as the last quarter of the 16th century and that the ideological roots of early Rosicrucianism lie with Simon Studion, Julius Sperber, and Aegidius Gutmann.[37] 'Why', he asks, 'was the term "Rose Cross" not used by these writers but suddenly appears all at once in writings with an attested existence around 1610?'[38] (The simple answer—apart from the fact that the writings in question were circulating in manuscript before that date—is that the originators of these ideas were *hermeticists*; for them nothing was more natural than to keep wisdom hidden in their own conventicles until its time had come; indeed, this is one of the central themes of the manifestos.) So Edighoffer locates Rosicrucian origins in the circle of Andreae's friends, focusing particularly on Dr. Tobias Hess.

> Toutes ces constatations d'ordre psychologique, appuyées sur des textes et des documents d'époque, permettent d'établir de solides hypothèses quant à la genèse du mythe rosicrucien: le personnage de Christian Rose-Croix, peut-être né très tôt dans l'imagination du tout jeune étudiant, aurait pris consistance et vie à la suite du procès de la pasquinade, donc vers la fin de

---

[33] Ibid., p. 450.
[34] Cf. ibid., p. 270–78, with *Cross and crucible*, I, p. 195–98.
[35] Edighoffer, *Rose-Croix et société idéale*, p. 288–96.
[36] Cf. ibid., p. 278–85, with *Cross and crucible*, I, p. 168–71, p. 198–200.
[37] *Cross and crucible*, I, p. 209–210, p. 232–35.
[38] Edighoffer, 'Andreana' (op. cit. in note 3 above), p. 288.

> 1607; le commerce avec Van der Linde, très versé dans les problèmes historiques et géographiqucs, aurait permis l'esquisse d'une biographie amusante et originale de l'éponyme. Le personnage et l'idée auraient alors séduit Hesz et Hölzel, qui s'en seraient emparés et leur auraient imprimé leur marque. Au début de 1610, un texte de la *Fama* aurait pris forme, et Abraham Hölzel, gentilhomme autrichien, l'aurait fait parvenir dans le Tyrol où Adam Haselmeyer en aurait eu connaissance. La *Confessio Fraternitatis* fut peut-être également esquissée à cette époque, sous l'influence déterminante de Tobias Hesz: sa grande piété s'accordait avec celle d'Andreae pour préconiser une lecture assidue et 'spirituelle' de la Bible, sa connaissance de la pansophie avait fait de lui un déchiffreur des caractères divins dans la nature, et ses contacts avec les oeuvres de Sperber, Studion et Brocardo avaient cultivé en lui la tendance millénariste.[39]

As for Andreae himself, his autobiographical assertion in later life that he had had nothing to do with the Rosicrucian mystification is, for Edighoffer, not unambiguous or unequivocal. Andreae confesses 'implicitement qu'il était aux sources du courant rosicrucien, qu'il fut surpris par sa puissance, et incapable de l'endiguer'.[40] Later, Andreae separated himself from this youthful pleasantry (*ludibrium*), and proceeded to write the *Theca* and the *Hochzeit*, thereby baptizing his earlier indiscretions.

> Malheureusement trop d'indiscrétions avaient été commises pour qu'il fût possible d'effacer le passé. Une seule solution élégante et honorable s'offrait à lui: assumer la Fraternité, reconnaître le personnage central, mais présenter par un nouvel écrit l'image du vrai Christian Rose-Croix, ainsi que sa propre conception de l'hermétisme, de l'alchimie, de la communauté rosicrucienne: tel est l'objet des *Noces chymiques* [. . .].[41]

And ultimately Andreae would whitewash Hess and give the impression in his autobiography that he had never been involved in the Rosicrucian mystification at all.[42]

Though he adroitly endeavors to dull the edge of the moral dilemma this poses for Andreae, Edighoffer, like Brecht, is left with a tarnished model of Reformation virtue. But, even taking this problem of Andreaean character weakness into account, what appears especially striking in Edighoffer's interpretation is its overall closeness to that set forth in *Cross*

---

[39] Edighoffer, *Rose-Croix et société idéale*, p. 234.
[40] Ibid., p. 381.
[41] Ibid., p. 391.
[42] For a neat and up-to-the-minute summary of Edighoffer's position, see his little book, *Les Rose-Croix* (Paris 1986²), p. 46–60.

and Crucible. Once Edighoffer concludes that Andreae was not an occultist but a genuine Lutheran social reformer, he necessarily finds himself reducing Andreae's role in the Rosicrucian mystification.

Indeed, no one denies, to use Professor Antoine Faivre's expression, that Andreae was in some sense at the *'carrefour'* of the mystification.[43] The question is: In what capacity? As promoter or opponent? Moreover, it is plain that Andreae was in contact with the ideology of the movement and knew individuals who were seduced by it; he tells us that himself. But was he merely *tempted* by the Rose Cross or did temptation become—even for a brief time in his life—*commitment*? One of Luther's favourite sayings concerning temptation is that you may not be able to prevent the birds from flying over your head, but you can certainly prevent them from nesting in your hair. Did the Rose Cross merely fly over Andreae's head or did it nest in his hair? Edighoffer would opt for the latter, and I believe in that respect he is wrong. Nevertheless, his total work carries Andreae scholarship farther in the direction it has long needed to move.

The Rosicrucian Issue

Limitations of space prohibit our reiterating the detailed argumentation of *Cross and Crucible* concerning Andreae's involvement (better, non-involvement) in the Rosicrucian mystification. It can certainly now be taken as established—Edighoffer's work arrives at precisely the same conclusions I do though by a different route—that Andreae's *Chymical Wedding* is a Christian corrective to the Rosicrucian manifestos. Thus, at least as early as 1616, Andreae had arrived at the world-view that would characterize his activity and writings thereafter. The only remaining question is: Had he initially been an adept? Here we shall do no more than let him speak for himself, relying on the fine legal principle that one is innocent until proven guilty beyond reasonable doubt.

In Andreae's autobiography, the following testimony introduces the author's ministry at Stuttgart:

> Testor S.S. Triadem ejusque immaculatam sponsam ecclesiam Evangelico-Lutheranam Christiana et Germana fide, me [...] risisse semper Rosae-Crucianam fabulam, et curiositatis fraterculos fuisse insectatum.

Note, first of all,[44] that this is a testimony under the strongest possible oath. Andreae, a clergyman of the Lutheran church, swears, 'as a faithful

---

[43] Antoine Faivre, Preface to Edighoffer, *Rose-Croix et société idéale*, p. IV.
[44] For a fuller discussion of this key passage, see *Cross and crucible*, I, p. 178 ff.

Christian and German, by the Most Holy Trinity and his immaculate spouse the Evangelical Lutheran Church', that he has 'always laughed at the Rosicrucian fable and combatted the little curiosity-brothers'. For Andreae to have lied under these circumstances would have meant a denial of the whole theological basis of his life. Secondly, Andreae's use of 'spousal' language in this passage recalls his *Chymical Wedding*, whose content provided a specific Christian corrective to the Rosicrucian manifestos. Thirdly, Andreae's declaration could hardly be more unambiguous: he tells us that he had *always (semper)* not only rejected the Rosicrucian myth but also opposed those associated with it. Edighoffer bruises the clear meaning of the passage when he argues that the *'curiositatis fraterculi'* opposed by Andreae were the crude alchemical 'puffers' and not 'les hypothétiques adeptes de la 'Fraternité'.[45] The specific mention of the 'Rosicrucian fable' in the immediately preceding phrase belies such an interpretation. Finally, what possible motive would Andreae have had to prevaricate—or even equivocate—in this autobiography? He never in his lifetime sought its publication, and it was not in fact published in the Latin original until 1849!

Andreae's testimony—fully in accord with his consistent, lifelong denial of involvement in the creation of the Rosicrucian mystification[46]—also weighs heavily against the notion that his close friends were the founders of the movement or authors of its manifestos. The most that can be said is that Tobias Hess flirted with Simon Studion's Naometrian prophetic vagaries, but at the end of Hess's life Andreae gave him a clean theological bill-of-health.[47] And, as we have seen, Christoph Besold had no personal knowledge of the authorship of the *Fama*, though he was a prominent member of Andreae's circle.[48] In colloquial terms, contemporary Andreae scholarship is barking up the wrong tree when it tries, by innuendo and conjecture, to locate Rosicrucian origins in Andreae or in his immediate friends of Tübingen days. An understanding of Andreae's alchemical perspective will make this plain fact if possible even plainer.

The Gospel vs. Hermeticism

Johann Valentin Andreae's overarching commitment to the theology of the Lutheran Reformation is being more and more widely acknowledged.

---

[45] Edighoffer, *Rose-Croix et société idéale*, p. 379.
[46] *Cross and crucible*, I, p. 180–88.
[47] Ibid., p. 201–209.
[48] See above, the text of this present essay at notes 16–18. Cf. also *Cross and crucible*, I, p. 232–33, note 234.

4. The World View of Johann Valentin Andreae

We have seen that Professors Brecht and Edighoffer are convinced of it, whatever they may believe about Andreae's youthful Rosicrucian involvements. Dr. Gerhard Schäfer has recently mined that central Lutheran vein of Andreae's personal character in an eloquent essay.[49]

What did Andreae's theological commitment specifically mean for his great work of literary alchemy, the *Chymical Wedding*? Henry Corbin rightly emphasizes that all alchemy is a 'liturgy'[50]; for Andreae in particular, what was being celebrated? Simply stated, the scriptural gospel of our Lord and Savior Jesus Christ. In the *Chymical Wedding*, salvation is understood not in occult, gnostic terms[51]—as man's esoteric quest to manipulate Nature so as to achieve personal wholeness (Hemingway's Santiago!), but in biblical, evangelical terms—as the product of God's historical revelation of himself through the death of his Son on the Cross for our sins and his Resurrection for our justification. The Philosopher's Stone becomes the biblical 'Stone that the builders rejected': Christ himself, who alone can achieve the conjunction of opposites in the individual soul and in the cosmos (the 'chemical marriage' of Sulphur and Mercury representing the Marriage Supper of the Lamb).[52] The radical differences between Andreae's Reformation alchemy and that of esoteric Paracelsian nature-mysticism may be illustrated by the following chart:

---

[49] Gerhard Schäfer, 'Johann Valentin Andreae. Im Zeichen von Kreuz und Rose – Der Calwer Dekan', in: *Der Landkreis Calw. Ein Jahrbuch 1984* (Bad Liebenzell 1984), p. 99–110.

[50] Henry Corbin, *L'Alchimie comme art hiératique* (Paris 1986), p. 12.

[51] 'It remains uncertain whether the Fraternity of the Rosy Cross ever had more than a symbolic existence, but its values were familiar: they went back to the ancient traditions of gnosis', Keith Thomas, *Religion and the Decline of Magic* (Harmondsworth, Middlesex 1978), p. 320–21. Cf. John Warwick Montgomery (ed.), *Demon Possession. A Medical, Historical, Anthropological and Theological Symposium* (Minneapolis 1976), passim.

[52] See John Warwick Montgomery, *Principalities and Powers. The world of the occult* (Minneapolis 1973), p. 96–107 (in the expanded but now out-of-print edition of 1975, this material appears on p. 90–99).

	Basis of Salvation	Mechanism of Salvation
Gnostic, Occult, Alchemy →	REPEATABLE MYTH	HUMAN WORKS
Andreae's Lutheran Alchemy →	ONCE FOR ALL HISTORICAL ACTS (*HEILSGESCHICHTE*)	GRACE THROUGH FAITH

The entire text of the *Chymical Wedding* demonstrates how fully Andreae believed that alchemy ought to reinforce, not the belief of the esoterists that man can become God by way of nature, but the central Christian affirmation that the eternal God became man to save and hallow nature. 'Natural philosophy' interested Andreae because it could point men to Jesus Christ. For him, the ideal natural philosopher was not an anthropocentric Paracelsian, spinning personal, scientific, and social salvation out of the womb of his own human potentiality, but a theocentric Christian who is drawn by God's creative and redemptive work to the 'transcendent perfections and excellencies' of Christ. This is how Andreae described the natural philosopher of his *Christianae Societatis imago*, and we cannot do better than to end this commemorative essay with his words:

> The Philosopher [is] of the sect of those old Philosophers, who by glimmering of nature came to the light of heaven: He, as the Divine hath the written word, hath the printed word, and in contemplation of this visible world finds the Creatour, and worships him: his study is subjectated in nature and the Creatures, whence he observes the changes and conflicts of life and death, light and darknesse, truth and falsehood, and discernes them by the rayes of Christian Religion. Moreover he weighes the endeavours, proceedings and labours of those admired wits, to whom it was given in mid-darknesse, to see somewhat, especially he examines that desired tranquillity of the mind, & draws it to Christ, in whose transcendent perfections and excellencies he stands amazed.[53]

The author does not wish to conclude his essay without acknowledging the fine bibliographical service provided by the Württembergische Landesbibliothek, Stuttgart, and particularly by Stefan Strohm of its staff. Attention should be drawn to

---

[53] Johann Valentin Andreae, 'A Modell of a Christian Society', ed. George H. Turnbull, in: *Zeitschrift für Deutsche Philologie* (1955), p. 158–59. Cf. *Cross and crucible*, I, p. 241–55 ('Andreae and the hermetic philosophy').

4. The World View of Johann Valentin Andreae

Strohm's learned study, Die Kupferbibel Matthäus Merians von 1630 *(Stuttgart 1985), which contains valuable iconographical discussion of some of Andreae's early printed works issued by the printing house of Lazarus Zetzner in Strasbourg (p. 53-75).*

5. John Arndt Revisited

My doctoral dissertation in theology at the University of Strasbourg dealt with one of the greatest Lutheran scholars and littérateurs of the early 17th century, Johann Valentin Andreae. The three-volume thesis was published in two volumes in the distinguished monographic series, the International Archives of the History of Ideas, edited by the late Professor Paul Dibon of the Sorbonne.[1]

One of Andreae's favourite authors was John Arndt, a transition figure between scholastic Lutheran orthodoxy and pietism.

> In 1615, Andreae published a summary of Johann Arndt's famous devotional work, *True Christianity*. Andreae's s high opinion of Arndt is evident from the fact that in 1621 he published still another anthology of *True Christianity*, and in 1644 he included both of these digests in his *Summa doctrinae christianae trigemina*. ... It is not difficult to see why Arndt appealed to Andreae ...: Arndt was firmly committed to orthodox Lutheranism (he had studied under Pappus at Strasbourg and had given his allegiance to the *Formula of Concord*); ... and his entire career was spent in an effort to make the truths of Lutheran theology live in the personal experience of believers.[2]

I myself included an edition of Arndt's *Devotions and Prayers*[3] in my list of "100 Select Devotional Works" published in an early number of *Christianity Today*.[4]

But all this is not to say that there are no problems with John Arndt's ideological orientation.

First, Arndt's concessions to *alchemical mysticism*. Arndt was fascinated by Heinrich Khunrath's quasi-occult *Amphitheatrum sapientiae aeternae* (1609),[5] and there is good evidence of personal contact between Khunrath

---

[1] John Warwick Montgomery, *Cross and Crucible: Johann Valentin Andreae (1586-1654), Phoenix of the Theologians* (The Hague: Martinus Nijhoff, 1973). The 2-vol. set is available from Nijhoff's successor publisher in The Netherlands.
[2] *Ibid.*, I, 55-56.
[3] Selected and translated by John Joseph Stoudt (Baker).
[4] Reprinted in Montgomery, *The Suicide of Christian Theology* (Minneapolis: Bethany, 1975), pp. 475–79.
[5] *Cross and Crucible, op. cit.*, I, 18.

and Arndt.⁶ Indeed, a short commentary on the *Amphitheatrum* has been attributed to Arndt by at least two authorities.⁷ This brief commentary is titled, *Judicium und Bericht eines Erfahrnen Cabalisten und Philosophen über die 4 Figuren dess grossen Amphitheatru D. Heinrici Khunradi*—"The Judgment and Commentary of an Experienced Cabalist and Philosopher concerning the Four Figures of Doctor Heinrich Khunrath's Great Amphitheatrum." Its German text is found appended to Khunrath's *De igne magorum philosophorumque secreto externo et visibili, das ist Philosophische Erklärung* (1783). It has been translated into English in an obscure publication of 250 copies only: *The Amphitheatre Engravings of Heinrich Khunrath*.⁸

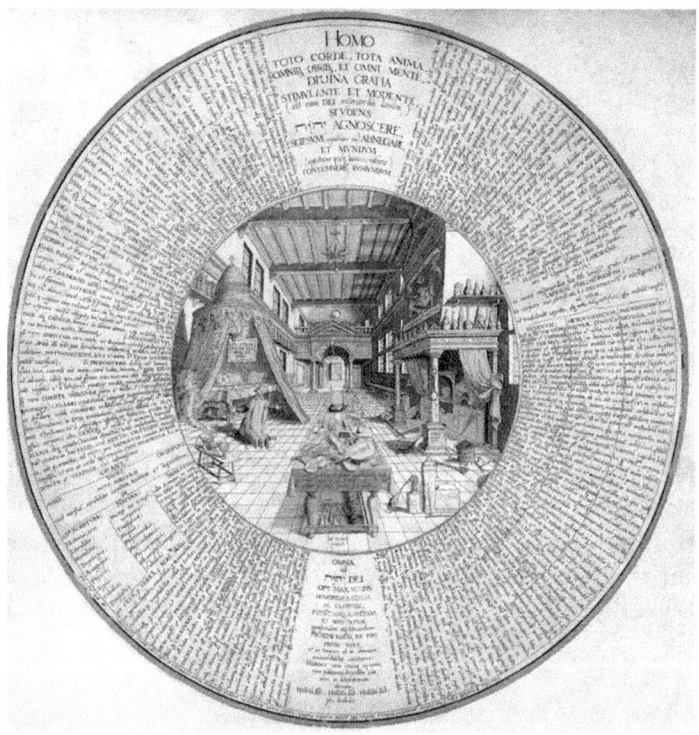

---

6   Peter J. Forshaw, "Unexpected in the Octagon: Heinrich Khunrath's Presentation Copy to Erasmus Wolfart," pp. 78–80; accessed 1 March 2019 at: *https://www.academia.edu/30459656/Unexpected_in_the_Octagon_Heinrich_Khunrath_s_Presentation_Copy_to_Erasmus_Wolfart*

7   Adam Friedrich Böhmen (1747 and 1783) and Carlos Gilly (1986).

8   Trans. Patricia Tahil, ed. Adam McLean (Edinburgh, Scotland: Magnum Opus Hermetic Sourceworks, 1981), pp. 81–84. My signed copy is no. 108.

Arndt deals with only the first four complex illustrations in Khunrath's book. Here is his general comment on the illustrations one through three:

> In all three Air is as a Spirit (distilled essence), just as in the natural world of Water, Fire and Air, the same is her spirit and life. Microcosmically, these three are called Spirit, Soul and Body. First, the Spirit, for which a Body is prepared, and then thirdly the Soul is the "perfected" and refined and purified (enlightened) life.[9]

Though Arndt stresses that Khunrath's foundation is the biblical principle "the fear of the Lord is the beginning of wisdom," it seems clear that he has no problem with the human attainment of enlightenment through some kind of spiritual ascent.

A recent scholarly commentator has written:

> In the *Judicium*, Arndt declares that Khunrath intends to show how Solomon, the Biblical Books of Proverbs and Wisdom, "laid the groundwork and foundations of Natural *Magic*, supernatural *Cabala* and Divine *Theology*. This knowledge is connected with "three lights and spirits: *Magic* is the natural light and the natural spirit; *Cabala* is a supernatural light and spirit, an angelic spirit; *Theology* is the light of God, the Holy Ghost. The first magical light is equated with the Paracelsian "Light of Nature" while the second Cabalistic light with the radiance and light in the breast-plate of the high-priests.[10]

What is the problem here? Though Arndt certainly intended to remain faithful to Lutheran (and New Testament) soteriology, it is painfully evident that he moves from a theocentric, Christocentric view of salvation and sanctification to an anthropocentric perspective. One rises to holiness and an ideal relationship with God through human attainment. The direction is *upwards*, whereas in the theology of the New Testament, sin makes this impossible and salvation is the product of God's movement *downwards* to a fallen race through the incarnation, death, and resurrection of His Son, Jesus Christ.

Reformation alchemy, as exemplified in Andreae's *Chymical Wedding*, is the very opposite of Paracelsian nature mysticism: salvation is by grace alone, not by the manipulation of natural, magical, or supernatural forces.

> The ideal natural philosopher was not an anthropocentric Paracelsian, spinning personal, scientific, and social salvation out of the womb of his own

---

[9] *Ibid.*, p. 84.
[10] Forshaw, *op. cit.*, p. 77.

human potentiality, but a theocentric Christian who is drawn by God's creative and redemptive work to the "transcendent perfections and excellencies" of Christ.[11]

Secondly, there is a real problem with Arndt's *pietism*. Arndt's mystical anthropocentrism connects directly with his pietistic orientation.[12] "The father of Lutheran Pietism is not Spener but John Arndt. ... Arndt was an effective preacher whose chief objective was to edify and confirm the heart rather than to inform the head.[13]

Unfortunately, the lack of emphasis on "informing the head" often resulted in an absence of adequate doctrinal instruction. Arndt's successors (Spener, Francke, *et al.*) moved Lutheran theology away from the solid confessional teaching that had characterized Luther's theological style and that of his 16th- and 17th-century orthodox Lutheran successors.

This move was away from the classic Lutheran insistence that the entire gospel is *extra nos*—outside of the person, a product solely of God's revelation of himself in Scripture and in the incarnate Christ. The church's focus changed from the gracious reception of objective truth to a satisfaction with subjective experience.

And since subjective experience resided within the individual, truth was seen more and more as the natural product of human rationality. From Pietism, the ideological pendulum swung to rationalism. The 18th-century's so-called Enlightenment was surely a progeny of 17th-century Pietism. Kant and many other leading lights of the new rationalism had pietistic backgrounds.

To be sure, Arndt's interest in natural magic and mystical alchemy was doubtless motivated by a desire to connect theology with the latest "science" of his day and thus to provide a bridge for the personal conversion of unsaved intellectuals. But this laudable motivation must always be tempered by the absolute need to retain sound biblical teaching—particularly the way of salvation as set forth in the written word and centered on Christ, the living Word. Apologetics and "contemporary relevance" must never obscure the eternal message of the gospel—Christ the same, yesterday, today and forever.

---

[11] Montgomery, "The World-View of Johann Valentin Andreae," in: *Das Erbe des Christian Rosenkreuz* (Amsterdam: In de Pelikaan, 1988). pp. 152–69, at 167; reprinted in this volume (*supra*).

[12] Cf. Avalon Swenson, "Johann Arndt & Paracelsus: Natural Science in Early Pietism," accessed 1 March 2019 at: https://conservancy.umn.edu/handle/11299/190889

[13] Fred Ernest Stoeffler, *The Rise of Evangelical Pietism* (Leiden: Brill, 1971), pp. 201–210.

6. Choosing Books for a Theological Library

Apologia for the Present Study: The Need for a Normative Approach

Chaucer's Clerk, we read, "looked holwe" and "ful thredbare was his overeste courtepy," because

> For hym was levere have at his beddes heed
> Twenty bookes, clad in blak or reed.

This fourteenth-century bibliophile, whatever else may be said of him, clearly lacked a sound book-acquisition policy; he was not successful in determining what portion of his total income should be used for books and what portion should not. This failing places the Clerk in a vast company both of laity and of clergy, both of individual persons and of corporate persons. The need for adequate book-acquisition criteria has existed among virtually all book collectors (not merely those suffering from Dibdin's disease) since the time the number of books in existence became too great for a collector to own all of them; and this event apparently occurred quite some time ago, for Koheleth laments that even in his day עֲשׂוֹת סְפָרִים הַרְבֵּה אֵין קֵץ (Ecc. 12:12).

The continually increasing quantity of graphic records across the centuries has made book selection the fundamental problem of librarianship in every age. The first formal treatise on library organization and administration, Gabriel Naudé's *Avis pour dresser une bibliothèque* (1627), devotes its longest chapter by far to advice on "selecting the books." Lt. Col. Frank Rogers of the National Library of Medicine stated the issue accurately for librarians from Naudé's day to our own when he wrote in 1956:

> Acquisition is the first process, in a sequence of processes, in which a library engages. The acquiring of material is, therefore, basic, in the fundamental sense that it precedes other processes. Books not acquired need not be cataloged, bound, stored or serviced; neither can they be used in the answering of reference queries. The problem of what books to try to acquire, out of the vast number it is possible to acquire, is a problem of very great importance to every library, of whatever kind.[1]

---

[1] Frank B. Rogers, "Introduction and Statement of the Problem," *Acquisitions Policy of the National Medical Library; Proceedings of a Symposium Held 12 April 1956* (Washington: National Library of Medicine, 1957), p. 1.

In the twentieth century particularly, the need for sound book selection principles has become acute. Whether or not one fully agrees with the statistics of Fremont Rider's assertion that university libraries double their holdings every sixteen years, it is clear beyond all doubt that most research libraries today are experiencing what Vosper has termed "elephantiasis of the bookstacks."[2] The Yale Library's changed attitude toward acquisitions may be taken as typical of many research libraries in recent years:

> The general policy of the Yale librarians before the second World War was to collect as much of the printed and manuscript output of the world as was needed and would be useful to a university with extensive research programs and teaching at the graduate level. It is safe to say, I believe, that our policy was to keep any book and most periodicals that came our way, and I am sure that since our acquisitiveness was almost omnivorous, largely because of the American custom of keeping up with the Joneses, our shelves are weighted down with many books and periodicals that we easily could do without. We were ambitious to be a library of record, that is, to have one copy of every book of any importance. This is a highly questionable ambition, impossible of attainment, and based on lack of, or fear to use, judgment on the part of librarians.... A new policy for the libraries at Yale now exists, and to be successful must be adopted by all the libraries at Yale: selective instead of all-embracing; selective acquisition; selective retention or storage.[3]

Any program of selective acquisition in a library leads almost inevitably to the question of an explicit book selection policy. This is true because

> all libraries have acquisition policies, whether they are recognized or not, and ... the extent to which a library fails to recognize the kinds of policies which it is following may possibly be a measure of the potential inadequacies of its collection over a long period of time.[4]

But the creation of a meaningful book selection policy is more easily contemplated than executed, especially in a research library. Professor James Hart well points this out by example:

---

[2] Robert Vosper, "Acquisition Policy–Fact or Fancy?," *College and Research Libraries*, XIV (October, 1953).

[3] James T. Babb, "The Future of the Research Library and the Book Collector," *Books and Publishing Lecture Series*, Vol. I (Boston: Simmons College School of Library Science, 1954), pp. 1,3.

[4] Herman H. Fussler, "Acquisition Policy: the Larger University Library," *College and Research Libraries*, XIV (October, 1953), 363.

6. Choosing Books for a Theological Library

> A ... student was able to place Emerson's theories of education in context and show them to be less novel than supposed; this was done by comparing Emerson's statements with those that contemporaries enunciated in obscure addresses at commencement and Phi Beta Kappa exercises in the 1840's. ... If such diverse materials were needed for productive scholarship by ... graduate students, where can one draw the line for appropriate acquisitions by a research library?[5]

In spite of the overt success of some acquisition policies—the John Crerar's being notable in this regard—widespread frustration seems to characterize discussions where this vital matter is the center of attention. There appears to be a praiseworthy willingness to deal with the flood of printed matter from the important (but certainly secondary) angles of storage policy, cooperative acquisition, and interlibrary loan; but the central issue of what in fact deserves to be obtained *per se* does not receive the consideration it warrants.

If the problem of quantity of publication vs. limitations of space and budget plagues research libraries as a genus, the same must be said even more emphatically of the theological library as a species of research collection. Unlike most other intellectual disciplines, Christian theology has had a continuous and active publishing life of twenty centuries, and theological writing constituted practically all of the significant Western literary production during more centuries of the Christian era than modern man generally recognizes. Most of this vast body of material is relevant to the theology of Protestantism; and if the literature of comparative religion is also included, the result is a truly staggering bibliographic load. In his *Manuductio ad Ministerium*, the Puritan divine Cotton Mather expressed bewilderment over this very problem:

> You may Expect, that I should more Positively say, What English Treatises of Practical Divinity, I would commend unto you. But here I am encumbred as Hevelius was, when he would have so partitioned his accurate Selenography as to have done Justice unto the Names of all the more Illustrious Astronomers. Yea, so Great is the Army of them who have published the True Gospel, that I cannot pretend unto the long List of them that have come to the Help of the Lord.[6]

---

[5] James D. Hart, "What a Scholar Expects of Acquisitions," *Problems and Prospects of the Research Library*, ed. by Edwin E. Williams (New Brunswick, N. J.: Scarecrow Press for the Association of Research Libraries, 1955), p. 61.

[6] Cotton Mather, *Manuductio ad Ministerium; Directions for a Candidate of the Ministry*, ed. Thomas J. Holmes and Kenneth B. Murdock (New York: Columbia University Press for the Facsimile Text Society, 1933), p. 9, *et al.*

These statements were made in 1726, and although during the last two hundred years the proportion of theological to secular literature published has diminished, the actual quantity of theological material issued each year has multiplied beyond anything Dr. Mather could have imagined. That theological libraries have not been able to keep pace with publication in their field becomes quite evident when we note that a recent authoritative article on theological libraries lists only ten American seminary libraries with quality collections of over one hundred thousand volumes, and only one of these exceeds three hundred thousand volumes in size.[7] One must not assume that the European situation is ideal by contrast; Burke, after a personal inspection of Catholic theological libraries in Germany, wrote: "Even today Germany is still rich in traditional works, rare books, incunabula and manuscripts . . . but there is a tremendous gap in the contemporary holdings of seminary libraries."[8]

The very fact that so many theological libraries are small in size and have no Farmington-Plan type of cooperative acquisition program with other libraries, means that selective acquisition has been carried on for some time in these institutions; the question is, consequently, what principles have guided the selection? The dearth of theological librarians with competent training both in librarianship and in theology makes one naturally suspicious of implicit book acquisition methods in American seminaries, and explicit statements of policy are few and far between. The late appearance on the scene of a professional association for theological librarians (the American Theological Library Association was founded in 1947) is but another indication that the problem of book acquisition policy for theological institutions has been neglected far too long, and deserves immediate and close attention.

---

[7] Kenneth S. Gapp, "Theological Libraries," *Twentieth Century Encyclopedia of Religious Knowledge; an Extension of the New Schaff-Herzog Encyclopedia of Religious Knowledge*, ed. Lefferts A. Loetscher (Grand Rapids: Baker Book House, 1955), Vol. 2, p. 1101. It is of course true that some seminary libraries are departments within large university library structures, and as such benefit from the holdings of the entire library systems of which they are a part, but this does not alter the fact that the specifically theological holdings of these institutions are relatively small in quantity.

[8] Redmond A. Burke, *Report on a Survey of German Philosophical-Theological Libraries* (Bad Nauheim, Germany: Author mimeographed, 1949), p. 24, *et al.*

Preliminary Analysis of the Problem

The Difficulties with Existing Book Selection Policies

A logical starting point for determining the requirements of an adequate book acquisition policy is the examination of existing policies and proposals for the establishment of policies. Two main inadequacies are seen to be present in a good number of these statements; we shall take up each in turn.

Many book selection policies are like poor Bible commentaries; they thoroughly explain the obvious while leaving the complex unanalyzed. This is probably the greatest failing of existing policies, and can be illustrated with reference to virtually any type of library. In its section on the selecting of religious publications, the Enoch Pratt Free Library Policy (recognized generally as one of the finest in the public library realm), states that

> it is especially important that the Library maintain an impartial recognition of conflicting points of view in this field. It attempts to provide authoritative and objective presentations, avoiding inflammatory, extreme, or unfair statements and highly emotional treatments.[9]

Few people, one readily admits, would attempt to argue against these sentiments (as in the case of sin, most of us are against it),[10] but the latitude of choice within the limits here set is still so great that the surface of the selection problem has hardly been scratched. In the university library field, Harvard asserts that, together with its Farmington responsibilities, it will maintain "research coverage" of "church history ... other than American and modern, and Hebraic materials" and "reference coverage" of "religion, aside from the subdivisions listed above."[11] Granting Harvard's appreciable book budget, one still suspects that the University has to do considerable

---

[9] *Book Selection Policies and Procedures; Pt. I: Policies*, ed. Marion Hawes and Dorothy Sinclair (Baltimore: Enoch Pratt Free Library mimeographed, 1950), pp. 55–56.

[10] It should be noted, however, that not a few of the world's great religious writings have been not only "inflammatory," but even "extreme," "emotional," and "unfair." The lack of precise definition of terms in such statements as the one quoted complicates unnecessarily the already complex problem of book acquisition standards.

[11] Keyes D. Metcalf and Edwin E. Williams, "Acquisition Policies of the Harvard Library," *Harvard Library Bulletin*, VI (Winter, 1952), 21–22.

(undefined) selection within these specified limits. Hart has criticized the Library of Congress acquisition policy for a similar lack of specificity:

> The Library of Congress ... in 1940 declared that in addition to the bibliothecal materials necessary to the Congress and the officers of the government, and in addition to materials recording the life and achievements of the people of the United States, it "should possess, in some useful form, the material parts of the records of other societies, past and present." But how is one to define "material parts" or state the extent of these material parts appropriate to our national library as against those appropriate to our other research libraries?[12]

The acquisition statement included in the accrediting standards of the American Association of Theological Schools, though expressly intended for Protestant seminaries in general, is nonetheless deserving of censure for its lack of preciseness (note especially points b, c, d, and g):

> Acquisition policy should be governed by the following considerations: a) the theological curriculum, b) the research and teaching needs of the faculty, c) the need to understand contemporary culture nationally and internationally, d) the need to understand persons, e) the accessibility of materials in other libraries, f) the possibility of cooperative acquisitions policies with other libraries and g) the long-range development of the school with reference to degree programs and research interests.[13]

In light of the examples here presented, one is compelled to agree with Fussler's assertion that "libraries inevitably must ... become more selective in their acquisition policies than they are now."[14]

A second fundamental difficulty in many existing book selection policies is the presence in them of the age-old logical fallacy of *petitio principii*. Whereas they purport to offer objective canons of selection which will obviate, or at worst sharply diminish, reliance upon the subjective judgment of authorities, they frequently depend for their effectiveness upon just such subjective, authoritarian judgments. In the university library acquisition policies, wide areas of collecting are not infrequently left, without

---

[12] Hart, *op. cit.*

[13] Quoted in *Aids to a Theological School Library*, (rev. ed.; Dayton, Ohio: American Association of Theological Schools, 1958), p. 39.

[14] Herman H. Fussler, "Readjustments by the Librarian," *Librarians, Scholars and Booksellers at Mid-Century; Papers Presented before the Sixteenth Annual Conference of the Graduate Library School of the University of Chicago*, ed. Pierce Butler (Chicago: University of Chicago Press, 1953), p. 64.

further definition, to the "specialized" knowledge of faculty members; where this occurs, the degree of subjectivity involved prevents the acquisition policy from being a very meaningful "policy" at all. The same seems to be true in seminary book collecting, where a slavish reliance upon professorial authority is often encountered.[15] One readily grants that "to look at an acquisition policy as a potential formula into which one can feed the author, title, date, language, and subject matter of any book and come out with a priority rating indicating how much should be spent for it and whether it should be bought instantly, later, or not at all, is to ask for disappointment and frustration."[16] However, it is clear that unless an acquisition policy establishes clear principles by which those who are empowered to select do the selecting (rather than relying upon the selectors to operate by their own implicit principles), it can fulfil only inadequately the proper functions of a policy worthy of the name.[17]

Prolegomena to an Adequate Book Acquisition Policy for Theology

If we agree with Dr. Homer W. Smith's Pauline-flavored dictum, "to those who think that a library should be all things to all men, I can only say nonsense,"[18] and likewise agree that explicit statements of acquisition policy are to be preferred to subjective, undefined methods of book selection, we are brought to the point of asking: On what basis can a specific, non-question-begging selection policy for theological libraries be constructed? To answer this key question we must enter a very sensitive area: that of the theological librarian's understanding of his own role. For not a few theo-

---

[15] Note, for example, the paper by Elton E. Shell in the *Proceedings of the American Theological Library Association*, X (1956), 36–37.
[16] Fussler, "Acquisition Policy: the Larger University Library," *College and Research Libraries*, XIV (October, 1953), 366.
[17] Wilson and Tauber, in their widely-used text on university library administration, rightly separate the problem of "what materials should be acquired" from the questions as to "who should participate in the selection" (but unfortunately spend no appreciable time dealing with the former); see Louis Round Wilson and Maurice F. Tauber, *The University Library*, (2d ed.; New York: Columbia University Press, 1956), p. 349. It cannot be too strongly emphasized that an answer, however adequate, to one of these two questions does not *ipso facto* provide an answer to the other.
[18] Homer W. Smith, "The Problem from the Viewpoint of Medical Research," *Acquisitions Policy of the National Medical Library; Proceedings of a Symposium Held 12 April 1956*, p. 25.

logical librarians the problem of explicit book selection policy is non-existent because these librarians do not consider book selection—much less the setting of selection policy—as their proper function. They would concede that they have a responsibility to select general reference materials needed by the library, but they would point out that in the theological area their knowledge is necessarily so inferior to that of the teaching faculty that they must defer to the latter in all matters of book acquisition.

Let us take a hypothetical (but concrete) example of what happens when this philosophy of theological librarianship is applied in practice. On Monday morning, Professor A arrives at the library with an antiquarian dealer's catalog in which he has checked about thirty items, totaling roughly $300. These thirty items are Russian and Spanish books dealing with the Bogomile heresy. Says Professor A: "Telegraph at once for these books. What a fabulous find! You know the importance of this material; as I've said so many times in my published works, orthodoxy is the death of the church—the heresies are the true life of Christendom, for they show us the beliefs of the sensitive minority." The librarian, who recognizes that Professor A has forgotten more about Bogomilism than he, the librarian, will ever know, promptly telegraphs for the thirty items, thus spending $300 of the $1200 seminary book budget for the year. On Wednesday, enter Professor B, in a state of considerable agitation. "I just heard that we spent a full one-fourth of our year's book budget on some early heresy—Bultmannism, I think they said. What's that got to do with the practical work of the body of Christ? Does it aid in increasing the membership roles? In enlarging apportionments? Fortunately, I have just learned how we can rectify this excess. Old Pastor Sumppump, D.D., passed away last year, and, as you well know, he had collected the best private library of sermon illustration books in this part of the country—1000 volumes—including all published editions of *Seven Thousand Snappy Sermon Starters*. His widow will give us the whole lot for only $500! Think of it—just fifty cents a volume. Get on that phone before we lose the whole collection to the Methodists." The librarian gets on the phone, and by three o'clock the same afternoon two-thirds of the year's book budget has been spent. Six months later, the librarian cannot understand why he seems unable to obtain even minimal balance and coverage in his book acquisitions. "Obviously," he concludes, "the trouble is in the mediocre book budget. Next year I'll try to increase it to $1500."

The trouble? Not primarily the budget, but the librarian himself, who is no professional regardless of degrees or official status at his institution. This librarian is a mere *technician*, carrying out routine ordering instructions given by others. Note also (and this is of even greater importance)

6. Choosing Books for a Theological Library 175

that because the librarian has no explicit personal policy of selection, he is at the mercy of the divergent and implicit policies of the faculty. Faculty member A sees the entire theological task through the colored lens of his own pet thesis; faculty member B—whose understanding of the goal of the church is radically different from that of faculty member A—does the same thing from his own presuppositional viewpoint. The result: chaos.

Satisfactory theological book selection will never come about until the librarian sees his own role not as that of a technician who follows externally-set policy, but as that of the *creator* of policy. Because he is not committed to a single teaching area, he has a perspective which no teaching faculty member can have to the same degree: a generalist's perspective on the whole theological field and on its relation to other fields. Naturally this presupposes adequate theological training for the librarian. I believe that as a general rule (and there are, of course, exceptions) any person without the minimum of a B.D. is a positive menace in a theological library position; it is the non-theologically trained librarians in seminary libraries who have contributed most to removal of book selection from the librarian's control, to lack of faculty status for theological librarians, and to the common view of seminary faculty that the librarian is a technician and not a professional (which is precisely the case in theological librarianship if the librarian doesn't know theology). But the possession of the B.D. will not automatically solve the acquisition problem, needless to say; the theologically-trained librarian must have the intellectual courage to take the reins in book selection, and this means setting explicit policy. And how is policy to be set? One possible approach may be termed "descriptive," another "normative."

The descriptive approach to book acquisition policy is widely employed at the present time. In brief, it attempts to determine what a given library ought to acquire by analyzing the past needs of the library's clientele or by anticipating what their future needs will be. A concise statement of this approach is given by Phelps in an article on book selection for special libraries: "It is vital . . . that the special librarian should be aware of the specialized requirements of his organization, its current and anticipated needs."[19] A similar statement from the pen of a theological librarian is the following:

> After the immediate problems of teaching materials are fulfilled, build selected primary source material which will strengthen the scholarly trend of

---

[19] Ralph H. Phelps, "Selecting Material for Science-Technology Libraries," *Special Libraries*, XLIV (March, 1953), 89.

the institution. Trends in fact or anticipation provide the framework of the library's selection program.[20]

The difficulty of anticipating future needs has generally led to a concentration on past needs. Ranganathan writes:

> If book selection can be based on the present wants by ascertaining individual wants and integrating them it would be ideal. But it is not easy. ... A method which is more easily workable and is in actual use is to ascertain past wants.[21]

A complex and sophisticated technique for determining past wants of a research faculty is suggested by McAnally's doctoral dissertation, *Characteristics of Materials Used in Research in United States History*;[22] just as McAnally attempted to ascertain by source analysis what materials had been employed by scholars of American history, so it would be possible by source analysis of the writings of a theological faculty to determine the types of materials which they have in the past utilized in their scholarly endeavors. A more broadly-based approach to selection (but one still essentially descriptive in character) involves the analysis of the current general trends in a field, and the types of literature associated with or stemming from these trends. In the case of theology, works similar to Nash's *Protestant Thought in the Twentieth Century*[23] can serve as a guide to publications of special interest in the present theological milieu.

The fact that descriptively-oriented approaches to book selection are so readily and uncritically accepted by today's librarian is in part a tribute to the social-science interpretation of librarianship so effectively set forth by Pierce Butler over twenty-five years ago. That a library's book collection should reflect the needs of its clientele and the social patterns of the time has been widely accepted as axiomatic since Butler wrote:

---

[20] Decherd Turner, Jr., "Book Selection and Instruction," *Proceedings of the American Theological Library Association*, VI (1952), 19.

[21] S. R. Ranganathan, *Library Book Selection* (Delhi: Indian Library Association; London: G. Blunt, 1952), p. 127.

[22] Arthur Monroe McAnally, *Characteristics of Materials Used in Research in United States History* (Chicago: University of Chicago Graduate Library School, unpublished Ph.D. dissertation, 1951).

[23] Arnold S. Nash (ed.), *Protestant Thought in the Twentieth Century; Whence & Whither?* (New York: Macmillan,1951).

6. Choosing Books for a Theological Library

> In the library no less than in the school curriculum selection with reference to the kind of people served is the sole criterion of social efficiency. A continuous sociological study of group characteristics and activities is the only safe guide to a successful reformation of either institution.[24]

Although one hates to violate Plutarch's injunction that "de mortuis nil nisi bonum," it is necessary to point out that the descriptive, Butlerian approach to book acquisition turns the library into a chameleonic institution with no power to resist negative social trends. With respect to academic libraries, and the theological library in particular, we should carefully weigh, the words of Ralph Beals:

> Mr. Crane Brinton referred to the fact that there are unquestionably waves of fashion in scholarship. I sometimes think that they are as capricious as the waves of fashion which govern trends in women's hats. If one looks at the research library of this year in relation to the research library at the turn of the century, there are certain unmistakable differences some of which we certainly should facilitate, some of which we should resist.[25]

If the research interests of the faculty at a seminary are accepted as the prime determinant for book selection in that seminary library, the collection will necessarily become a hodgepodge, for faculty members come and go at any institution, and the research interests of the individual faculty member can vary widely and change frequently during his career. Moreover, faculty members do not necessarily concentrate on the most significant aspects of their field when engaging in research; many are the theological libraries, I venture to say, which contain quantities of material on, say, infralapsarianism, because of a faculty member's burning interest in the subject, and correspondingly few publications dealing with, say, the sacraments, due to a lack of research pressure to obtain them. It should also be stressed that the theological library which ties its acquisition wagon to the star of current theological trends is not much better off. True, contemporary research interests are likely to be less erratic than those of a single seminary faculty, but any one acquainted with the history of doctrine knows that stupifying overbalance has occurred in theological research during certain epochs. The late nineteenth, early twentieth century

---

[24] Pierce Butler, *An Introduction to Library Science* (Chicago: University of Chicago Press, 1933), p. 51. Dr. Herman Fussler informs me that Butler moved away from this thoroughgoing descriptivism before his death.

[25] Ralph A. Beals, in *Changing Patterns of Scholarship and the Future of Research Libraries: a Symposium* (Philadelphia: University of Pennsylvania Press, 1951), p. 19.

constitutes an excellent example of this, as a matter of fact, for under the impact of Ritschl, Fosdick, etc., emphasis was shifted from the objective Biblical and doctrinal account of what God had done for men in Jesus Christ, to a subjective "social gospel" which was interested in little more than what men could do for God through functional activism. The literary result was a tremendous quantity of cheap and ephemeral publications describing practical techniques for organizing auxiliary groups in the church, incorporating boy scout troops in the total program of the church, and so forth. Solid theological research suffered greatly during this period, but most theological libraries leaped on the bandwagon (forgetting, apparently, St. Paul's warning not to be carried about παντὶ ἀνέμῳ τῆς διδασκαλίας Eph. 4:14), collected great amounts of this type of material, and neglected more basic research works on the ground that they were behind-the-times and unfaithful to the contemporary *Zeitgeist*.

No research library worthy of the name can be indifferent to the specific needs of its clientele, or oblivious to the publication trends in its fields of subject interest, but it should appear clear from the foregoing that these considerations must assume a subordinate place in the drafting of book selection policies. What, then, ought to be the prime factor? Immanuel Kant demonstrated with finality that the descriptive cannot logically give rise to the normative. What ought to be done can never be derived from what has been done or from what is contemplated (the popular impression of the Kinsey reports notwithstanding). To discover what materials are necessary to support research in theology, it is necessary, therefore, to analyse the nature of the theological discipline—to determine how the various aspects of the subject ideally relate to each other; and then to see what the implications of this analysis are for the acquisition of library materials. Such a fundamental analysis is absolutely essential where theology is concerned, for theology was not born yesterday, and the theological trends of today may—when set against the total stream of Christian history—constitute deviations of serious proportion. In theology it is certainly true that, as Bernard of Chartres put it: "Nous sommes comme des nains assis sur les épaules de géants. Nous voyons donc plus de choses que les Anciens, et de plus lointaines, mais ce n'est ni par l'acuité de notre vue, ni par la hauteur de notre taille, c'est seulement qu'ils nous portent et nous haussent de leur hauteur gigantesque."[26]

---

[26] Quoted in Etienne Gilson, *L'esprit de la philosophie médiévale* (2d. ed.; Paris: Librairie Philosophique J. Vrin, 1944), p. 402.

A Morphology of the Theological Field as a Basis for Seminary Book Aquisition

Analysis of the Subject Matter and Literature of Theology

Although the words "religion" and "theology" are often used interchangeably in common parlance, it is important that they be distinguished at the outset of this analysis. "Religion" (from the Latin *religio*, "Conscientiousness/conscience/respect for and worship of what is sacred") is a general and anthropocentric term; as Webster puts it, it refers to "the service and adoration of God or a god as expressed in forms of worship." In contrast, "theology" (from the Greek θεός and λόγος, "speaking about God") is specific and theocentric in its connotations; it takes a particular Divine Being (rather than man's experience of or reaction to Him) as a starting-point, assumes that this Deity has revealed Himself to man in a definite and meaningful way, and sets itself the task of studying that revelation and all its implications. Christian theology, in the Protestant sense, may therefore be defined and described as

> the entire body of knowledge pertaining to the understanding and exposition of the Bible. This knowledge is commonly divided into four groups: 1) exegetical theology, which includes Biblical isagogics and the history of the canon and translations, hermeneutics and textual criticism, exegesis of the Old and the New Testament, and a study of modern translations; 2) systematic theology, which embraces dogmatics or doctrinal theology, the study of the Symbolical Books, moral philosophy and Christian ethics, and often also apologetics and polemics; 3) historical theology, which includes church history and archaeology and its various periods, the history of dogma and confessions, and patristics; 4) practical theology, with subdivision of pastoral theology and church polity, catechetics, homiletics, diaconics and missions, liturgies and hymnology, and Christian art and architecture.[27]

---

[27] *Lutheran Cyclopedia*, ed. Erwin L. Lueker (St. Louis: Concordia Publishing House, 1954), p. 1051. Note that this definition presupposes a qualitative distinction between special (Biblical) revelation and general revelation. My appreciation to Mr. Edward Hunter, formerly my assistant at the University of Chicago Divinity School Library, and now on the library staff of the Methodist Theological School in Ohio, who engaged in stimulating dialogue with me on the legitimacy of employing this historical approach.

The order in which the four main divisions of theology are listed in the above definition is not a capricious one, for theology is a pyramidal discipline. Exegetical theology constitutes the base of the pyramid, since it investigates the content of the Biblical revelation, and thereby provides the fundamental data for the other three theological fields. Systematic theology rests directly upon exegetical theology, for it organizes systematically and cogently the data provided by exegetical theology, thus supporting the historical and practical divisions. Historical theology studies the activities of the church through the centuries; its chief concern is to discover how the Biblical truths set forth by systematic theology have been understood and applied by Christian believers. Practical theology, because of its functional character, has a position at the apex of the pyramid; it sets forth no new Christian truth, but seeks to relate and apply the insights of the other three branches of theology to the life and work of the contemporary church and to secular culture.

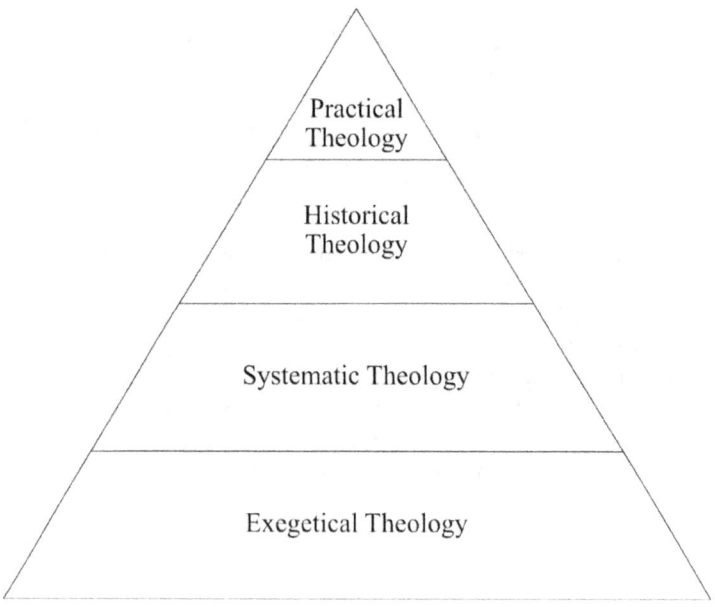

THE THEOLOGICAL PYRAMID

In spite of the twentieth-century proliferation of sub-branches in the theological field (e.g. psychology of religion, religion and art), the basic four-step structure of Protestant theology remains constant—as, in fact, it must,

6. Choosing Books for a Theological Library

if theology is to retain its essential character as a discipline.[28] Since the criteria for sound research materials differ within these four branches of theology, it is essential to treat them separately for the purposes of the present study. The reader should not, however, lose sight of the total theological picture; nor should he forget that, while great care is to be exercised in all aspects of theological book selection, the ramifications of poor selection become greater as one approaches the base of the pyramid. A theological library having a poor stock of Biblical materials is in actuality a poor theological library in all areas, for researchers in systematic, historical, and practical theology are in no position in such a library to check the accuracy of materials in their specific fields. On the other hand, a library inadequately stocked with practical theology works, though inadequate in that particular, is not thereby seriously crippled as a research tool in exegetical, systematic, or historical theology.[29]

With the general theological *Gestalt* clearly in mind, one can proceed to analyze the structure and literature of each of the four major divisions of theology, in order to determine the relative importance of each of the parts to the whole. Such an analysis must be simple enough that it can readily be applied when selecting books via the available book selection tools; yet it must be specific enough to provide definite, objective guidance for the selector. The analytical technique presented below involves applying to each of the theological disciplines three or four factors ("types of material in the field," "depth of treatment," "language," and sometimes "coverage of material"), and the grading of the results on the basis of relative importance. To employ this technique in practice, the selector should assign to a book under consideration grades corresponding to each of the above-mentioned factors, and then multiply the three or four grades together so as to obtain a single score for each book. The score which a book

---

[28] It will be noted that in this paper theology is consistently treated from the historic, Protestant, Reformation viewpoint. Readers with other religious orientations, or librarians in institutions where other religious positions are taken as definitive, must therefore adapt the material here given to their particular situations. In the book selection charts to follow, such readers will undoubtedly wish to alter some of the grading coefficients employed; this can readily be done without destroying the usefulness of the approach.

[29] This is not to say, of course, that disciplines higher on the pyramid (e.g., practical theology) do not occasionally offer theological insights to students working in more fundamental areas (e.g., exegetical theology); but it must be recognized that if the Scriptures are the sole *principium cognoscendi* of theology (as historic Protestantism has always claimed), then such insights must be tested for truth value by the theological disciplines underlying them, and are therefore in reality reflections or reverberations of truths already present in those more central disciplines.

receives provides a basis for comparing that book with other possible purchases. If a book attains a score of 1 (which it can attain only if it receives the highest possible grades across the board), it should be considered a "must" item—an item which is of the greatest importance to a theological library. If the book scores from 2 through 4, it is a high quality work, in a class of which most items could well be obtained.[30] If the book receives a score of 5 or higher, it falls in the category of less desirable works, of which some, but not most, need be purchased for the theological library. It will be noted that this procedure will not *per se* determine what books are to be accepted and what books rejected in the given theological library situation; if it purported to do so, it would by that very fact be highly suspect. Several other important factors must be brought into play in order to attain a full-orbed selection policy. These will be discussed as soon as the factors related to the four theological disciplines have been set forth.

---

[30] The reader will observe, on studying the grading system employed that a score of 2–4 can be obtained only if the individual grades which the item receives are (1)(1)(1)(2), or (1)(1)(1)(3), or (1)(1)(1)(4), or (1)(1)(2)(2).

6. Choosing Books for a Theological Library

Exegetical theology. Books in the Biblical field should be evaluated according to the following scheme:

Types of Material in the Field	Depth	Coverage	Language
1 Reference works (texts, atlases, dictionaries, léxica, grammars, etc.)	1 Based on original language	1 Whole Bible	1 English
	2 Based on version language	1 O. T.	2 German, Latin
		1 Messianic portions	3 French
	5 Based on modern language		4 Other Romance languages, Dutch, the Scandinavian languages
2 Introductory works		2 Portions especially relevant: to N.T. (e.g. Pentateuch, Prophets)	
1 Canon			
2 Textual criticism			5 Other languages
3 Higher criticism		2 Books quoted in N.T.	
1 Inspiration		3 Books not quoted in N.T.	
1 Hermeneutics		1 N. T.	
3 Biblical background		1 Gospels, parables, miracles, Sermon on Mount	
1 Exegetical (interpretative) works		1 Pauline epistles	
2 Biblical theology		2 Other epistles	
		2 Acts	
		1 Johannine writings	
		2 Revelation	
		4 Apocrypha & pseudepigrapha	

The reasons for most of the specific grading in this chart and the others below will be evident to those acquainted with the theological field. However, some aspects of the grading deserve clarification. In the "types of material in the field," it is assumed that works dealing with the revelatory character of Scripture (canon, inspiration), or its interpretation (hermeneutics, exegesis), and general reference works on the Bible are of paramount theological importance; of secondary significance are works dealing with the text and human authorship of Scripture (textual criticism, Biblical "introduction"), and works of Biblical theology;[31] of tertiary value are works relating the Bible to the cultural setting in which it appeared (Biblical background), and books presenting (highly speculative) opinions of higher critics. The "depth" of a work in the area of exegetical theology depends upon its linguistic basis; the most important works are based upon the Hebrew, Aramaic, or Greek texts of Scripture; next come those based upon early versions (such as the Latin); and of far less significance are those which do not penetrate beyond the level of a modern translation of the Bible. "Language" refers to the language of the book which is being evaluated, and the grading is based both upon the linguistic attainments of American Biblical scholars, and upon the relative importance of Biblical literature in various languages.

---

[31] Thayer, the great N.T. Greek lexicographer, wrote: "Works on Biblical theology ... rather than on exegesis ... contain ... much that is suggestive exegetically. They often put old texts in a new light. But ... the very fact that they are dominated by a theory foredooms them in all probability to serious re-adjustment. They take up into themselves altogether too much of those little systems that have their day and cease to be. One does not have to live very long to outlive books which in their time were thought to contain the last word on these debated Biblical topics" (Joseph Henry Thayer, *Books and Their Use: an Address* (Boston, Houghton, Mifflin, 1893), pp. 19–20.

6. Choosing Books for a Theological Library 185

Systematic theology. Works of systematic theology are to be judged by the following criteria:

Types of Material in the Field	Depth	Language

1 Reference works and general treatments
1 Dogmatics
  1 Bibliology
  1 Theology
  2 Anthropology
  1 Soteriology
  3 Eschatology
3 Ethics
2 Apologetics
	1 Employment of sound exegesis and competent use of philosophical material
	2 Employment of sound exegesis
	5 Competent use of philosophical material
	5 Popularizations
		1 English
		2 German, Latin
		3 French, Swedish, Dutch
		4 Other Romance languages, other Scandinavian languages
		5 Other languages

Under "types of material in the field," the traditional major divisions of systematic theology have been listed;[32] as in the case of the other branches of theology, subdivision can be carried out to a much greater extent than has been done here, but in practical book selection this will seldom be necessary. Dogmatics is the fundamental area of systematic theology, and thus deserves a higher grade level than apologetics (which defends the assertions made by dogmatics) or ethics (which derives its principles directly from dogmatics). Within dogmatics, the most important material is concerned with the Bible, God, and salvation; the doctrine of man is secondary, and the material in eschatology (being the farthest removed from immediate application) is to be placed on a tertiary level.[33] The "depth" of a systematic theology book is related primarily to its use of the data pro-

---

[32] They are well explained and related in Karl Hase's *Hutterus Redivivus* (10. ed.; Leipzig: Breitkopf and Härtel, 1862). "Theology" as a subdivision of dogmatics treats the doctrine of God; "bibliology," the doctrine of the Bible; "anthropology," the doctrine of man; "soteriology," the doctrine of salvation; and "eschatology," the doctrine of "the last things" (the second coming of Christ, the general resurrection, etc.).

[33] We are of course referring here to "futuristic" eschatology (the historic meaning of the term) and not to "realized" eschatology (in the Bultmannian sense, e.g.). Realized eschatology is in actuality a variety of soteriology, as Otto Piper has shown in his trenchant critique of Bultmann.

vided by exegetical theology; if it is solidly grounded in these data, it deserves high commendation; if not, it is of questionable value. A work of systematic theology ought also to be philosophically sophisticated, but a lack in this regard is not of overwhelming consequence. It will be noted that Dutch and Swedish are given relatively high ratings among the languages of systematic theology; this is because of the important Calvinistic works emanating from Holland, and the Lutheran publications coming from the Lundensian and other theological schools-of-thought-in Sweden.

Historical theology. The evaluation schema for the historical area of theology is as follows:

Types of Material in the Field	Depth	Coverage	Language

1 Reference works
1 Continental church history-general treatments
  1 Ancient church history (to ca. 500)
  2 Medieval church history (ca. 500–1400)
  2 Renaissance
  1 Reformation
  3 Age of "orthodoxy" (ca. 1580–1750)
  3 Age of "romanticism" (ca. 1815–1900)
  1 Twentieth century
	1 Related to exegetical & systematic foundation; reliance upon primary source materials
	2 Related to exegetical & systematic foundation; reliance upon secondary source materials
	3 Reliance upon primary source materials, but little relation of material to exegetical & systematic foundation
	5 Reliance upon secondary source materials; little relation of material to exegetical & systematic foundation
		Non-biographical works
		1 Concerned with more than one major Protestant ecclesiastical movement (Lutherans, Calvinists, Episcopalians, etc.) or with ecumenical relations.
		2 Concerned with only one major Protestant ecclesiastical movement
		2 Concerned with more than one segment of a major Protestant ecclesiastical movement (Presbyterian U.S., Missouri Lutherans, etc.)
		3 Concerned with one segment of
			1 English
			2 German, French, Latin
			4 Other Romance languages, Scandinavian languages, Dutch
			5 Other languages

1 American church history-general treatments		a major Protestant ecclesiastical movement	
3 Colonial and early national period (to ca. 1790)		3 Concerned with Roman Catholic or Eastern Orthodox churches in general	
2 Westward expansion (ca. 1790–1830)		4 Concerned with segments of the Roman Catholic or Eastern Orthodox churches (Jesuits, etc.)	
3 Civil War period (ca. 1830–1870)			
2 Era of "big business" (ca. 1870–1910)		5 Concerned with the sects and cults	
1 Contemporary		Biographical works*	
1 Foreign missionary materials		1 Concerned with key figure in general church history (Augustine, Luther, Calvin, etc.)	
		2 Concerned with person associated with key figure in general church history (Melanchthon, etc.)	
		4 Concerned with important figure in history of a minor denomination	
		5 Concerned with minor figure in church history	

* Also to be included here are creative writings and sermons of churchmen (unless their nature requires them to be evaluated as exegetical, systematic, or practical theology works), but (1) depth factor is not to be applied to such creative works, (2) for language categories given above substitute: 1 Original language, 1 English (or German, French—but only if original language is other than English, German, or a Romance language, and English translation is not available; or other Romance language—but only if original language is other than English, German, or a Romance language, and neither an English, nor a German, nor a French translation is available), 4 Other languages.

In historical theology, the "types of material in the field" generally relate to the widely-used (and in some cases admittedly doubtful) historical categories. Where a book includes material dealing with more than one historical epoch, it should be given the highest (i.e., numerically lowest) applicable grade. The grading of the epochs has been based upon their relative importance in the total history of the church; no intention exists here to evaluate these epochs from a secular standpoint. In order to anticipate the historian's inevitable criticism of this grading of epochs, we quote Shera's sane assertions:

> Because the tradition is widely accepted among historians that no generalization should be advanced unless all the available evidence has been examined, no stone left unturned, every witness summoned, they have urged the preservation of not only the more important records but the indiscriminate preservation of everything. ... In the past there have been just enough examples of the value of this omnivorous collecting to give the argument substantial weight, but ... as the discipline itself matures, the historian should, indeed must ... abandon the false and impossible goal of "completeness."[34]

A theological library is not a general historical library, and if it attempts to collect indiscriminately all material bearing on the history of Western Christendom, the result will be an appalling bibliothecal mess. "Depth" in historical theology is concerned with the familiar primary source-secondary source distinction, and with the relating of historical theology material to its Biblical and systematic foundations.

Practical Theology. The selection of materials in the practical theology area should be based upon the following considerations:

---

[34] Jesse Hauk Shera, *Historians, Books and Libraries* (Cleveland: Western Reserve University Press, 1953).

Types of Material in the Field	Depth	Language

1 Reference works
1 Psychology of religion
1 Sociology of religion
1 Religion and art
1 Liturgies and devotional writings
1 Religious education
   1 Theory
   3 Curriculum materials
1 Church administration
1 Homiletics (for sermons of notable churchmen, see above under Historical theology)
   1 Homiletic theory
   3 Exemplary sermons and sermon outlines
   5 Sermon illustrations
	1 Sound relation to exegetical, systematic, and historical theology: sound application of appropriate related discipline (psychology, sociology, art & architecture, church history, education, administrative theory, speech)
	
	5 Little attempt to relate material to exegetical, systematic and historical foundation; of little attempt to apply insights of appropriate related discipline
		Apply to all "types of material" except Church administration and Homiletics:
		1 English
		2 German, French (and Italian for Religion and art, and Latin for Liturgies and devotional writings)
		5 Other Romance languages
		5 Other languages
		
		Apply to Homiletics and Church administration:
		1 English
		5 Other languages

In practical theology the strict application of the "depth" criterion is of crucial importance. Great quantities of practical theology materials are being produced at the present time (as, in fact, disproportionately large amounts have been published throughout Christian history). Many of these publications are deceptively alluring, and a theological library can soon become engulfed with ephemera if it does not keep clearly in mind that a quality work in practical theology must (1) reflect the cumulative wisdom of exegetical, systematic, and historical theology (acquaintance with *all three* of these is ideal), and (2) apply the best insights of the discipline related to the practical field involved (psychology in the case of psychology of religion, administrative theory in the case of church administration, etc.).[35]

---

[35] An article on theological librarianship which almost completely misunderstands the relationship between practical theology and the other theological areas is Theodore Trost's "The Seminary Curriculum, the Library, and the Librarian," *Proceedings of the American Theological Library Association*, III (1949), pp. 29–37.

Some essential considerations. Now that specific selection criteria for the four major theological disciplines have been presented,[36] we are in a position to set forth a number of selection factors by which the results of the

---

[36] A theological area not covered in the preceding discussion is that of "comparative religion," which, strictly speaking, is not a field within Christian theology, but an attempt to understand other systems of belief with which the Christian faith comes into contact. In some theological school curricula, comparative religion is not taught as a separate subject, but appropriate aspects of it are dealt with in the courses in apologetics, missions, etc. For purposes of theological book selection in comparative religion, the following scheme will be found helpful; it will be noted that the closer the relationship of a given religion to the Christian tradition, the higher is the grade level assigned to it:

Types of Material in the Field	Depth	Coverage	Language
1 Reference works and general treatments 1 Judaism 2 Mohammedanism 3 Major Eastern religions (Buddhism,* Hinduism, Jainism, Shinto, Confucianism, etc.) 4 "Dead" religions of classical times Other religions (Polynesian religions, African faiths, etc.)	1 Material presented in relation to the Christian faith; based on primary sources 2 Material presented in relation to the Christian faith; based on secondary sources 2 Reliance on primary sources, but material not presented in relation to the Christian faith 4 Reliance on secondary sources, and material not presented in relation to the Christian faith	1 General 1 Emphasis on scriptures and doctrines of the group 2 Emphasis on history of the group 2 Biographies of important religious leaders of the group 3 Biographies of minor religious figures in the group 4 Emphasis on the practices of the group 5 Other emphases	1 English (and original language of religious scriptures) 2 German, French 4 Other Romance languages 5 Other languages

6. Choosing Books for a Theological Library 191

above grading system can be related to a particular theological library situation. These factors are to be applied by the selector in such a way that his final acquisition decisions will harmonize both with his book budget and with the other local conditions under which he is working. The size of the given book budget will obviously determine how heavily these factors need to be brought to bear in a specific library situation.

The first of the factors requiring attention here has implicitly been considered to some extent in the above grading process; it is the matter of *author and publisher*. Since the selector is seldom able to peruse the books themselves before choosing them, and since in many instances he does not even have the benefit of critical reviews at the time he makes his decisions on acquisition, he must frequently induce the depth (if not the content) of a volume largely from the name of the author and the name of the publisher. However, it should be emphasized that, wherever possible, author and publisher should be considered separately from the above grading, since an author or publisher whose work has generally been of a certain type or quality in the past need not forever or consistently conform to a previous pattern. This is a particularly important fact to keep in mind in theological book selection, where there is a tendency to stereotype authors and publishers as "fundamentalist," "modernist," etc., and to ignore the works issued by certain denominational publishing houses. This is not to deny that "es preciso conocer la orientación de las distintas casas editoras para tener así un dato útil para la valoración del libro";[37] but care must be taken not to allow *ad hominem* selection to displace selection based on an accurate evaluation of the quality of publications themselves. In the case of authorship, the question is not essentially the abstract one of "Is the author distinguished?," but the specific one, "Is the author's background sufficient to support what he has written in this particular book?" In the religious realm, where a great number of famous people apparently feel compelled to record their religious views in print, and where persons with little training in a given theological discipline cannot resist writing

---

* I.e., Hinayana Buddhism; Mahayana Buddhism, because of its closer relation to the central Christian doctrine of grace, should be given a grade level of 2.

[37] María Teresa Freyre de Andrade, *El Servicio de Bibliografía y Referencia, y la Adquisición de Libros en una Biblioteca* (La Habana: Asociación Bibliotecaria Cubana, 1942), p. 21. I have noticed an almost pathological prejudice on the part of some ill-informed theological librarians against the publications of Eerdmans, Zondervan, and Baker; it cannot be emphasized too strongly that these houses are not "fundamentalist"—they are conservative Calvinist, and issue a great deal of very valuable and important literature.

tomes on that subject, the selector must clearly recognize the distinction between eminence and theological competence.

Secondly, one must take into account *the numerous minor criteria which characterize particular subject disciplines*. In historical works, for example, the presence of bibliographic footnotes is more important than in the case of sermonic materials. In biography, treatments of living persons (all other things being equal) are not to be rated as highly as treatments of individuals whose lives have been completed. Criteria of this variety should be common knowledge to selectors with good cultural and theological backgrounds and competent library training; limitations of space prevent us from going beyond mere mention of them here.[38]

A third factor is *the already existing library collection*. A theological library which is weak in particular subject areas should presumably make special effort to strengthen those areas. However, such weakness should not appreciably influence current selection. The extent of the weakness will determine what proportion of the current book budget is to be spent in buying older materials, and what portion can be freed for the acquisition of new publications. It is important that the latter not be slighted in favour of the former, or the problem of "gaps" in the collection will simply be compounded or extended over a greater length of time. It is preferable, wherever possible, to obtain special funds for dealing with weaknesses in the collection, instead of allowing the past continually to strangle the present.

Fourthly, *the availability of materials in other libraries* must be considered. It has been assumed throughout the present analysis that the theological library will depend upon general (university, college, public, etc.) libraries for non-theological materials. Where such libraries are not present or suitable, the theological library must utilize a part of its own book budget for

---

[38] A work which is particularly helpful in setting forth such criteria in the religious realm is Lester Asheim's *The Humanities and the Library* (Chicago: American Library Association, 1957), chap. 1. An example of a publication which acts as a guide to criteria in a particular sub-area within theology is R. Pierce Beaver's "Building a Basic Missions Collection in a Theological Seminary Library," *Missionary Research Library Occasional Bulletin*, VI:5 (June 20, 1955). Because so many "minor" criteria are bibliographical in character, I have the opportunity of adding another *caveat* to my earlier remarks on the menace produced by theological librarians without the B. D.: seminary librarians without at least graduate B. L. S. training are generally menaces also—though slightly less severe ones.

important non-theological publications.[39] In some cases, the theological library will be able to depend upon other theological collections for particular items or subject areas, and will not therefore need to purchase certain works which it would otherwise have to buy. The present paper has not concerned itself at all with the matter of cooperative acquisitions among theological libraries, but, needless to say, such cooperation ought strongly to be encouraged as an aid in covering the vast field of theological publication.

A fifth consideration is the *faculty specialization at the particular institution*. Such specialization manifests itself both in the instructional materials and in the research works which the faculty requests the library to purchase. In most cases (if we assume that the given faculty is a sound one), these requests will be in line with the normal library acquisition program, since the latter is based primarily upon the character and structure of the theological discipline. However, the specialist almost always tends to overrate the value of his specialty, so some conflict of interest is inevitable. Depending upon the nature of the local situation, the theological library may well give greater than normal stress to certain subjects because of the research specialties of particular faculty members; and it is common practice for institutional emphases to skew collecting in certain areas (e.g., Baptist history in a Baptist seminary). However, the selector must be continually vigilant in these matters, for otherwise the seminary library can become virtually a personal library in the hands of those who are able to exercise the strongest pressure.

---

[39] Researchers in theology must maintain contact with non-theological areas of thought. "Originality depends on new and striking combinations of ideas. It is obvious therefore that the more a man knows the greater scope he has for arriving at striking combinations. And not only the more he knows about his own subject but the more he knows beyond it of other subjects" (Rosamond E. M. Harding, *An Anatomy of Inspiration* (Cambridge: Heffer, 1948), p. 3). The degree to which theologians have in the past employed non-theological materials is a subject well worth investigating, perhaps by means of the source analysis technique. Until such studies are made, it is difficult to determine the type or amount of non-theological literature which the theological researcher should have at his disposal. However, it goes almost without saying that non-theological reference and bibliographical works must be acquired, for without them the theologian has no sound access to subject materials outside of his own field. For a basic list of non-theological (as well as theological) reference works essential to the seminary library, see my booklet, *The Writing of Research Papers in Theology* (Ann Arbor: Edwards Bros, for the U. Chicago Divinity School, 1959).

A final selection factor, closely related to the previous one, is *the current trends in theology*. These deserve more attention than faculty research emphases at the given institution, but, even when this has been granted, one should observe that a theological library collection can be seriously overbalanced through naive concession to such trends. To cite a contemporary example: the Dead Sea scroll discoveries are of tremendous consequence in the present theological scene, but if they are allowed to eat up great quantities of a seminary book budget, other equally (or, in long-term perspective, more?) significant publications will have to be neglected.

The six considerations just discussed will be applied by the selector to the results of the subject scoring as outlined previously. When this is intelligently done, in light of the inevitable budgetary limiting factor, the consequence should be a theological book selection procedure which (to use Plato's expression) "cuts at the joints." Now let us conclude with an example illustrating the practical application of this technique.

An Illustration of the Theological Book Acquisition Method Presented Here

We shall assume the existence of three theological libraries, A, B, and C, with total yearly book budgets (exclusive of binding and periodical appropriations) of $4,500, $3,500, and $2,500 respectively.[40] It will further be assumed that all three of these libraries have competent collections of basic theological reference works (as listed by the American Association of Theological Schools), and that all three have decided that weaknesses in their collections require them to devote one-fifth of their yearly book budget to non-current acquisitions. Each seminary will be hypothetically located close enough to a good university or public library so that non-theological materials will not enter into the acquisition problem. Seminary A will be considered Baptist; seminary B will have on its faculty a specialist in the parabolic teaching of Scripture; and seminary C will have as one of its faculty members an eminent scholar who has devoted his life to Methodist

---

[40] These figures compare favorably with the budgets of American seminary libraries of varying sizes, as shown by American Association of Theological School figures. We are not concerned in this illustration with the periodical budget, but it should be obvious that periodicals ought to be selected by much the same subject grading system as is applied to monographs, and that relative allocations of periodical and book funds should be made subsequent, nor prior, to such grading. (Note that the book budgets and pricing given illustratively in the present article are now ancient history; the reader must, it should go without saying, employ the same methodology to current library budgets and book and periodical pricing.)

6. Choosing Books for a Theological Library

local history. In all three schools, instructional requests from faculty average one book ($3.50) per week throughout the year. The problem to be solved is: Taking a single week in isolation,[41] what current publications are to be purchased by each of these libraries in order to further theological research at the given institutions?

It will be apparent from the data just given that A has $65.50 to spend on current research materials in any single week, B has $50.50, and C, $34.50. If we take $3.50 as the average library purchase price of a current theological work, A can buy approximately 19 books per week; B, 14 books per week; and C, 10 books per week. We shall assume that the three libraries employ the national and trade bibliographies as their sole selection tools for current materials; and in order to simplify our illustration even further, we shall, for the week in question, deal only with *Publishers' Weekly* and the *British National Bibliography*.[42] Which books listed in these publications, then, should the three libraries purchase in a specified week? The following thirty-five religious books are cited in PW for April 20, 1959, and BNB for April 1, 1959;[43] each book has been rated according to the charts given previously:

Title	Category	Score
1. Boyd, Jesse L. *A History of Baptists in America prior to 1845*. 205 pp. (5 p. bibl.) il. New York, American Press.	Hist.	(2) (1) (2) (1) = 4
2. Buttrick, George Arthur. *Sermons Preached in a University Church*. 222 pp. (12 p. bibl. notes) Nashville, Abingdon Press.	Hist. (biog.)	(1) ( ) (2) (1) = 2

---

[41] In reality, of course, a single week's selection cannot be isolated from monthly selection, quarterly selection, yearly selection, or from past selection as a whole. However, for purposes of simplicity, the isolated week is being assumed in our illustration.

[42] A theological library worthy of the name will not neglect review articles or publisher's announcements, but there is little doubt that the more comprehensive the library's use of national and trade bibliography, the less reliance will have to be placed on blurbs and reviews as firsthand sources of information on new publications. My former professor, LeRoy Merritt, has shown in his studies that reviews often provide a very questionable basis for sound book selection.

[43] BNB arrives at American libraries later than PW, so issues of the two publications for the same week will not normally be consulted concurrently.

3.	De Blank, Joost, abp. *Uncomfortable Words*; foreword by the Bishop of London. 120 pp. New York, Longmans.	Hist. (biog.)	(1) ( ) (2) (1) = 2
4.	Ford, Ruth Sykes. *A History of the First Methodist Church of Hutitsville, Alabama, 1808-1958.* 127 pp. (bibl. notes) il., map. Huntsville, First Methodist Church. (One of the first churches to be established in Alabama.)	Hist.	(1) (2) (4) (1) = 8
5.	Hastings, James, ed. *The Great Texts of the Bible: Genesis-Numbers.* 457 pp. (bibls. and bibl. footnotes) Grand Rapids, Eerdmans.	Exeg.	(1) (1) (2) (1) = 2
6.	_____. _____: St. Luke. 487 pp.	Exeg.	(1) (1) (1) (1) = 1
7.	Heschel, Abraham Joshua. *Between God and Man; an Interpretation of Judaism.* 279 pp. (4p. bibl. and bibl. notes) New York, Harper.	Comp. Rel.	(1) (2) (1) (1) = 2
8.	Heslop, William Greene. *Nuggets from Numbers.* 192 pp. Butler, Indiana, Higley Press. (Authorisan evangelist minister.)	Exeg.	(1) (5) (2) (1) = 10
9.	Howie, Carl Gordon. *God in the Eternal Present.* 128 pp. Richmond, Virginia, John Knox Press. (Presbyterian clergyman discusses the character of God, sin, heaven, good works.)	Sys.	(1) (5) ( ) (1) = 5
10.	Linden, James V. *The Catholic Church Invites You.* 127 pp. St. Louis, Herder.	Sys.	(2) (5) ( ) (1) = 10
11.	Lockyer, Herbert. *The Mystery and Ministry of Angels.* 96 pp. Grand Rapids, Eerdmans.	Sys.	(3) (1) ( ) (1) = 3

6. Choosing Books for a Theological Library

12. Maus, Cynthia Pearl. *Christ and the Fine Arts*, rev. ed. 821 pp. il. New York, Harper.	Prac.	(1) (5) ( ) (1) = 5
13. *Meditations for the Monthly Retreats; for the Use of the Daughters of Charity.* 359 pp. Westminster, Md., Newman Press.	Prac.	(1) (5) ( ) (1) = 5
14. Murphy, Francis Xavier. *Pope John XXIII Comes to the Vatican.* 257 pp. il. N.Y., McBride.	Hist. (biog.)	(1) (3) (2) (1) = 6
15. Owen, George Frederick. *The Shepherd Psalm of Palestine.* 84 pp. (bibl.) Grand Rapids, Eerdmans. (Photographs of the Palestinian shepherd and his flocks accompany each of the meditations.)	Exeg.	(1) (5) (2) (1) = 10
16. Pearson, Roy Messer. *The Ministry of Preaching.* 127 pp. (bibl. notes) N.Y., Harper. (Author is dean of Andover-Newton Theological School.)	Prac.	(1) (1) ( ) (1) = 1
17. Thompson, William Taliaferro. *Adventures in Parenthood; Christian Family Living.* 155 pp. (6 p. bibl. Notes) Richmond, Virginia, John Knox Press.	Prac.	(1) (5) ( ) (1) = 5
18. Turnbull, Ralph G. *Sermon Substance.* 224 pp. Grand Rapids, Baker Book House. (104 tested sermon outlines by the pastor of the 1st Presbyterian Church in Seattle, Washington)	Prac.	(3) (5) ( ) (1) = 15
19. White, Reginald E. O. *Prayer is the Secret; the Prayer Experience of the Apostles and Church Fathers.* 143 pp. N.Y., Harper. (Author is pastor of the Grange Baptist Church in Birkenhead, England.)	Prac.	(1) (5) ( ) (1) = 5

198 Part Two: Theology, the Future, and the Occult

20. Wickenden, Arthur Consaul. *The Concerns of Religion*. 185 pp. (3 p. bibl.) N.Y., Harper. (Rev. ed. of "Youth Looks at Religion.")	Prac.	(1) (5) ( ) (1) = 5
BNB Listings		
21. Lambeth Conference, 1958. *The Holy Bible, its Authority and Message*. London, S.P.C.K. 30 pp.	Exeg.	(1) (1) (1) (1) = 1
22. Filas, Francis Lad. *The Parables of Jesus: a Popular Explanation*. N.Y., Macmillan. 172 pp.	Exeg.	(1) (5) (1) (1) = 5
23. Diem, Hermann. *Dogmatics*, tr. from the German. Edinburgh, Oliver & Boyd. 375 pp.	Sys.	(1) (1) ( ) (1) = 1
24. Watt, William Montgomery. *The Cure for Human Troubles: a Statement of the Christian Message in Modern Terms*. London, S.P.C.K. 159 pp.	Sys.	(1) (5) ( ) (1) = 5
25. Guirdham, Arthur. *Christ and Freud: a Study of Religious Experience and Observance*. London, Allen & Unwin. 194 pp.	Prac.	(1) (1) ( ) (1) = 1
26. Heim, Karl. *Jesus the Lord*, tr. from the German. Edinburgh, Oliver & Boyd. 192 pp.	Sys.	(1) (1) ( ) (1) = 1
27. Rooney, Gerard. *The Mystery of Calvary*. N.Y., McGraw-Hill. 131 pp.	Sys.	(1) (2) ( ) (1) = 2
28. Saywell, George Frederick. *Christian Confidence*. London, Clarke. 142 pp. (Articles reprinted from *The Times*, 1939–45.)	Prac.	(1) (5) ( ) (1) = 5
29. Martin, Celine, Sister. *A Memoir of My Sister, St. Therese* (1873–1897), tr. from the French. Dublin, Gill. 249 pp. il.	Hist. (biog.)	(3) (1) (5) (1) = 15

6. Choosing Books for a Theological Library

30. Kühner, Hans. *Encyclopedia of the Papacy*, tr. from the German. London, Owen. 249 pp. il. bibl.	Hist.	(1) (1) (3) (1) = 3
31. Carpenter, Spencer Cecil. *Eighteenth Century Church and People*. London, Murray. 290 pp.	Hist.	(3) (1) (2) (1) = 6
32. Church in Wales. *Official Handbook*. Cardiff, Author. 463 pp. (Previous issue 1939.)	Hist.	(1) (3) (4) (1) = 12
33. Payne, Ernest Alexander. *The Baptist Union; a Short History*. London, Carey Kingsgate. 317 pp. il. bibl.	Hist.	(1) (3) (4) (1) = 12
34. *Jewish Travel Guide*. London, Jewish Chronicle Publications. 303 pp.	Comp. Rel.	(1) (2) (5) (1) = 10
35. *Encyclopaedia of Islam*, new ed. Leiden, Brill. Vol. 1, fase. 15.	Comp. Rel.	(2) (1) (1) (1) = 2

The thirty-five publications may now be classed as follows: those with a score of 1: 6, 16, 21, 23, 25, 26; those with a score of 2–4: 1, 2, 3, 5, 7, 11, 27, 30, 35; those with a score of 5 or more: 4, 8, 9, 10, 12, 13, 14, 15, 17, 18, 19, 20, 22, 24, 28, 29, 31, 32, 33, 34. A number of these books may be eliminated from further consideration because their authorship is not of sufficient stature to support the subject matter involved (nos. 8, 9, 10, 13, 15, 19, 20, 27, 28).[44] One of the books (no. 14) may be dropped at this point because it is a biography of a living person about whom more data will certainly be available later.

Library C, which can purchase ten books, will then select the six books having a score of 1, item no. 4 (concerned with Methodist local history), item no. 5 (in a series with item no. 6, which has a score of 1), and in all probability two high ranking items from the 2–4 class—perhaps item no. 30 (a reference work, but not involving the pecuniary outlay of no. 35, for which *The Shorter Encyclopaedia of Islam* would readily substitute in a small theological library) and item 2 (the sermons of one of the most eminent university pastors of our time.)

---

[44] To be sure, such works may be purchased at a later time, if their authors become more widely recognized or if the selector discovers new evidence concerning the quality of the books.

Library B, which can select fourteen books from the list of thirty-five, will purchase the six books scoring 1, item no, 22 (on Jesus' parables), and presumably all the items scoring 2–4 with the exception of item 1 (of more limited denominational interest) and 27 (eliminated above.)

Library A, whose purchases can extend to nineteen books per week, will obtain all the books having scores of 1–4 (again with the exception of no. 27), and five books from the 5≠ class (certainly including item no. 33, which is of special interest to Baptists, and probably also items 17, 22, 24, and 31—which have relatively high scores, are of reasonably general interest, and are not later editions of widely-available books as in the case of item 12).

* * *

The preceding illustration will have demonstrated to the reader how the theological book selection procedure set forth in this paper can be applied in a practical seminary library situation.[45] It is hoped that this subject-oriented technique can also be adapted to disciplines other than theology.

---

[45] Note the major advantages of this technique: (1) Subject selection factors have a constant weight in relation to each other; thus the method provides far greater objectivity than is possible in ordinary selection—where one factor is allowed to have great value in one selection decision and little value in another, or where "snap" decisions are frequently made without considering the gamut of factors; (2) The technique can be taught by one librarian to other members of his staff or to interested faculty, thus bringing the same specific acquisition method to bear on all selection carried on in a given institution; (3) The grading technique makes it possible for a library to keep a detailed record of past selection decisions for comparison with and as an aid to current selection; thus consistency of selection policy can be maintained. Moreover, the rating technique employed here has another possible use in the evaluation of existing theological book collections. Such an evaluation of the eschatology section of a large interdenominational seminary library was quite revealing. The library possessed (as of May 1, 1959) 333 books classified in eschatology by the Library of Congress system (BT 819–90), out of a total of some 5,440 systematic theology works (class BT). Since eschatology is a relatively minor division of systematic theology, this cannot be considered a bad proportion. However, when these 333 books were rated by the present method, only 16 fell into the 2–4 category. A total of 115 received scores of 5≠ and 202 were rejected outright because of their highly dubious character of authorship (e.g., Joseph Wilkins' *The Voice of Inspiration on the Seven Last Things of Prophecy; or What Saith the Scriptures on the Coming of the Lord* (London: 1872). If it is argued that this library may have purchased a good cross-section of the available eschatological publications, I would argue (1) trash is trash, and should not be purchased even if it is the only thing available, (2) the given library in fact lacks a number of

6. Choosing Books for a Theological Library 201

But wherever the method is employed, it is clear that great responsibility devolves upon the selector, for the subject-evaluation charts (which are at the center of this acquisition method) can be effectively utilized only by those who are thoroughly conversant with the subject matter evaluated on these charts. We do not here lamely forsake objectivity by giving free reign to a selector's subjectivity; rather, we present a technique for objectively channeling the energies of those selectors who realize, with Naudé, that

> a man may acquit himself worthily of this responsibility if his judgment is not perverted, rash, filled with absurdities, or clouded by puerile opinions, which cause many to despise and reject all that is not to their taste, as if one should govern himself according to the whims of his fancy, or as if it were not the duty of a wise and prudent man to consider all things impartially and never to judge them by the prejudices of others but only by weighing thoughtfully their actual character and usefulness.[46]

---

the eschatological works listed in Wilbur M. Smith's standard *Preliminary Bibliography for the Study of Biblical Prophecy* (Boston: W. A. Wilde, 1952.)

[46] Gabriel Naudé, *Advice on Establishing a Library*, with an Introduction by Archer Taylor (Berkeley: University of California Press, 1950), p. 46.

PART THREE: CASTING A WIDE SWATH

1. Transhumanism?

Just before Easter (2019), I attended a seminar sponsored by the Paris bar on the subject—I translate—"Transhumanism: the Human Being Raised to a New Level."

The speakers included impressive scientific experts in the realms of cerebral stimulation, exoskeletal research, and genetic manipulation.

You may well ask why generally conservative lawyers would be flirting with such a subject. The answer, aside from the legal implications of the topic (more on that later), is probably—at least in part—that these days everyone wants to be on the cutting edge of futuristic ideas. "Of making many books"—and mod seminars—"there is no end."

One would have thought that the impending Easter celebration might have suggested at least a word about fallen human nature (the first Adam) and the new creation instituted by the incarnation and the conquest of death by the Second Adam, the resurrected Lord Jesus Christ.

Ah, no. Instead, we were presented with theories of human transformation. The evolutionary process, based on natural selection, is just too slow. Humans must take control, thereby moving beyond humanity as is to a hyper-humanity—a stage beyond mankind as we have known it (him? her?). By the application of the scientific wonders of our time, illness can be a thing of the past; perhaps death itself can be conquered.

A half-century ago, secular humanist Julian Huxley put it this way:

> Up till now human life has generally been, as Hobbes described it, "nasty, brutish and short"; the great majority of human beings (if they have not already died young) have been afflicted with misery in one form or another—poverty, disease, ill-health, over-work, cruelty, or oppression. They have attempted to lighten their misery by means of their hopes and their ideals. The trouble has been that the hopes have generally been unjustified, the ideals have generally failed to correspond with reality.
>
> The zestful but scientific exploration of possibilities and of the techniques for realizing them will make our hopes rational, and will set our ideals within the framework of reality, by showing how much of them are indeed realizable. Already, we can justifiably hold the belief that these lands of possibility exist, and that the present limitations and miserable frustrations of our existence could be in large measure surmounted. We are already justified in the conviction that human life as we know it in history is a wretched makeshift, rooted in ignorance; and that it could be transcended

by a state of existence based on the illumination of knowledge and comprehension, just as our modern control of physical nature based on science transcends the tentative fumblings of our ancestors, that were rooted in superstition and professional secrecy....

The human species can, if it wishes, transcend itself —not just sporadically, an individual here in one way, an individual there in another way, but in its entirety, as humanity.[1]

In fairness, at least two of the invited speakers at the Bar conference expressed concern as to the possible negative effects of messing with humanity as such. There were reminders of Hitlerian experimentation on death-camp inmates to justify the Third Reich's conviction that Aryans were superior to, for example, Jews and other minorities.

Far more, however, should have been said about the horrors of all eugenic philosophies—for example, the sad history in the Commonwealth of Virginia where interracial marriage was prohibited by law to ensure "racial purity." It would also have been enlightening if the established historical connection had been pointed up between Darwinian evolutionary theory and eugenic racism.

But what about genetic engineering? From an ethical standpoint, how should it be evaluated? Here are a series of propositions that, in this author's view, should govern this difficult area.

1. No genetic manipulation is ever justified if it entails the destruction of embryos or fetuses, since they are actual, not just potential, human beings. The end never (pace Lenin and Joseph Fletcher) justifies the means.[2]
2. If no human life is destroyed by genetic modifications, *and* where there is adequate evidence based on responsible animal experimentation, etc. of the absence of negative side effects, there is no reason to condemn the human application of the methodology *per se*.[3]

---

[1] Julian Huxley, *New Bottles for New Wine* (London: Chatto & Windus, 1957), pp. 13–17.

[2] I have written much on this subject. See, for example, my book, Slaughter of the Innocents, relevant material in my *Christ Our Advocate and Christ As Centre and Circumference*, and my public debate with Joseph Fletcher (Situation Ethics—available as a transcript and in audio format).

[3] Cf. S. Patra, A. A. Andrew, Human, Social, and Environmental Impacts of Human Genetic Engineering. J Biomedical Sci. 2015, 4:2. DOI:10.4172/2254-609X.100014.

3. If the conditions just set out are fulfilled, and genetic manipulation is likely to cure or mollify an identifiable negative medical condition unable to be corrected by less intrusive means, it should be encouraged.
4. If the conditions set forth above are fulfilled, there should be no *a priori* objection to genetic manipulation the purpose of which is to *improve* the lot of a human being (for example, if IQ could be raised). But the creation of "designer babies"—such as apparently produced a few years ago by Chinese doctor He Jiankui employing the new germinal technique (CRISPR-Cas9) to alter existing DNA by way of "genetic scissors"—and any and all efforts to implement racial preferences genetically must be unqualifiedly condemned.
5. Serious sanctions must be incorporated into domestic and international law to deter practices that would, with no medical benefit, genetically modify the human being and his/her progeny. (The European Commission's Directive 2001/18/EC and the even more restrictive French legislation on genetically modified foods is surely a step in the right direction, but a great deal more needs to be done to protect the human being from irresponsible experimentation. In Canada, it is illegal for researchers to alter the human genome in any way that could be inherited; if convicted, the defendant faces up to ten years in prison.)

These principles are grounded in a biblical view of man—that the human being, as created by God Almighty, must not be turned into something else. There is nothing the matter with reducing the effects of original sin insofar as a fallen race is capable of doing so; but there is everything wrong with thinking that we are our own gods and can do a better job than the Creator through fashioning a new humanity.

We must never forget the miseries imposed on the modern world by the atheistic, humanistic Marxist belief in a "Soviet New Man" to appear as soon as the proletarian ownership of the means of production in society brings about the end of capitalism and the magical appearance of a classless society.

The work of Mary Shelley's Dr Frankenstein has always been described as the creation of a *monster*—for good reason.

If we are really dissatisfied with humanity as is (and there is generally good reason to be dissatisfied, especially when we look into the mirror), the answer is indeed a "new creation." But that is not available in the laboratory. "If any man be in Christ, he is a new creature: old things are passed away; behold, all things are become new" (II Corinthians 5:17).

2. Muslims As Two-Faced

My legal specialty is international human rights law and I have defended with success religious liberties—in particular, the rights of Christians to evangelise—before the European Court of Human Rights: three consolidated cases against Greece (*Larissis et al.*) and *Bessarabian Orthodox Church v Moldova*. The Bessarabian Church case was regarded by a former President of the Court as the most important religious liberties case to come before the ECHR at that time (2001).

I therefore keep a close eye on cases involving Article 9 rights as guaranteed by the European Convention on Human Rights. Recently, a series of three lectures at Lincoln's Inn (English barristers must be members of an Inn—a medieval guild) provided updates on the case-law of the ECHR. The lectures were given by a former Judge of the Court, Egbert Myjer, a distinguished Dutch jurist. (*En passant,* I cannot resist mentioning the irrelevant fact that, though called to the English bar at Middle Temple, I soon joined Lincoln's Inn, owing to [1] its fine library, and [2] its superb wine cellar.)

In discussing recent cases under Article 9—the article protecting freedom of thought, conscience and religion—Judge Myjer focused on *Osmanoglu and Kocabas v. Switzerland* (Judgment of 10 January 2017).

In this case, Mr Osmanoglu, born in Turkey but brought up in Switzerland, returned as an adult to Turkey to deepen his knowledge of Islam. Whilst there, he married, and then returned to Switzerland. His pre-adolescent daughter was enrolled in a primary school requiring swimming lessons for all the children. The pupils were not separated by sex for these lessons, and Mr Osmanoglu objected on religious grounds. He lost at every level in the Swiss courts and, having "exhausted domestic remedies," took his complaint to the European Court of Human Rights.

The Court conceded that he had a genuine religious complaint, even though the Qur'an demands the separation of the sexes only post-puberty under such conditions. But it decided for the Swiss government—on the grounds of "the margin of appreciation" and "proportionality"—that, in light of Article 9's qualification that religious liberties can be limited where there are reasonable and legal grounds to do so for the public good. In the instant case, it was asking too much that the country provide separate swimming facilities or modify its educational curricula in primary schools to satisfy the concerns of hyper-devout Muslims.

As I contemplated this case, I immediately thought of the current, 18-month incarceration of an American evangelist in Turkey. In 2016, Pastor

Andrew Brunson, an American citizen who has lived in Turkey for 23 years, was arrested and charged with complicity against the Turkish regime by way of alleged support for a Muslim cleric in the United States, one Fethullah Gülen, who wants to overthrow the current, radically Islamic and oppressive Turkish presidency of Recep Erdogan. If convicted, Brunson could face a 35-year prison sentence or even life imprisonment for treason and terrorism. Without success, Pastor Brunson has testified that he has no connections whatever with Gülen or his outlawed Kurdistan Workers Party (PKK), has no political agenda whatever, and has been jailed simply for his Christian testimony. The charge against Brunson includes the specific claim that Turkey is a traditionally Muslim country and to encourage people to become Christians is effectively a treasonable activity—this, in spite of Turkey's ratification of the European Convention on Human Rights, guaranteeing religious freedom and right to change one's religion! (In discussing this matter with Judge Myjer, I was told that there are currently no less than 150 human rights cases pending against Turkey at the ECHR.)

Since no judgment has yet come down in the Brunson matter, domestic remedies have not been exhausted and the case cannot be taken to the ECHR. Pastor Brunson must cool his heels in jail, and he was recently transferred to a jail with a particularly bad reputation for the ill treatment of prisoners. Erdogan has obliquely suggested that the solution might be the U.S.'s willingness to extradite Gülen—as a kind of prisoner exchange.

Now what lesson can be derived from the two cases just described? In *Osmanoglu*, a Muslim living in an open, Western society attempts to use the freedoms guaranteed in that society to obtain special privileges for his religion, to the disadvantage of non-Muslims. In the Brunson matter, occurring in a Muslim country, even basic religious freedoms are curtailed with no regard for evidence or the rule of law.

The Muslim religion is two-faced. It wants religious liberty for itself and, given the opportunity, curtails it for everyone else. When Western thinkers endeavor to present Islam as just another example of fine religiosity, this truth deserves to be taken into account. In point of fact, Islam and human rights are simply incompatible.

Further reading on the subject: Montgomery, "A Non-Politically-Correct Remedy to Muslim Terrorist Immigration," in his *Defending the Gospel in Legal Style* (Bonn, Germany: Verlag für Kultur und Wissenschaft, 2017).

3. The Stereotypic Clergyman

If you love theatre, the place to go is Paris. There are literally hundreds of productions every week, owing to the French government's subsidizing of the arts. True, this is not an unqualified good, since it allows some perfectly dreadful pieces to be staged, but it does mean that there are always fine productions to see.

A recent example of the latter is a new staging of Georges Feydeau's *La Dame de Chez Maxim*. This boulevard comedy, first produced in 1899, has been cleverly updated by the director, Alain Sachs, who moves it back and forth from the 21st- to the 19th-century. The actors are superb comedians whose timing is impossible to fault. The play is one of Feydeau's best vaudeville productions, since he received considerable artistic inspiration at Maxim's famed restaurant—whilst managing to lose a great deal of money gambling there. (You can still eat at Maxim's, but the gambling is long gone.)

The plot hinges on mistaken identity: the wife of one character is assumed to be the wife of another character, and vice versa. Present through most of this is the local priest. Amidst the often hilarious confusion and *quiproquos*, the priest maintains an insipid, ingratiating smile in an obvious attempt to cater to the nobility around him. When something off-color is said, his facial expression simply changes to neutral—never a word of criticism, much less a frown that might offend.

If one were to do a survey of the clergy in films and contemporary drama, I venture to say that the result would be much the same: the clergy are portrayed as ineffective sycophants, going along with the status quo and hoping, at all costs, to be accepted by those of influence around them.

To be sure, this failing has been recognized in church circles. The liberal answer is to strive for innovation: new theologies, new political campaigns, new methods of social salvation. Ironically, this has turned out to be just another form of accommodation, since the endeavors to modernize have invariably been instances of political correctness. (The society approves of homosexual relationships and practices? Lo, the liberal clergyman creates new theology by jumping on the secular bandwagon.)

But surely the conservative clergy do not make such a mistake? Do they not oppose the contemporary mindset by their orthodox doctrinal positions?

In point of fact, the evangelicals, whilst in principle holding to the full authority of Scripture, make sure that they avoid those biblical teachings that particularly irritate the secular society. For example, they do not take a rigorous approach to divorce (permitted in Scripture only in cases of adultery and malicious desertion). Sermons are legalistic and moralistic, suggesting that salvation is principally a matter of works, not the cross of Christ. Worship styles are a painful imitation of cheap, secular, teenage music ("I'm so happy" sung umpteen times to a melody with only three or four notes). Meanwhile, Bach and Mendelssohn go out the window, as do the great chorales and hymns of the Reformation period with their solid biblical content.

And the conservatives have no trouble aping the administrative style of large corporations: high (often obscene) salaries for the top administrators, coupled with low regard and low salaries for the average parish pastor. The financing of missionary work is sacrificed for continually enlarging bureaucratic operations (more personnel at church headquarters, irrelevant conferences, insipid church publications that no one reads—since they present only the leadership's party line).

Add to this a worship of the church structures (the Synod, the seminaries, *et al.*) rather than a recognition that *the gospel*, not the bylaws, should be central to everything the church does.

And one notices not a few clergy lifting themselves up through grand titles ("presiding bishop," etc.) and a non-Protestant view of ordination (the "indelible stamp" that presumably gives the clergy the right to run everything their way). What a contrast with Walther's wonderful sermon title, "The Sheep Judge Their Shepherds." So much for congregational polity.

The clergy—and the church—must take on a prophetic, non-politically-correct stance. Sucking up to secularism has always, in the long run, made the church, its pastors, and its message irrelevant. Once the church becomes another Microsoft and its clergy quasi-presidents of the Moose lodge, any meaningful reason to join is destroyed. Biblical evangelism goes out the window. After all, Microsoft and the Moose will always be more fun than the church. Every pastor needs to see clearly that the purpose of the church and one's personal ministry is not "fun" but the cosmic task of saving souls, who, in turn—by way of the eternal gospel—constitute the only route to saving society.

Feydeau, inadvertently, by common grace—like much secular art and literature—opens the door to good teaching by bad example.

4. On Innovative Theologians

We begin by introducing you to a learned Sufi of the 13th century, Nasreddin Hodja, who has provided humorous and bizarre stories to generations within and beyond Turkey and the Islamic world.[1] Why? You will find out at the end of this short paper. For the moment, listen to two typical tales of the Hodja:

> One day, Hodja lost his donkey. While looking for it he was also rejoicing. When the people saw him, they couldn't figure out why he was so happy, and they wanted to find out the reason for this. So the Hodja told them:
> I'm happy because I wasn't riding the donkey when it got lost. If I had been I'd be lost now, too.[2]
> One hot summer's day the Hodja dismounted from his donkey and lay down to rest in the shade of a walnut-tree at the edge of an egg-plant patch. He began to think.
> 'How strange of God it is,' he mused, 'that he should cause a large fruit like the egg-plant to grow on the end of a tiny stalk, and a small fruit like a walnut to grow on an enormous tree. Surely it would have been better if walnuts grew on little stalks, and egg-plants on trees.'
> At that moment a walnut fell from the tree and hit the Hodja, small as it was, hard on the top of the head. The Hodja ruefully rubbed his skull.
> 'All is for the best in this world,' he thought. 'If egg-plants grew on trees, my head would have been smashed to pieces!'[3]

We note (the year is 2018) a messy theological situation at, of all places, the Moody Bible Institute. I have been a fan of Moody (Church and Institute) ever since becoming a Christian as an undergraduate at Cornell University. Evangelist Dwight Moody was the Billy Graham of his time (or, rather, Billy Graham was the Dwight Moody of our time). I presented one of my "Defending the Biblical Gospel" seminars at Moody Church and its just-retired, long-time senior pastor was Erwin Lutzer, my graduate student at the

---

[1] Efforts, more or less successful, have been made to identify a historical Hodja. The oldest manuscript of Nasreddin dates to 1571. The earlier tales have been expanded and added to across the centuries, both in Muslim and in western literatures.
[2] *202 Jokes of Nasreddin Hodja* (Istanbul, Turkey: Minyatür Yayinlari, n.d.), No. 71.
[3] *Tales of the Hodja,* ed. Charles Downing (London: Oxford University Press, 1964), p. 54.

Trinity Evangelical Divinity School and later recipient of an honorary doctorate at the Simon Greenleaf School of Law when I was its Dean. In short, theological trouble at Moody *really disturbs me*—and should be a deep concern to evangelicalism in general.

The issue is—ignoring the politics—whether to tolerate postmodern philosophies of truth that are uncomfortable with "truth as correspondence." Why a discomfort by evangelicals drinking at the founts of postmodernism? Because if the truth of Scripture entails comparing biblical statements with the facts of the world, then any apparent discrepancies must be resolved or inerrancy goes down the drain. Substituting a non-correspondence view of truth, in postmodern fashion, eliminates the awkward business of factually defending what the Bible asserts and presumably (if one jettisons all common sense) allows a "true" Scripture to contain factual errors.

In *Alice in Wonderland*, Humpty Dumpty pontificates: "When I use a word, it means just what I choose it to mean—neither more nor less." "The question is," responds Alice, "whether you can make words mean so many different things." Of course you can, but you will need to pay extra for doing so. And where truth is concerned, the additional payment to achieve effective communication and a satisfactory view of the world is far too excessive for theology—or society in general—to tolerate. Think of George Orwell's cacotopian novel, *1984,* where the totalitarian Party controls everything by making truth whatever the rulers wish to promote. Truth as correspondence is an underlying assumption of all attempts to understand the external world as it really is and what can be found in it.

Examples:

It is the case that an elephant is sleeping in the bedroom. False—why? We check, even under the bed and in the closets, and find no elephant.

It is the case that light has the properties of both wave and particle. True—why? Because solid physical experiments show this to be the nature of light.

The Genesis flood was an actual event. True, for Jesus, seen to be God incarnate by fulfilled prophecies and his resurrection from the dead, held it to be so (Mt 24, Lk 17).

I [Jesus] *am the truth* (Jn 14). "Personal—existential—truth," not correspondence? Hardly. Unless what the New Testament account says corresponds to what Jesus in fact said—and unless there was historically a Jesus who said it, any "relationship with him" is utterly chimerical, like believing in the Tooth Fairy.

And consider the following little computer program. (I prepared it on a Tandy Color Computer 3, but this simple Basic program can be compiled

4. On Innovative Theologians 215

and run on most computers—such as the Apple 2 or the Apple gs—with few if any modifications:

```
10 CLS
20 B=(6+8)>(3+4)
30 C=(9+2)<((SQR(4)+SQR(9))
40 IF B THEN PRINT "B IS TRUE, F
OR IT CORRESPONDS TO LOGICAL REA
LITY." ELSE PRINT "B IS FALSE, S
INCE IT DOES NOT CORRESPOND TO L
OGICAL REALITY."
50 IF C THEN PRINT "C IS TRUE, F
OR IT CORRESPONDS TO LOGICAL REA
LITY." ELSE PRINT "C IS FALSE, S
INCE IT DOES NOT CORRESPOND TO L
OGICAL REALITY."
```

If you compile and run this program, proposition B will turn out to be true and proposition C, false. Why? Because B is a correct mathematical assertion, corresponding to reality, whilst C is not.

Ah, you say, "But mathematics is a purely formal system, and we are concerned with *theological* truth.' Obvious response: It makes no difference whatsoever the *sphere* of the truth. Pigs is pigs. Truth is truth—whether is has to do with mathematics, geology, the location of the nearest McDonald's, or God's revelation to us. (See this author's *Tractatus Logico-Theologicus*, sec. 3.28 for a detailed discussion of the correspondence theory, followed by a refutation of postmodernist epistemology.)

The late Prof. Dr Robert Preus offered a list of proof texts to show that the correspondence approach to truth is assumed throughout Holy Scripture. He is eminently worth quoting here (from his essay in my *Crisis in Lutheran Theology* [3rd ed., 3 vols.; New Reformation Press/1517 Legacy, 2017], Vol. 2):

> It has been conjectured that the Bible does not operate with a correspondence theory of truth, and therefore it would be quite meaningless to claim that Scripture reveals truth in the sense of statements. This desperate position seems to lie behind the allegation (Abba) that "there is no biblical warrant for making inerrancy a corollary of inspiration." We should not waste much time answering such a conjecture. The purpose of declarative statements is to make words correspond to fact (except in the case of deliberate lies). Without the correspondence theory of truth there can be no such thing as *infonnative* language or *factual* meaning. The eighth commandment entirely breaks down unless predicated upon the correspondence theory of truth. So much for the logical impossibility of the above theory. As a matter of fact Scripture is replete with evidence that it operates throughout with the correspondence idea of truth (cf. Eph. 4:25; John 8:44-46; I Ki. 8:26; Gen. 42:16, 20; Zech. 8:16; Deut. 18:22; John 5:31 ff.; Ps. 119:163; I Ki. 22:16, 22 ff.;

Dan. 2:9; Prov. 14:25; I Tim. 1:15; Acts 24: 8, 11). It is utterly irrelevant when Brunner counters that Scripture teaches a *Wahrheit als Begegnung* (which is the title of one of his books). This is only to confuse truth (which pertains to statements) with certitude. So too is it irrelevant to point out that *aletheia* and *emeth* often refer to something more deep than mere correspondence to fact, that they refer to God and His faithfulness. God is true (faithful) simply because future events (fulfillment) *corresponds* to His word of promise, and His word is true for the same reason.

Of course, divine truth goes beyond mere correspondence. Any truth with a personal dimension (marriage, for example) transcends correspondence ("I love her," "she loves me"). However: *if there is no underlying correspondence with reality,* the relationship—the love—is just a fantasm, not something real and true, to say nothing of potentially or actually salvatory.

Leaving aside these miseries at the Moody Bible Institute, we move to the so-called "radical Lutheranism" of the late Gerhard Forde. Forde argued that the Reformation doctrines of grace alone and faith alone are enough to transform Christendom. He denied the sanctifying "Third Use of the Law" and effectively reduced all of Christian theology to the doctrine of justification. Interestingly, he did not hold to classic bibliology—the *de facto* inerrancy of Holy Scripture. Here is a typical quotation presenting his viewpoint:

> Inspiration in this view refers to the entire activity of the Spirit by which he dwells in the Church and attends the proclamation of the Word. In the older theory, inspiration is too static and finally too anemic. It seems to assume that the Spirit can convince of the truth only through a book without errors. The Spirit has a much more powerful means than this at his disposal, namely the "two-edged sword of the Word" through which he creates faith. The question, therefore, of whether or not there may be human errors of one sort or another in scripture is of no particular importance. Just as the pastor on Sunday morning may make errors of one sort or another in preaching and still preach the Word so also with scripture. . . .
>
> Often the question is asked of this method, "If you admit that there are errors in the little things how do you know that they didn't make errors in the big things as well, i.e., once you start admitting errors, where do you stop?" To this the only answer is . . . the faith born out of the law-gospel experience.[4]

---

[4] Gerhard Forde, "Law and Gospel As the Methodological Principle of Theology," in Theological Perspectives: A Discussion of Contemporary Issues in Lutheran Theology (Decorah, Iowa: Luther College Press [1962]), p. 65. Cf. Montgomery, *Crisis in*

4. On Innovative Theologians

Can one, then, simply believe the gospel without worrying about its grounding in real history? The great lay Roman Catholic theologian Jean Guitton provided the definitive answer in his description of his conversations with a certain Dr Couchoud who declared, "I believe everything in the Apostles' Creed except the phrase, 'He suffered *under Pontius Pilate.*'" In the true spirit of Gnosticism, Couchoud thought that he was thereby making Christianity invulnerable to historical criticism. "Invulnerable, perhaps," replied Guitton, "but totally evacuated of meaning. What you reject is the heart of Christianity: the mystery of a *real* incarnation."[5]

Why is the factual inerrancy of the Scriptures so important? Is it not really enough to "believe the gospel"—or, if one is a confessional Protestant, just believe what the Confessions say? Isn't Forde's "radical Lutheranism" sufficient? The obvious answer is that the gospel and the creeds are dependent on the factuality of the biblical record. There is no value in the Nicene Creed (or the Lutheran *Book of Concord*) if there was no historical Jesus or if we cannot rely on what he taught as set forth in the New Testament. If you think so, you might as well be Muslim (with a book full of historical errors concerning events of the Old and New Testament)—or Mormon (with no historical foundation for the claims in Joseph Smith's *Book of Mormon*)—or member of some other religion or cult. The truth of the gospel depends squarely on the truth of the New Testament record—and Jesus there put his divine *imprimatur* on the entire text of the Old Testament. *No reliable Bible, no reliable (or saving) Christ.*

So we return to the Hodja.

> Nasr Eddin even at a young age received the dignity of becoming a mullah—learned in theology and sacred law—and could thereafter instruct at a theological seminary.
>
> One morning, wanting to reach a book on a rather high shelf of the library, he climbed on a stack of Qur'ans. One of his colleagues was scandalized.
>
> By Allah, Nasr Eddin! You are really impudent. Aren't you afraid of soiling the holy scriptures?

Lutheran Theology (3d ed., 3 vols.; 1517: Irvine, CA: The Legacy Project/New Reformation Press, 2017), I, 95 ff.

[5] Jean Guitton, *Journal, 1952-1955* (Paris: Librairie Plon, 1959), pp. 19-21. Cf. Montgomery, *Where Is History Going?* (Minneapolis: Bethany, 1969), p. [7].

That was something I was previously afraid of, replied the Hodja. But now that I am a mullah, it's the Qur'an that should be afraid of me.[6]

Though the modern theologian does not any longer fear the Christian Scriptures, the Bible has every reason to fear the modern theologian. Scripture is at the theologian's mercy when he no longer believes in its inerrant, once-for-all revelatory character. It becomes (to use Luther's felicitous analogy) a "waxed nose" that can be twisted in any direction according to the interests of the innovating theologian. After all, if one cannot find a new theology there, how can one ever obtain one's doctorate or become famous as a thinker of new theological thoughts? If one believes that theological fame and fortune depend on innovation rather than on fidelity to the revealed Word, one is a danger not just to oneself but simultaneously to the entire Christian church.

---

[6] *Les Aventures de l'incomparable Nasr Eddin Hodja*, ed. Jean-Louis Maunoury (Paris: Editions J'ai Lu, 2008), p. 346 (my translation). Numerous collections of the tales are available in English and in French.

5. Racism in American Lutheranism

You will suppose that this short article deals with some form of anti-Semitism—or perhaps with indifference toward the plight of the American Indian. Not so. Your only recourse is to read on to understand the article's title.

Winston Churchill is currently receiving much attention and praise in Europe—even in France, remarkably, where most French consider the UK's departure from the European Union (BREXIT) as utter folly. On French movie screens this first week of January, 2018, appears Joe Wright's intelligent and thought-provoking Winstonian film, "*Les Heures sombres*" (English title: "Darkest Hour").

A columnist for *Le Figaro Magazine*, 5 January, in discussing Churchill's uphill struggle to declare war on Hitler's Germany, makes the important point that Churchill, in opposing a policy of appeasement (think of Chamberlain at Munich in 1938) had the English powers-that-be dead against him. Why? because of the powerful historical connections between the German and English aristocracies. In the 18th and 19th centuries, German blood filled the veins of the British monarchy. The Hanovers occupied the throne from 1714 until the death of Queen Victoria. Victoria's first language was German, and she regularly spoke it with her husband Prince Albert. The Windsors, who succeeded the Hanovers, were originally the Saxe-Coburg and Gotha family—name changed at the time of the First World War—quite understandably. (Reminds me of my teaching at Waterloo Lutheran University in Kitchener, Ontario, Canada; before WWI, Kitchener was "Berlin, Ontario.").

In the early 1930s, the English aristocracy saw opposition to Germany as favouring France. Churchill, however, recognised the appalling danger of a consolidated Europe under the Nazi boot, and *refused to allow historical and racial alignments to obscure the ideological horrors of Nazism. For him, ideas were thicker than blood.* And, by his unique and unforgettable rhetoric, he convinced the nation—a truly populist victory over an aristocratic oligarchy.

In American Lutheran theological circles, the German connection is primary, and has been so for well over a century. The American university was transformed in the 19th century on the model of the hierarchical German universities. Read Mark Twain's hilarious *A Tramp Abroad* (with Appendix: "The Awful German Language"), together with its two sequels; also: Alexander McCall Smith's **Professor Dr** von Igelfeld series (*Portuguese Irregular Verbs*, etc.). The Germany of the so-called Enlightenment was the crucible in which the 19th- and 20th-century higher criticism of the Old and New Testaments bubbled up: Graf, Kuenen, Wellhausen; Rudolf Bultmann and the post-Bultmannians.

So where do American Lutheran seminary graduates go for doctorates? Generally to universities where the theological faculties have swallowed German higher criticism hook, line, and sinker, and often ape the authoritarianism of the German professorial class (who brook little opposition to their presuppositions and methodologies).

After all, it took the Lutheran Church-Missouri Synod almost a hundred years to shift from the German language to English and to realize that one could not evangelise in a language the American populace did not speak or understand. The easy solution was, of course, not to evangelise but simply to conduct services for immigrant German-speakers—thereby sadly reducing the universal application of the Great Commission to an audience of Germanic extraction.

A further deleterious consequence of this perspective on the part of Lutheran theologians and theological students has been an avoidance of contact with English-speaking American conservative denominations. This ostrich-like behaviour has been excused by cries of "unionism" against the few in American Lutheranism who have benefitted from the work of other conservative denominations in defense of biblical reliability and classic, creedal Christianity. At the time of the modernist-fundamentalist controversy, Lutherans could, for example, have learned much from the work of B. B. Warfield, James Orr, and many others who contributed to the monographic series, *The Fundamentals*. And, today, how many Lutheran theologians are members of the Evangelical Theological Society, whose brief doctrinal statement requires commitment to the total truth of Scripture?

May we suggest that in Lutheran circles racism has prevailed over ideology? Seminarians and faculties of theology should be asking, not whether a Germanic atmosphere is more comfortable and maximally prestigious, but whether the theology available there is *compatible with Holy Scripture and the Confessions*. A generation ago, Kurt Marquart showed the sheer impossibility of reconciling even a mild literary higher criticism with classic Lutheranism. Today, we are told by American Lutheran seminarians that the underlying principles of liberal biblical criticism are accepted as a matter of course in even the more conservative theological seminaries.

The late, great Presbyterian theologian John Gerstner—whom I knew well—spent his career endeavoring to persuade his church body and their seminaries to refuse the higher criticism and remain true to the Reformed

Confessions. He did not succeed; the ecclesiastical bureaucrats and consumers of European liberal theology won the day. (See Jeffrey S. McDonald's recently published biography of Gerstner in the Princeton Theological Monograph Series, published by Pickwick/Wipf & Stock.)

I personally do not want to live to see the day when this tragedy repeats itself in those few contemporary conservative Lutheran bodies officially committed to an inerrant Scripture. There is a call for "21st-century Luthers." I would be satisfied with a 21st-century theological Churchill.

6. Do Christian Children lose Contact with Reality?

A recent research article has caused a flap in the media. Its title: "Judgments About Fact and Fiction by Children from Religious and Nonreligious Backgrounds" (*Cognitive Science* [2014], 1–30).

The three researchers—two from university Education departments and the third a social scientist—carried out two studies of five- and six-year-old children, providing them stories of three kinds: "realistic" stories with no miraculous or magical elements; religious stories involving divine intervention; and fantastic stories containing magical elements but no intervention by deity. The children consisted of four groups, one lacking religious background, the other three having such (children attending parochial school, children of churchgoing families, and children who both attended church with their families and were enrolled in parochial school). Result: the "secular" children, far more successfully than the children with religious background, recognized and classed as fiction characters in the religious and fantastical stories (categories two and three). All of the religious children were of Christian background and the researchers modeled their "divine intervention" and "fantastical" stories on biblical accounts of miraculous events.

The researchers do not anywhere in their study explicitly state their own worldviews—whether they are religious believers or unbelievers. But it is not difficult to determine their stance. In the Abstract of their paper, they use the following language: "The results suggest that exposure to religious ideas has a powerful impact on children's differentiation between *reality and fiction*" (our italics). Clearly, the authors see divine intervention and magic as *unreal*. The Keywords list following the Abstract include "Religion," "Fantasy," and "*Impossibility*"—the latter term surely indicating that for the authors some things accepted by the religious children fall into the category not just of unreality, but of impossibility. The only philosophical citation among the references at the end of their study is to David Hume's refutation of the miraculous in his *Enquiry concerning Human Understanding*—an argument thoroughly refuted today by many, even non-Christian, philosophers.[1] And consonant with their Humean perspective,

---

[1] E.g., John Earman, *Hume's Abject Failure: The Argument Against Miracles* (New York: Oxford University Press, 2000). Needless to say, the authors of the study we are discussing make no reference whatever to such treatments.

the authors declare (p. 13): "It is possible that religious teaching, especially exposure to miracle stories, leads children to *a more generic receptivity toward the impossible*, that is, a more wide-ranging acceptance that *the impossible can happen in defiance of ordinary causal regularities*" (italics ours).

Even more revealing of the researchers' biases is the following conclusion they present (p. 21): "Religious children are likely to see God as connected to their everyday lives and are prepared to view religious stories containing miracles as *similar to realistic stories*. They judge the characters in those stories to be real, and they frequently appeal to God in justifying those categorizations. Thus, for these children, God is part of the *real world* and stories that refer to God can properly be regarded as *realistic*" (italics ours). In the metaphysic of our authors, the theological and the fantastic are not to be classified as "reality."

How should such a study be evaluated? Some interesting perspectives do arise. For example, the authors point out that their results appear to put paid to the argument offered by some scholars that children are "hard-wired" to believe (J. L. Barrett: children are "born believers"; J. M. Bering: children possess a "belief instinct"). In the study we are discussing, the children from non-religious backgrounds did not demonstrate any such tendency to "believe" when presented with miraculous or fantastic material, whereas the children of religious background did.

To be sure, it is always possible that the non-religious children reacted as they did because of the conditioning they had received from their unbelieving parents—so as to repress an inherent desire to believe! But the only way to test that would be to have a control group uninfluenced by anyone—which is obviously impossible—and reminds one of the inutility of seeking answers from "feral children"—children allegedly brought up by animals (the Romulus/Remus scenario).

In general, however, the study we considering here does little more than confirm common sense—namely that children influenced by biblical narratives will consider such material factual and will apply that insight when they view other, analogous narratives; children without that background will not do so. (How very many "empirical" studies in the educational realm expend immense amounts of time, energy, and money demonstrating the obvious and even the tautological!)

The essential question to be faced is surely *whether the biblical material is in fact fictional or realistic*. The authors simply assume that miracles in the Bible do not reflect reality, and consequently that the children of non-religious background have a better grip on reality than do the religious children. In a contingent universe, the authors might be correct—but *the case for the facticity of biblical narrative and biblical events would have to be investigated to establish this—and this the authors have not done.* They simply engage in circular reasoning, based upon their own view of what constitutes and what does not constitute reality.

If God has revealed himself in history, as the Bible declares from cover to cover, then the children from Christian backgrounds have a tremendous advantage: their view of the world is far more consonant with reality than is a rationalistic metaphysic. The researchers dimly perceive this toward the end of their study. They say, *inter alia*: "Religious children have a broader conception of what can actually happen" (p. 22). "A religious upbringing overcomes children's pre-existing doubts about whether ordinarily impossible events can occur" (p. 23). "It is possible that religious instruction helps children to engage in . . . imaginative reflection with respect to impossible events" (p. 24). "Religious children approach unfamiliar, fantastical stories flexibly" (p. 25).

And why, we ask, shouldn't they? Ours is a mysterious universe in which God does—in reality—intervene. Fantasy is often a reflection of such—and writers such as George MacDonald, C. S. Lewis, and J. R. R. Tolkien have shown the connections between the world of Fairie and the factual Christian gospel.[2] The child who benefits from a biblical perspective thus has a properly "flexible" take on our physical universe, governed by relativity, where anything can theoretically happen; on the wondrous range of fantasy literature, where magic can reflect the supernatural realm behind our prosaic, daily existence; and on the most important of all factual truths that God has loved a fallen race so much that he miraculously enters it to save us from narrow self-centeredness and closed-minded rationalisms.

As I have written elsewhere in analyzing the realm of the supernatural: "If we are members of the secular scientific community, we should do all that we can to counter the mind-set of scientistic prejudice and strive for greater openness in an Einsteinian universe where no possibility can be ruled out *a priori*. With Gardner Murphy we should recognize that 'in science we are not unused to discoveries of considerable magnitude; and if, after due scrutiny facts become compulsory, men of science must be ready to enlarge their scheme of the universe so as to admit them.' In the aphoristic words of Charles Robert Richet, recipient of the Nobel prize in psychology and medicine (1913): 'Je ne dirai pas que cela est possible; je dis

---

[2] See John Warwick Montgomery (ed.), *Myth, Allegory, and Gospel* (Minneapolis: Bethany, 1974).

seulement que c'est vrai' [I shall not say that something is *possible*; I say merely that it is *true*]."³

Perhaps the genuine lessons of the study we have been analyzing are the very opposite of those implied by its authors. The valid conclusions would appear to be: (1) Enroll your child in parochial school and give him or her the benefits of a churchgoing family. (2) If parochial school is not practicable, at least offer him or her a consistent church experience. (3) In the child's religious education, stress the factual nature of everything in Scripture, particularly its miracles, and provide a strong apologetic to back this up. (4) In the secular schools—and this in no way violates the separation of church and state—raise questions of facticity where religious literature and fantasy are taught, thereby introducing the child to the open universe in which we all live.

---

[3] John Warwick Montgomery, *Principalities and Powers: The World of the Occult* (Minneapolis: Bethany, 1973), p. 46 (2d ed.; Minneapolis: Dimension Books, 1975), p. 42.

7. Those Who Have Not Heard the Gospel: A Construct

> ["T]he Chinese heathen refused to let her inject him because if Josef had also been bitten, he wanted Josef to have the serum: If Josef was allowed to live, he reasoned, he could save many children's lives, and he was only a farmer who didn't even have a farm anymore." ...
> 'Josef said he was so frightened he didn't even consider rejecting the offer. ... He asked the nurse to inquire whether the Chinese heathen had heard of Jesus. She didn't even have time to pose the question. ... He died within seconds."
> "So the man is burning in hell now?"
> "According to Josef's understanding of the Bible, yes. However, Josef has renounced religion now."
> "So that was the reason he lost his faith and left the country?"
> "That was what he told me."
> — Jo Nesbø, *The Redeemer*, trans. (from the Norwegian) by Don Bartlett (New York: Vintage, 2014), p. 140-41.

What about those millions of people who have never heard the name of Christ—or those who, owing to prejudicial backgrounds or upbringing, such as many in the Jewish tradition—have never been able to understand or appreciate the gospel message? As in the above narrative, not a few unbelievers and former believers have used the argument that they are damned as sufficient ground to reject the truth of Christian faith as such.

The standard Roman Catholic solution to the problem—shared by most liberal Christians—is that if heathens act in accord with the best light they possess and/or lead honest, moral lives, they shall be saved even without knowledge or acceptance of Christ.[1] This viewpoint, however, must surely be rejected on clear biblical grounds: no one is saved by good works (Romans 3; Ephesians 2:8-9), and faith in Christ, the only Redeemer, is the sole route to heaven (John 14:6; Acts 4:12).

So are we compelled to say that those who have not heard the gospel message or have been unable to understand it are damned? This seems in

---

[1] "Those who, through no fault of their own, do not know the Gospel of Christ or his Church, but who nevertheless seek God with a sincere heart, and, moved by grace, try in their actions to do his will as they know it through the dictates of their conscience—those too may achieve eternal salvation" (*Catechism of the Catholic Church* [1992], # 847).

direct tension with the biblical affirmations that God "wants all people to be saved and to come to a knowledge of the truth" (I Timothy 2:4) and that only refusal to accept Christ is the source of eternal loss (Matthew 23;37; Luke 13;34). Is there any way to reconcile these passages of Holy Writ with those cited above?

Constructs are employed in science, law, and other fields as a means of offering explanations when the data do not themselves provide solutions. The test of a good construct is that it best explains recalcitrant data. The construct never has the force of the original data; its value lies solely in its explanatory value.[2] Let us offer a construct in the matter at hand.

Suppose that at the moment of death—neither before nor after—but at the dividing line between the two, the individual who has never had an opportunity to meet Christ or meaningfully hear and understand his gospel were to be confronted by the Savior. At that point Christ and his way of salvation would need to be accepted or rejected; no neutrality would be possible.

Observe: such a decision-situation would be neither a "second chance" (since there had never been a first chance) nor a salvation-after-death contrary to Hebrews 9:27, for the meeting with Christ by grace alone (note well) would occur on the margin between this life and the next.

As a literary parallel, one thinks of the story by Ambrose Bierce of the Civil War soldier whose highly detailed but imagined reunion with his wife occurs in the split-second of his death by hanging.

In any event, the construct here is offered for apologetics purposes—to assist in dealing with those who would reject the faith because of frequently-heard claims of the damnation of the heathen that almost certainly impugn God's justice and love. The proffered construct must never be elevated to the level of doctrine, since it is not expressly taught in the Scriptures.

This means that such a construct cannot be used as an excuse for lessening the missionary effort: since Scripture is silent on the ultimate fate of those who have not heard (as it likewise is in the case of unbaptized infants), the church must go on the assumption that, just as baptism is to be carried out as responsibly as possible, so also missionary efforts are to be

---

[2] Cf. Montgomery, "The Theologian's Craft: A Discussion of Theory Formation and Theory Testing in Theology," in his *Suicide or Christian Theology* (Minneapolis: Bethany, 1970), pp. 267–313; and in his *Christ As Centre and Circumference* (Bonn, Germany: Verlag für Kultur und Wissenschaft. 2012), pp. 40–77.

7. Those Who Have Not Heard the Gospel: A Construct

maximized—thereby fulfilling the Great Commission to go baptizing all nations and preaching the gospel to every creature.[3]

In sum: the construct we have been suggesting (1) appears not to contradict any biblical affirmations and (2) offers an explanation that conjoins with the overall biblical picture of a God of infinite love who would not condemn his creatures because of accidents of time or place but only because of a conscious rejection of the salvation he has provided in Christ.[4] That being the case, the construct presented here may be of utility as we present God's truth to a secular and doubting age.

---

[3] Matthew 28:19; Romans 10:14.
[4] Cf. Montgomery, "The Freewill Issue in Theological Perspective," in his *Christ As Centre and Circumference* (op. cit.), pp. 270–85.

8. Freedom of Expression and Respect for Beliefs in France

An important colloquy took place on February 17, 2015 at the headquarters and under the sponsorship of the Paris bar in the wake of the Charlie Hebdo murders by Islamic terrorists a month before. Titled, "Liberté d'expression et respect des croyances," the conference featured two major speakers, Michel de Salvia, speaking on the case law of the European Court of Human Rights, and Jean-Yves Dupeux, discussing relevant French case law. The issue was the tension between freedom of speech and the protection of religious belief in a democratic society.

Athough that tension is certainly present in all western societies, it is particularly acute in France, where the Revolution against the Old Regime eliminated blasphemy law but where, in 1905, the separation of church and state was achieved—not, as in the United States, to protect religions from government interference, but to reduce as much as possible the influence of the church in French public life.

Indeed, the history of the tension between free speech and religious belief in France has created a checkered legal scene, making one think of the radical extremes of French politics in general across the centuries: from the autocracy of the Ancien Régime to the radicalism of the Revolution (in which the second-generation revolutionaries guillotined the first generation revolutionaries) to the autocracy of Napoleon; from the chaos of the Days of May, 1968, to the return of Charles de Gaulle to even greater central power thereafter. All of which confirms the aphorism of the sixteenth-century Protestant Reformer Martin Luther that the history of a fallen face is "the history of a drunk, reeling from one wall to the other."

The immediate aftermath of the Charlie Hebdo atrocities on 7 January was a universal outcry against the terrorists who had killed the editors and cartoonists of the satirical journal for their depictions of Muhammad and swipes at Islam. I was myself in Paris at the time and could hardly make my train connections because of the massive street demonstrations. Virtually everyone identified with the magazine; the cry "Je suis Charlie" was (and is) present almost everywhere in the country.

There were, of course, dissenters—some claiming that the satires in *Charlie Hebdo* had gone beyond the limits of good taste (which, as a matter of fact, they had—but that was consistent with a long tradition of nasty French satire in print and in film). Those dissenters found themselves in deep trouble, not a few of them receiving stiff fines and even prison sentences for "inciting to terrorism." Thus, a black comedian, Dieudonné, who has long been a thorn-in-the-flesh to the politically-correct establishment, and has been regarded as an anti-Semite, was indicted for putting on his Facebook page "Je me sens Charlie Coulibaly" (Coulibaly being one of the terrorists); for this "apology for terrorism" he was given a two-month suspended sentence, and could have received a sentence of seven years imprisonment and a fine of €100,000. (Cf Alexander Stille, "Why French Law Treats Dieudonné and Charlie Hebdo Differently," *New Yorker*, January 15, 2015.)

One thinks of other, parallel instances of criminal and civil actions in France against those critiquing religious positions. Most striking is the legal history of former femme fatale Brigitte Bardot's verbal attacks on Islam for its ritual slaughters of sheep. She has been fined five times, the latest conviction requiring her to pay €15,000, for inciting racial hatred against Muslims. In 2005, Jean-Marie Le Pen, former head of the conservative Front National political party, having made strongly negative statements about the consequences of Muslim immigration in comments to the national newspaper *Le Monde*, was convicted of inciting racial hatred.

What is the legal basis of such convictions? Press freedoms are guaranteed by the 29 July 1881 Press Law; section 14 of this comprehensive act, however, condemns hate speech—incitement to racial discrimination, hatred, or violence on the basis of one's origin or membership (or nonmembership) in an ethic, national, racial, or religious group. The Code Pénal, 625-7, R.624-3 and R.624-4, also makes it an offense to engage in such defamatory or injurious conduct via private communication.

In November, 2014, a French counterterrorism law was passed by Parlement. Its effect is to move "incitement" and "defence of terrorism" from the Press Law to the Criminal Code. Penalties are a five-year maximum prison sentence (seven years if posting online is involved) and €45,000 (€100,000 if there is online posting).

Significantly, in an unsuccessful attempt in France to ban the Martin Scorsese film, "The Last Temptation of Christ" (1988), the French court nonetheless declared that "respect for beliefs" was legally on the very same level as "freedom of expression."

The difficulty, as M. Dupeux rightly pointed out, is that there is no proper definition of such terms as "provocation" or "defamation" or "injury" in these areas, so the result is that the French judge is left to decisions based on little more than naked subjectivity.

The European Court of Human Rights has, in general, been pro-government in its handling of freedom of expression cases that involve a religious

8. Freedom of Expression and Respect for Beliefs in France   233

dimension. The court has stated on several occasions, even when it has sided with the applicant, that it cannot rely upon a single, common European moral or religious position, owing to the pluralism and the variation of belief amongst the European States-Parties to the Convention (see, for example, *Otto-Preminger-Institut v Austria I* [application 13470/87; judgment 20 September 1994], para 50). The Strasbourg court therefore generally relies on an individual nation's "margin of appreciation" to determine what in fact constitutes incitement to religious hatred, apology for terrorism, etc. What would constitute a genuine offence in one European country would not necessarily be so categorised in another.

The case of *Leroy v France* (application no 36109/03; judgment of October 2, 2008) is illustrative of the manner in which the ECHR generally exempts from the protection of freedom of expression law those prosecuted for hate speech. In that case, the court considered that the cartoonist who published a drawing showing the attacks on the Twin Towers on September 11, 2001, with the caption, "We all dreamt about it ... Hamas did it," was rightly condemned for complicity in defence of terrorism. The court stated: "In conclusion, the domestic court could reasonably consider that the interference with the applicant's exercise of his right to freedom of expression was necessary in a democratic society within the meaning of Article 10 of the Convention. There was therefore no violation of this provision."

The contrast with the Anglo-American common-law tradition could hardly be greater. The US Supreme Court has repeatedly refused to condemn hate speech as such. It has even allowed provocative action in situations where great offence was given to a given religious group—the classic example being the pro-Nazi march in Skokie, Illinois—a predominately Jewish community in the Chicago area (see *National Socialist Party of America v Village of Skokie* [432 U.S. 43 (1977)]). Only if the hate speech or action is on the level of "crying 'fire' in a crowded theatre"—productive of riot or affray—will freedom of speech or action be prohibited. American law has regarded First Amendment freedoms as too important to be curtailed in a democratic society unless (and it is very rarely the case) that the provable consequences are so severe as to outweigh the exercise of those freedoms.

To be sure, America, unlike Europe, has never suffered the horrors of bombings, the Nazi regime or the death camps, but the central jurisprudential question remains: How important is freedom of expression in general and freedom to assert and to critique religious positions in particular? The American view is that such freedoms are of paramount significance and that any compromise of those freedoms can only reduce genuine democracy and lead to an abridgment of human rights. Freedom of expression is a tender plant: it must be protected against every effort to limit it, whatever the best intentions of those desiring to do so.

A mature society must tolerate dissenting opinions—even those of an obnoxious character. If one's cherished beliefs are attacked and ridiculed, in an open society one has the facilities to respond. The American society is often regarded by Europeans as childish and immature. But in regard to "hate speech," it is Europe (and the French) who display gross immaturity by their efforts to protect their citizenry—regarded as children—from insult and corresponding emotional distress. It was Voltaire (surely French) who declared: "I do not agree with what you say, but I shall defend to the death your right to say it." Would that contemporary French law paid closer attention to that *bon mot*.

9. Terrorism and Revolution: Are They Ever Justified?

Ours is a messy world. Ethical decisions are often very difficult, particularly for Christians who want to follow biblical mandates and avoid violating revealed law. Classic illustration: Corrie ten Boom's "hiding place" scenario: Nazis at the door during the occupation of the Netherlands in World War II; does she prevaricate to save from the concentration camp Jews concealed in her house? She does, thereby lying—a sin (John 8:44). Some theologians, such as Norman Geisler solve the ethicals problem by arguing that one only sins if one chooses to obey the less important command (here, refusing to lie) rather than the more important biblical teaching (regard for one's neighbor—Matt. 22:37; Luke 10:27). That ethical theory, known as hierarchialism, is favoured by Roman Catholic casuists (Geisler, though an evangelical, took his doctorate in philosophy at a Roman Catholic institution), but also by followers of John Wesley—both theological viewpoints maintaining that true holiness and ethical perfection are achievable in this life.

Reformation theology, however, takes with utter seriousness the scriptural principle that before God no sin is less important than another (James 2:10). *Any* sin is sufficient for divine condemnation. In this sinful world, one must often choose between evils, endeavoring to go with the lesser-of-evils. And it is essential to see that a lesser evil will always remain an evil, requiring us to admit our sinful condition and to seek forgiveness. As Luther well put it, the believer must go to the Cross daily.

But what about revolution against unjust government? We are told in the Bible that God hates injustice (the prophetic teachings of the Old and New Testaments), but also that we are to be "subject to the governing authorities, for there is no authority except that which God has established" (Romans 13). Most American Christians believe that the 18th-century American Revolution was justified on the grounds that a government that would engage in taxation without representation could subsequently even force on everyone a single national church. On the other hand, loyalists argued that such slippery-slope reasoning was insufficient, and future Parliaments could reverse existing legislation.

The French Revolution of 1789 has been shown by impressive modern scholarship to have produced dreadful consequences in many spheres of life, from the economic to the religious (it marked the end of Christianity's dominance of French culture). The 20th-century Russian Revolution led to horrors from which Europe is still recovering. The trouble with most revolutions is that one cannot readily predict whether the new government (and no one but Robinson Crusoe lives government-less) will be worse than the existing state of affairs.

As for terrorism, a recent Italian-French film (*Dopo la guerra*—"After the War") forces serious ethical thinking on the issue. Sadly, the film will probably not reach the United States, since it boasts no celebrated actors and the dialogue is entirely in French and Italian, with subtitling only in those languages.

The film is a fictionalized account based closely on the activities of student activists and the Communist Red Brigades in Italy during the first decade of the present century. In 2002, Marco Biagi, an Italian university economist and consultant to the government was gunned down for his support of changes in labor legislation that were believed by many on the left to be hurtful to the working classes. (This theme makes the film particularly contemporaneous in Europe, since at the moment—Spring, 2012—the French labor unions are planning massive strikes to force the Macron government to give up badly-needed revisions of the *Code de Travail*—the existing labor legislation that makes it almost impossible to fire incompetent workers and grants unjustifiable privileges to certain classes of workers, such as railway employees.)

The plot focuses on one Mario (note the indirect reference to the actual victim), who is the leader of a 2002 terrorist cell that assassinates a Bologna university professor and government consultant. In the film, the victim is also a judge, and the motivation for his execution includes the fact that he has sentenced members of the cell to prison terms. Mario, who may himself have been the assailant, escapes to France, taking his young daughter Viola with him. He thus intends to benefit from President Mitterand's policy (bad political relations existing between Italy and France at the time) not to allow the extradition of politically-motivated terrorists from France to Italy. In this he is successful and lives in France with his daughter for the ensuing years.

Two decades later, with a change in the political climate, the Mitterand policy is reversed, and the Italian government—owing to an interview Mario unwisely gives to a French journalist in which he argues that the Italy should grant amnesty to the Red Brigades' extremists—now seeks Marco's extradition. That would mean immediate incarceration, since by Italian law Marco is an escaped felon. So Marco obtains fake passports for himself and his daughter, now 16, to settle in Nicaragua. Viola had not wanted to leave Italy two decades earlier, and she cannot stomach the thought of another displacement. While Marco and Viola are driving away from Bologna, Viola throws their passports out of the car window. Marco brakes, leaves the car, and searches for the passports in the brush at the side of the highway. He finds them, but in returning to the car does not see another car coming and is killed instantly. In the final scene of the film, the plane carrying Viola, accompanied with her father's casket, lands at the Bologna airport, where her grandmother and other relatives are waiting for her.

The lesson of the film is clear: terrorism wreaks a dreadful toll also on those close to the terrorist. The life of Marco's mother, though having no political interests, is poisoned by the radicalism of her children: her other son has been killed by the police, and she has told Marco on his leaving Italy to stay in France even though she will never see him again, since "at least you will be alive." A distinguished family member who is an Italian judge and whose dream it was to become a chief prosecutor had to withdraw his candidacy owing to conflict of interest. Marco's daughter (note her name: Viola—violated?) had a promising life before her in gymnastics—a life destroyed by being taken away to France. Decades later, when Marco is ready to leave France for Nicaragua, the only language she speaks is French and she is desperate not to be uprooted again.

In Marco's interview, he is asked if he feels sorry for those left behind when the victim is killed. His answer: "There are innocent victims in every war." He is also entirely unaware of—or unmoved by—the consequences of his actions to the victims in his own family and immediate circle. To be sure, there are reasons for terrorism; Marco tells us that when his brother was killed, the brother had surrendered with his hands in the air, but the police shot him anyway and left his body in the street all night, "like a dog." But the lesser-of-evils calculus surely must also include that fact that in a democratic society there will be legal ways of dealing with corruption and bad government policies; only when democracy exists as a mere powerless sham can there be an argument for illegal violence (the plots to kill Hitler come to mind).

Among the neglected factors on the side of Romans 13—grounds for regarding terrorism and most revolutions as the greater of evils—is surely the devastating effects of such activities on those close to the terrorists and the revolutionaries themselves. Violence, like a stone thrown into the water, creates concentric circles of misery that spread far beyond the initial act.

10. Populism, Revolution and the Radical Reformation

If you are one of the (very rare) Americans who keep an eye on what is occurring elsewhere in the world, you will have read about the current "Yellow Vest" (*gilets jaunes*) protests in France. Since November, 2018, large numbers of protesters have repeatedly assembled in Paris and other major cities in general opposition to the status quo. The origin of the still unorganized, in large part spontaneous protests was a not unreasonable increase in fuel prices. Though the price increases occurred because of the oil market in the Gulf states, not owing the French economy at all, there was a considerable outcry over the fact that the French government did not reduce fuel taxes to lower the burden on the consumer (especially those dependent on driving to work). Soon the protests grew and motley bands of people with a diversity of grievances joined in, including thugs. As a consequence, there have been instances of property damage and looting—nothing on the scale of the 1968 student-led riots, finally brought under control by President de Gaulle, but enough to produce public concern and governmental response. Police action has been stepped up and President Macron has called for greater opportunities for the average Frenchman to air grievances and suggest changes through public meetings throughout the country.

What can be said of this? The problem is surely exacerbated by the right-to-strike clause in the French Constitution of 1946 (a clause reflecting the heritage of the French Revolution). But the issue with the Yellow Vests is not legal strikes. It is the illegal destruction of property and the idea that needed social change is achievable by going to the streets, screaming at the police, and pushing the forces of order to use batons and tear gas. Democracy, not just in France but in the civilized world in general, has structures in place for change to occur through civilized discussion and vote.

To be sure, the western world is suffering at the moment from a rise of populism, entailing general distrust of establishment in whatever form it manifests itself. The election of Donald Trump in the U.S. and the U.K.'s "Brexit" (Britain's leaving the European Union) are certainly reflections of a powerful anti-authoritarian spirit.

A little book (really a tractate of some 80 pages) recently published in France connects the "Yellow Vest" phenomenon with the Peasants' revolts of Luther's time: *La guerre des pauvres* ["The War of the Poor"] (Actes Sud,

2019), by Eric Vuillard, a popular author and journalist. The book centers historically on a positive treatment of the life and work of 16th-century radical reformer Thomas Müntzer and a justification of the kind of egalitarian society he strove (unsuccessfully) to create.

Müntzer obtained a respectable classical and theological education (master's degree in philosophy and bachelor's degree in biblical studies, both from the University of Frankfurt an der Oder) and, as a Roman Catholic priest, converted to Protestantism through the influence of Luther. He studied briefly at Wittenberg and had contact with Karlstadt and with Luther himself. Müntzer's life entailed wide and chaotic travels, largely in the German lands and with the Prague of the Hussites. He exchanged a number of letters with Luther (some of these have unfortunately been lost). From Müntzer's correspondence and writings, it is clear that he moved steadily to the left. In 1520, he can end a letter to Luther thusly: "Thomas Müntzer, whom you brought to birth by the gospel." But, just a few years later, in his *Sermon before the Princes,* Müntzer calls Luther "Brother Fatted Pig and Brother Soft Life" after Luther, not having personally undergone the social sufferings of the poor, condemned peasant radicalism. Luther finally penned a tract condemning Müntzer's theology in no uncertain terms: *A Terrible History and Judgement of God on Thomas Müntzer* (1525—after Müntzer's execution and death following the disastrous defeat of the Thuringian insurgents near Frankenhausen).[1]

What was Müntzer's position and why did he fall out with Luther?

Early in his travels, Müntzer became fascinated with the mystical theology of Johannes Tauler. From there, it was not a large step to the theology of *Schwärmerei*—the belief that the true source of God's revelation of his will lay not in Scripture but in inner experience. In arriving at that view, Müntzer was certainly influenced by the so-called Zwickau prophets (Nikolaus Storch, *et al.*) with whom he had personal contact. Müntzer declared: "If someone had never had sight or sound of the Bible at any time in his life, he could still hold the one true Christian faith because of the true teaching of the spirit, just like all those who composed the holy Scripture without any books at all." To which Luther, who had discovered the gospel by way of Holy Scripture *alone,* commented that he would not listen to Müntzer even if he had swallowed the Holy Ghost, "feathers and all."[2]

Müntzer's subjectivism was accompanied, quite logically, with a belief in dreams and visions. He offered himself to princes as a second Daniel, capable of interpreting their dreams in line with the "knowledge of God."

---

[1] WA, 18, 362–74.
[2] WA, 17, 1, 361–62.

10. Populism, Revolution and the Radical Reformation 241

And his personal mysticism led to an apocalyptic belief that the end times were at hand and the Peasant uprisings would usher in God's kingdom, of which he, Müntzer, was the prophet. One of the foremost scholarly specialists on Müntzer refers to his position as an "amorphous apocalyptic vision."[3]

Most of the poor peasants could not even read; Müntzer's replacement of the Bible by inner illumination doubtless had them in mind. Luther's solution was to translate the Scriptures into the vernacular—so that "every ploughboy could read God's word"—and to persuade civil government (the princes) to establish Christian schools.[4] Müntzer's answer was social leveling—absolute egalitarianism without the need for Scripture—and revolution against existing authority, both civil and ecclesiastical.

Fascinatingly (and we are not sure that Vuillard adequately appreciates the fact), Müntzer was the one Protestant Reformer lauded by the Marxists. During the cold-war days of East Germany (the misnamed DDR, the "German Democratic Republic"), when I took tours to Luther and Bach sites there, the state grudgingly acknowledged Luther, but made a hero of Müntzer. The reason: he promoted "proletarian revolution," and could therefore be regarded as a proto-Marxist.

In a sense, they had a point. When you allow the "inner spirit" to control, with no external, divine check upon it, anything is possible. You can ultimately get rid of God himself if you don't sense his presence (note the transmutation of Kierkegaard's Christian existentialism in the atheistic thought of Heidegger and Sartre). One needs to take a lesson from the sobering fact that the second generation of 18th-century French revolutionaries guillotined the first generation of revolutionaries.

What can be learned from all this? Several very important lessons for our day.

First, *theologically*. Luther was surely right that there must be an objective revelation by which to "test the spirits" (I John 4:1). So-called "natural revelation"—God's presence in nature—will never be specific enough or salvatory to give a fallen world what it needs. And if "special revelation"—God's verbal message to mankind is not *extra nos* ("outside of us"), it will be subject to all the vagaries of individual and societal human opinion. The

---

[3] Tom Scott, *Freiburg and the Breisgau: Town-Country Relations in the Age of the Reformation and Peasants' War* (1986); see also Scott's *Thomas Müntzer: Theology and Revolution in the German Reformation* (1989). Cf. Michael G. Baylor (ed.), *The Radical Reformation* (1991); and Peter Matheson (ed.), *The Collected Works of Thomas Müntzer* (1988).

[4] Cf. Montgomery, *In Defense of Martin Luther* (new ed.; New Reformation Press/1517: The Legacy Project, 2019).

classic Reformers, Lutheran and Calvinist, insisted that the Bible alone provided that special and final word of God. They were well aware that the absence of *sola Scriptura* in the Roman Church meant that the traditions of a sinful, fallen humanity would inevitably corrupt Scripture itself through wrongheaded biblical interpretation and foreign ideas entirely capable of overwhelming the scriptural text.[5]

Luther was also right in condemning the extremes of the Peasants' revolts (though, as usual, his language could have been tempered). Luther saw clearly that there is something far worse than bad government, namely, anarchy—where government as such disappears and nothing is left but will-to-power and might-makes-right. Luther took Romans 13 seriously, as must every Bible-believing Christian. Revolution can be justified only as a lesser-of-evils. It is sometimes necessary in a sinful, fallen world. But a lesser-of-evils never becomes a positive good. It is still an evil.[6]

Second, *culturally*. The American Founding Fathers were well aware of the dangers of uncontrolled populism. They had read and appreciated Plato's criticism of pure democracy as close to anarchy. This is why the American constitutional system is replete with checks and balances—to prevent any one branch of government from overwhelming the others. And fear of populism is the reason for the strange Electoral College, admittedly not of much value today, but originally designed to prevent horrible results as a result of popular idiocy corrupting presidential elections. Democracy needs to be *limited*. This is why we elect representatives to our legislatures. Our congressmen and their State equivalents are supposed to have knowledge and values so that their decisions will better represent the responsible will of the people than a simple counting of the noses of the population at large.

The Yellow Vests in France would accomplish far more if they got off the streets and focused on electing better government and supporting the sane politicians who do in fact work harder than we realize for the public weal. Americans would do far better if they stopped griping about the state of the Republican and Democratic parties and focused on encouraging the best young people to get into politics and the best lawyers to become judges. And all of us would do exceedingly better if we paid attention to such biblical passages as Romans 13 and the words of the great theologians such as Martin Luther who tell us rightly that we cannot save ourselves and that the entire gospel is *extra nos*.

---

[5] Cf. Regin Prenter, *Spiritus Creator* (1946 [in Danish], 1953 [English abridged ed]).

[6] See Montgomery's essays in *Christians in the Public Square* (Canadian Institute for Law, Theology and Public Policy, 1996).

Index of Names

Abraham 85, 86
Allis, O. T. 134
Ames, Dean 113
Ames, James Barr 113
Amis, K. 133
Andreae, Johann Valentin 14,
    145, 146, 147, 148, 149, 150, 151,
    152, 153, 154, 155, 156, 157, 158,
    159, 160, 161, 163, 165
Andrew, A. A. 206
Anselm of Canterbury 33, 36
Aquinas, Thomas 57
Aratus 25
Arndt, John 163, 164, 165, 166
Asheim, Lester 192
Atkin, Lord 115, 116
Augustine, St. 33, 57, 106, 121,
    130, 187
Aulén, Gustaf 59
Austin, John 107, 117
Ayer, A. J. 107
Babb, James T. 168
Babbage, Charles 31
Bach, J. S. 212, 241
Bailey, F. Lee 105
Bardot, Brigitte 232
Baring-Gould, S. 133
Barrett, J. L. 224
Barth, Karl 19, 20
Beals, Ralph A. 177
Beaver, Pierce 192
Becker, Carl 133
Bellers, Fettiplace 58
Bengel, J. A. 132
Bentham, Jeremy 107, 117
Benzmüller, Christoph 36
Bering, J. M. 224

Berkhof, L. 134
Bernard of Chartres 178
Bernoulli 44
Berry, G. R. 134
Besold, Christoph 150, 151, 158
Beyleveld, Deryck 116
Biagi, Marco 236, 237
Bibfeldt, Franz 87
Biederwolf, W. E. 125
Bierce, Ambrose 228
Biesterfeld, Wolfgang 147
Bittinger, Marvin L. 34
Black, Max 35
Blackstone, W. E. 136
Blaiklock, E. M. 24
Boettner, L. 135
Böhme, Jakob 132, 153
Böhmen, Adam Friedrich 164
Borst, Otto 152, 153
Bratke, E. 125
Brecht, Martin 146, 149, 151,
    152, 153, 156, 159
Bromiley, Geoffrey W. 13
Brown, B. H. 45
Brown, W. Adams 128
Brownsword, Roger 116
Bruce, F. F. 25
Bruell, Steven C. 65, 66
Bruno, Giordano 148
Bruns, Peter 140
Brunson, Andrew 210
Bultmann, Rudolf 20, 21, 87, 90,
    220
Burke, Redmond A. 170
Butler, Pierce 176, 177
Caesar 21, 74
Caiaphas 87

Calvin, John 131
Carroll, Lewis 87
Case, S. J. 135
Cathari 131
Catherine the Great 45
Catullus 74
Cephas 78
Cerinthus 130
Cesar Augustus 87
Chafer, L. S. 136
Charles, R. H. 126, 134
Churchill, Winston 219
Clark, H. B. 120
Cleanthes 25
Cobb, J. B. (Jr.) 135
Cohn, N. 131
Coleridge, Samuel 105
Comyns, Lord Ch. B. 114
Conzelmann, Hans 87
Cooper, Duff 119
Copeland, Jack 29
Corbin, Henry 159
Corredi, H. 137
Couchoud 217
Craig, William Lane ... 57, 58, 59, 61
Craven, E. R. 136
Crawley, J. Winston 66
Crerar, John 169
Crooks, Mark 13, 139, 142
Culver, R. D. 125, 136, 137
Daniélou, J. 129
Darby, J. N 132
Davenport, John 132
Davies, ... 139
Dawson, John W. (Jr.) 36
de Andrade, María Teresa
    Freyre 191
de Chardin, Teilhard 135
de Gaulle, Charles 94, 231, 239
de La Revellière-Lépeaux,
    Louis Marie 119

de Salvia, Michel 231
Dee, John 148
del Vecchio, Giorgio 107
Delecroix, Vincent 34
Denning, Lord 106, 109, 110, 121
Detmold, M. J. 108, 118
Devlin, Lord 103, 104
Dias, R. W. M. 108
Dibon, Paul 163
Diderot, Denis 45
Dillon, John 108, 109
Dionysius 129
Diplock, Lord 121
Dodgson, Charles 87
Downing, Charles 213
Dowrick, F. E. 109
Duchamp, Marcel 94
Dunaway, Faye 61
Dunham, William 43
Dupeux, Jean-Yves 231, 232
Dwight, Timothy 132
Dworkin, Ronald 116, 117, 119,
    121, 123
Earman, John 141, 223
Ebeling, Gerhard 87
Edighoffer, Roland 146, 149,
    151, 154, 155, 156, 157, 158, 159
Edwards, Jonathan 132
Ehlert, A. D. 137
Einstein, Albert 29
Eliade, M. 128
Emerson 169
English, E. S. 136
Epimenides 25
Erdogan, Recep 210
Euler, Leonhard 13, 43, 44, 45,
    46, 47, 48, 49, 50, 54, 55
Eusebius 129, 130
Fairbaim, P. 134
Faivre, Antoine 157
Falwell, Jerry 98

Index of Names

Farwell, J. 114
Feinberg, C. L. 136
Fellmann, Emil A. 45
Fermat, Pierre de 46
Festinger, L. 130
Feydeau, Georges 211, 212
Feynman, Richard 46, 47
Fibonacci (Leonardo of Pisa) 35, 41
Fletcher, Joseph 119, 206
Flew, Antony 27
Fodor, James 57
Forde, Gerhard 216
Foriers, P. 58
Forman, H. J. 130
Forshaw, Peter J. 164
Fosdick, Harry Emerson 178
Francke, August Hermann 166
Franklin, Ben 105
Franklin, H. B. 133
Frederick the Great 45
Freeman, Iris 110
Freiherr von Münchhausen, Hieronymus Karl Friedrich....89
Freud, Sigmund 31, 62
Friedrich of Württemberg 148
Froom, L. F. 137
Fuchs 87
Fuller, Lon L. 58
Fussler, Herman H. 168, 172, 173, 177
Gaebelein, A. C. 136
Gallagher, L. 133
Gangee, Sam 98
Gapp, Kenneth S. 170
Gaspar, L. 132
Gauss, Carl Friedrich 43
Geisler, Norman 235
Gergen, Kenneth J. 92
Gerstner, John 220
Gewirth, Alan 118
Gilson, Etienne 178
Gödel, Kurt 13, 36, 38, 41
Godet, F. 136
Goethe, J. W. 145, 153
Good, I. J. 141
Goodfield 130
Goodhart, A. L. 110
Goodwin, Thomas 132
Gordon, G. H. 107, 108
Gould, John 38
Goulding, K. 103
Graebner, T. C. 130
Graf 220
Graham, Billy 213
Guitton, Jean 217
Gülen, Fethullah 210
Gundry, Robert 86
Gutmann, Aegidius 155
Habermas, Gary 61
Hagenbach, K. R. 47
Hägerström, Axel 107
Hailsham, Lord 121
Hamilton, F. E. 134
Harding, Rosamond E. M. 193
Harnack, A. 134
Harrison, N. B. 136
Hart, H. L. A. 104, 117, 172
Hart, James D. 168, 169
Haug, M. 128
Hawes, Marion 171
Heartacre, Silvia 98
Hegel, Georg Wilhelm Friedrich 93
Heidegger, Martin 87, 93, 241
Heim, K. 136
Herod 87
Hess, Tobias 152, 155, 156, 158
Heward, Edmund 110
Hillegas, M. R. 133
Hippolytus 129
Hirst, P. 103

Hitler, Adolf 95, 98, 118, 142, 219, 237
Hobbes, Thomas 205
Hodge.........134
Hodja, Nasreddin.........213, 217
Höfener, Heiner.........147, 148
Hofmann, Melchior.........131
Hofstadter, Douglas 36
Holmes, O. W. (Jr.).........107, 113
Hume, David.........140
Hunter, Edward 179
Hunter, Henry.........48
Hus, Jan.........131
Hutten, K. 128
Huxley, Julian 205, 206
Ignatius.........130
Increase, Samuel 132
Irenaeus.........129, 137
Ironside, H. A. 136
Jacob.........86
Jacob, Nicolas.........120
Jacobson, Norman M..........66
James, the Apostle.........78
Janssen, F. A. 14, 145
Jerome, St. 129
Jiankui, He 207
Joachim of Fiore 131, 155
John, the Apostle......23, 74, 75, 81, 129
Johnson, Samuel.........98, 105
Joyce, James 94
Julius.........129
Justin Martyr 129
Kant, Immanuel.........106, 107, 108, 118, 166, 178
Kantonen, T. A. 137
Karlstadt.........240
Käsemann, Ernst.........87
Kateb, G..........133
Kelley, Edward.........148
Kelly, George A. 92

Kenyon, Lord 114
Kepler, Johannes 145
Khan, Ghengis 118
Khunrath, Heinrich 163, 165
Kienast.........147, 150
Kierkegaard, Søren 93, 241
Kik, J. M. 135
Kinsey.........178
Klyve, Dominic 48
Knox, R. A..........131
Koestler, Arthur 26
Kossmann, Bernhard.........147
Kuenen 220
Kuntsler, William 105
Lactantius 129
Ladd, G. E..........136
Lamont, W. D. 107
Lange, Joachim 132
LaSor, W. S. 137
Le Clère, Adrien.........48
Le Pen, Jean-Marie 232
Leonhard Euler, ...43
Leslie, Charles.........91
Lewinsohn, R. 130
Lewis, C. S..........18, 29, 57, 99, 225
Lewis, Geoffrey 116
Lichtenstein, A. 132
Liljegren, S. B..........133
Lincoln, Anraham 142
Llewellyn, Karl 107
Longenecker, Richard 25
Loopy, David.........98
Lueker, Erwin L. 179
Luke, the Evangelist 75, 79, 81
Luther, Martin....59, 62, 80, 93, 98, 131, 150, 152, 157, 166, 218, 231, 235, 239, 240, 241, 242
Lutzer, Erwin 213
Lyons, David 116
MacDonald, George.........225
Macron, President 239

Index of Names

Maestlin, Michael 145
Magdalene, Mary 69
Mager, Inge 147
Maine, Henry 113
Mains, G. P. 135
Mannheim, K. 133
Mansfield, Lord 112
Mark, the Evangelist 75, 81
Marquart, Kurt 220
Marquis de Condorcet ... 43, 47, 48, 49
Martin, J. P. 132
Marty, Martin 87
Masselink, W. 134
Mather, Cotton 132, 169, 170
Matheson, Peter 241
Matthew, the Apostle 75, 81
Maunoury, Jean-Louis 218
Mauro, P. 134
McAgony, Alister 98
McAnally, Arthur Monroe 176
McArthur, William G. 66
McCall Smith, Alexander 87, 219
McClain, A. J. 137
McDonald, Jeffrey S. 221
McEwen, R. W. 134
McGiffert, A. C. 130
McNamara 139
McPherson, N. S. 136
Mendelssohn 212
Menuge, Angus 57
Merritt, LeRoy 195
Metcalf, Keyes D. 171
Metzger, B. M. 127
Miller, F. D. 118
Milligan, W. W. 134
Mitchell, Basil 121, 122, 123
Mitterand, President 236
Mohammed 231
Molnar, T. 133
Moltmann, Jürgen 135
Moody, Dwight 213
Moore, G. E. 117
More, Henry 132
More, Thomas 133
Moreland, J. P. 57
Morris, J. H. C. 116
Moses 86
Müntzer, Thomas 240, 241
Murphy, Gardner 225
Murray, G. L. 134
Myjer, Egbert 209, 210
Nahin, Paul J. 47
Napoleon 231
Nash, Arnold S. 176
Naudé, Gabriel 167, 201
Neglcy, G. 137
Nerhot, Patrick 121
Nesbø, Jo 227
Newman, John Henry 103
Newton, Isaac 46
Nicodemus 79
Nietzsche, Friedrich 118
Nijhoff, Martinus 146, 163
Norrie, Alan 116
Novalis 153
Nozick, Robert 118
O'Connor, J. F. 112
Og 85, 86
Ogden, S. 135
Olivecrona, Karl 107
Orieux, Jean 119
Origen 129, 130
Orr, James 220
Orwell, George 94, 214
Osmanoglu 209
Otte, Wolf-Dieter 147
Paine, Thomas 44
Paleo, Bruno W. 36
Papias 129
Pappus 163
Paracelsus 153

Pascal, Blaise 54
Patra, S. 206
Paul, E. F. 118
Paul, J. 118
Paul, the Apostle 24, 25, 62, 71, 75, 77
Pauli, Wolfgang 68
Payne, J. B. 137
Pentecost, J. D. 136
Perelman, Ch. 58
Peter the Great 45
Peters, G. N. H. 131, 136, 137
Petry, R. C. 130
Peuckert 147
Pfeiffer, R. H. 126, 127
Pharaoh 86
Phelps, Ralph H. 175
Phillips, J. B. 29, 30, 75
Pieters, A. 134
Pilate 75, 81
Pittenger, N. 135
Pizarro 133
Plutarch 177
Polkinghorne, D. E. 92
Pollock, Frederick 113
Polycarp 130
Ponce de Leon 133
Pontius Pilate 217
Prenter, Regin 242
Prester John 133
Preus, Robert 215
Prevet, François 104
Princess of Anhalt-Dessau 45
Quasten, J. 137
Raimbault, Antoine 69
Randi 139
Ranganathan, S. R. 176
Raspe, Rudolf Erich 89
Rawls, John 118
Reese, A. 136
Rémy, Dominique 108

Reu, M. 131
Richeson, David S. 46
Richet, Charles Robert 225
Rider, Fremont 168
Ritman, Joseph R. 145
Ritschl 178
Robertson, A. T. 80
Robson, Peter 110
Rogers, Frank B. 167
Rooney, Andy 104
Ross, Alf 107
Roth, Andrew 105
Roth, Jonathan 105
Roux, J. P. 133
Rudolf II 148
Rutgers, W. H. 132
Ryrie, C. C. 136
Saarnivaara, U. 131, 137
Sachs, Alain 211
Sagan, Carl 140, 141
Salmond, S. D. F. 128, 134, 137
Sanceau, E. 133
Sandifer, C. Edward 47
Saphir, A. 137
Sartre, Jean-Paul 93, 94, 241
Sass, Louis A. 95
Schaeffer, Francis 95
Schäfer, Gerhard 145, 149, 159
Schaff, P. 132
Schick 147
Schickhardt, Wilhelm 145
Schillebeeckx 135
Schleiermacher, Friedrich D. E. 18
Schlonk, Alphonso 98
Schneider, G. Michael 65, 66
Scholtz 147
Scorsese, Martin 232
Scott, Tom 241
Seccombe, Thomas 89
Seiss, J. A. 136

Index of Names

Sewall, Samuel 132
Shagrir, Oron 29
Shedd 134
Shell, Elton E. 173
Shelley, Mary 207
Shera, Jesse Hauk 188
Sherlock, Thomas 76, 141, 142
Simpson, A. W. B. 112
Sinclair, Dorothy 171
Slesser, Henry 124
Smith, Homer W. 173
Smith, Joseph 142, 217
Smith, O. J. 130
Smith, Wilbur M. 125, 201
Söderblom, N. 128
Spener, J. C. 48
Spener, Philipp J. 132, 166
Sperber, Julius 155
Sperry, Willard L. 18
Sprevak, Mark 29
Stackhouse, John G. (Jr.) 91
Stalin, Josef 118
Stille, Alexander 232
Stoeffler, Fred Ernest 166
Stonehouse, N. B. 25
Storch, Nikolaus 240
Strobel, Lee 61, 62, 63
Strohm, Stefan 160
Strong 135
Studion, Simon 155, 158
Swenson, Avalon 166
Tacitus 74
Talleyrand 119
Tauber, Maurice F. 173
Tauler, Johannes 240
Taylor, Thomas Murray 120
ten Boom, Corrie 235
Tenney, M. C. 136
Tertullian 129
Thayer, Henry Joseph 184
Thévenin, R. 133

Thomas, Keith 159
Thomas, the Apostle 23, 24, 77
Tillich, Paul 25
Tolkien, J. R. R. 225
Torrance, T. F. 131
Toulmin 130
Tregelles, S. P. 136
Trendelenburg, Adolf 107
Troplong, M. 121
Trost, Theodore 189
Trump, Donald 239
Truzzi, Marcello 141
Turing, Alan 29
Turnbull, George H. 160
Turner, Decherd (Jr.) 176
Turretinus 59
Tuveson, E. L. 133
Twain, Mark 219
Twist, Oliver 98
Tyconius 130
Urban II 131
van Dülmen, Richard ... 149, 150, 151, 153
Vasilev, A. 131
Vecchio, Del 106
Venturini, Karl 73
Vergil 133
Vetluguin, Voldemar 104, 105
Victorinus 129
Viguier, Jacques 69, 70
Virgil 44
Voegelin, E. 133
Voltaire 44, 45, 234
von Döllinger, J. J. 131
von Igelfeld, Moritz-Maria 87
Vos, G. 134
Vosper, Robert 168
Vuillard, Eric 240, 241
Vulliaud, P. 128, 130, 131, 137
Walker, A. D. M. 104
Wallace, G. 104

Walsh, C. 133
Walther, C. F. W. 212
Walvoord, J. F. 136
Warfield, B. B. 135, 220
Warneck, Johannes 25
Watchman, Paul 110
Weber, F. 127
Wehr, Gerhard 153
Wellhausen, Julius 220
Wesley, John 132, 235
West, N. 136
Whately, Richard 74, 85
White, F. R. 133
Wilken, Todd 13
Wilkins, Joseph 200
Williams, David 119
Williams, Edwin E. 171
Williams, G. H. 132
Wilmot, J. 134
Wilson, Louis Round 173
Winfield, P. H. 113
Wisdom, John 27
Wittgenstein, Ludwig ... 31, 35, 118
Wood, A. J. 103
Wright, Joe 219
Wyclif, John 131
Xavier, Rodney 98
Yates, Frances A. 148, 149
Youschkevitch, A. P. 44
Zahn, T. 136
Zetzner, Lazarus 161
Ziltch, Methusula 98
Zoroaster 128

Index of Places

America 108, 122, 170, 172, 219, 233, 234, 242
Arc de Triomphe 61
Areopagus 24, 25
Athens 24, 25
Austria 233
Basel 44
Berlin 45, 219
Berlin Academy 45
Black Forest 145
Bologna 236, 237
Breisgau 241
British Academy 103
Champs-Elysées 61
Chicago 233
Corinth 25
Cornell University 213
Damascus 62, 71
Denver, Colorado 57
Edinburgh 57
England 76, 108, 110, 239
Europe 44, 58, 170, 219, 233, 234, 236
European Court of Human Rights 209, 231, 232
European Union 239
France 70, 108, 119, 219, 231, 232, 233, 235, 236, 237, 239, 242
Frankenhausen 240
Freiburg 241
Germany 45, 93, 108, 148, 219, 240, 241
Göttingen University 17, 21
Greece 209
Gulf states 239
Holland 186

Index of Places

Imperial Russian Academy
   of the Sciences 44
Israel 24
Italy 236, 237
Jonestown, Guyana 119
Judaea 75
London 94
Marburg 87
Methodist Theological
   School, Ohio 179
Middlesex University 103
Moody Bible Institute 213, 216
Munchhausen 89
Munich 219
National Library of Medicine .. 167
Netherlands 235
Nicaragua 237
Ontario, Canada 219
Open University in England 43
Oxford 87, 117
Paris 61, 205, 231, 239
Prague 148
Russia 108
San Francisco 105
Seine 48
Simon Greenleaf School
   of Law 214
Sodom and Gomorrah 60
Sorbonne 163
Spain 94
St Petersburg 44, 45
Strasbourg 61, 146, 163, 233

Stuttgart 145, 157
Sweden 186
Switzerland 209
Trinity Evangelical Divinity
   School 213
Tübingen 145, 152, 158
Tübinger Stift 151
Turkey 209, 210, 213
Twin Towers 233
UK 219
University of Auckland 24
University of Basel 44
University of British
   Columbia 74
University of Chicago 20
University of Chicago
   Divinity School Library 179
University of Frankfurt an
   der Oder 240
University of Strasbourg 163
University of Tübingen 151
US Supreme Court 233
Waco, Texas 119
Waterloo Lutheran
   University 219
Westmont College, Santa
   Barbara, California 86
Wittenberg 240
Württemberg 145, 148, 151
Yale Library 168
Zwickau 240

www.ingramcontent.com/pod-product-compliance
Lightning Source LLC
Chambersburg PA
CBHW070247230426
43664CB00014B/2432